St Petersburg

Nick Selby

L O N E L Y   P L A N E T   P U B L I C A T I O N S
Melbourne • Oakland • London • Paris

Map 1 ST PETERSBURG METRO САНКТ ПЕТЕРБУРГСКОЕ МЕТРО

Prospekt Prosveshchenia
Проспект Просвещения

Ozerki
Озерки

Udelnaya
Удельная

Pionerskaya
Пионерская

Chyornaya Rechka
Чёрная Речка

Petrogradskaya
Петроградская

Chkalovskaya
Чкаловская

Gorkovskaya
Горьковская

Sportivnaya
Спортивная

Primorskaya
Приморская

Vasileostrovskaya
Василеостровская

Gostiny Dvor/Nevsky Pr.
Гостиный Двор/Невский Пр.

Sadovaya/Sennaya Pl.
Садовая/Сенная Пл.

Tekhnologichesky Institut
Технологический Институт

Baltiyskaya
Балтийская

Narvskaya
Нарвская

Kirovsky Zavod
Кировский Завод

Avtovo
Автово

Leninsky Prospekt
Ленинский Проспект

Prospekt Veteranov
Проспект Ветеранов

Pushkinskaya
Пушкинская

Frunzenskaya
Фрунзенская

Elizavorskaya
Елизаровская

Moskovskie Vorota
Московские Ворота

Elektrosila
Электросила

Lomonosovskaya
Ломоносовская

Park Pobedy
Парк Победы

Moskovskaya
Московская

Proletarskaya
Пролетарская

Zvyozdnaya
Звёздная

Obukhovo
Обухово

Kupchino
Купчино

Rybatskoe
Рыбацкое

Devyatkino
Девяткино

Grazhdansky Prospect
Гражданский Проспект

Akademicheskaya
Академическая

Politekhnicheskaya
Политехническая

Bus No.80

Ploshchad Muzhestva
Площадь Мужества

Bus No.80

Lesnaya
Лесная

Vyborgskaya
Выборгская

Ploshchad Lenina
Площадь Ленина

Chernyshevskaya
Чернышевская

Ploshchad Vosstania/Mayakovskaya
Площадь Восстания/Маяковская

Vladimirskaya/Dostoevskaya
Владимирская/Достоевская

Ligovsky Prospekt
Лиговский Проспект

Pl. Aleksandra Nevskogo
Площадь Александра Невского

Novocherkasskaya
Новочеркасская

Ladozhskaya
Ладожская

Prospekt Bolshevikov
Проспект Большевиков

Ulitsa Dybenko
Улица Дыбенко

	Kirovsko-Vyborgskaya Line Кировско-Выборгская линия		Transfer Stations Станции пересадок
1		⬤	
2	Moskovsko-Petrogradskaya Line Московско-Петроградская линия	○	Metro Stations Станции метро
3	Nevsko-Vasileostrovskaya Line Невско-Василеостровская линия	🚆	Railway Stations Железнодорожные возкалы
4	Pravoberezhnaya Line Правобережная линия		

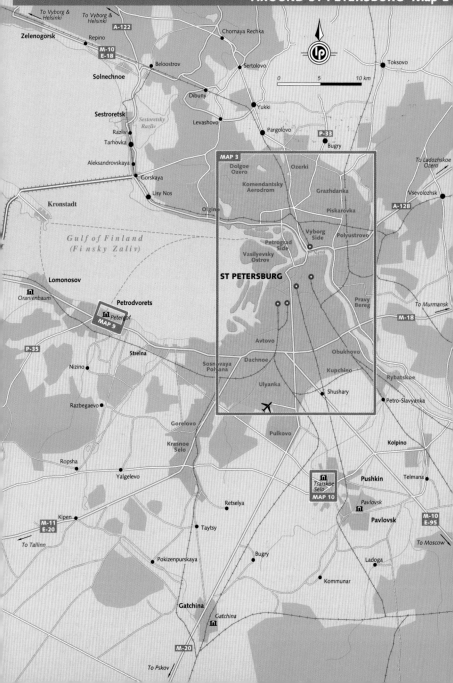

To Vyborg &
Helsinki

To Vyborg &
Helsinki

A-122

Zelenogorsk

Repino

Chornaya Rechka

Toksovo

M-10
E-18

Beloostrov

Sertolovo

Solnechnoe

Dibuny

Yukki

Sestroretsk

Sestoretsky
Razliv

Levashovo

Pargolovo

P-33

Razliv

Bugry

To Ladozhskoe
Ozero

Tarhovka

MAP 3

Aleksandrovskaya

Dolgoe
Ozero

Ozerki

Vsevolozhsk

Gorskaya

Komendantsky
Aerodrom

Grazhdanka

A-128

Lisy Nos

Piskarovka

Olgino

Kronstadt

Vyborg
Side

Polyustrovo

Gulf of Finland
(Finsky Zaliv)

Petrograd
Side

Vasilyevsky
Ostrov

Neva

ST PETERSBURG

Lomonosov

Pravy
Bereg

Oranienbaum

To Murmansk

Petrodvorets

M-18

Peterhof
MAP 9

Avtovo

Obukhovo

P-35

Strelna

Dachnoe

Kupchino

Rybatskoe

Nizino

Sosnovaya
Pol_ana

Ulyanka

Shushary

Petro-Slavyanka

Razbegaevo

Gorelovo

Pulkovo

Kolpino

Ropsha

Krasnoe
Selo

Yalgelevo

Tsarskoe
Selo

Pushkin

Telmana

MAP 10

M-11
E-20

Kipen

Retselya

Pavlovsk

Pavlovsk

M-10
E-95

To Tallinn

Taytsy

To Moscow

Pokizenpurskaya

Bugry

Ladoga

Kommunar

Gatchina

Gatchina

M-20

To Pskov

0   5   10 km

St Petersburg
2nd edition - February 1999
First published - February 1996

Published by
Lonely Planet Publications Pty Ltd A.C.N. 005 607 983
192 Burwood Rd, Hawthorn, Victoria 3122, Australia

Lonely Planet Offices
Australia PO Box 617, Hawthorn, Victoria 3122
USA 150 Linden St, Oakland, CA 94607
UK 10a Spring Place, London NW5 3BH
France 1 rue du Dahomey, 75011 Paris

Photographs
Roger Hayne, John Noble, Nick Selby, Georgi Shablovsky,
Georgy Skachkov
Some of the images in this guide are available for licensing from
Lonely Planet Images.
email: lpi@lonelyplanet.com.au

Front cover photograph
Beloselsky-Belozersky Palace in its prime, Nevsky Prospekt
(Nick Selby)

ISBN 0 86442 657 7

text & maps © Lonely Planet 1999
photos © photographers as indicated 1999

Printed by Colorcraft Ltd, Hong Kong

Contents

The Author

Nick Selby

Nick Selby was born and raised in New York City. An escaped sound engineer (he recorded rap 'music' at Walker & Six Recording and Chung King in New York; connected *Mofo The Psychic Gorilla* for Penn & Teller's Broadway show; worked 'mixing' 'music' and hauling cables on the soaps *As The World Turns* and *Guiding Light*, and mixing sound for CBS Sports), Nick DJ'd at Radio Zet, Warsaw's first independent radio station and moved to Russia in late 1991, where he wrote *The Visitor's Guide to the New St Petersburg*. Since then he's been travelling and working for Lonely Planet on a positively bizarre group of destinations including *Brazil*, *Florida* and *Miami* (with his wife Corinna), *Germany*, *Russia*, *St Petersburg*, and *Texas*. He and Corinna live in Tarifa, Spain (Europe's southernmost point). This marks the seventh time Nick has permanently left Russia.

FROM THE AUTHOR

Hearty thanks again to Elena Vvedenskaya, and to Shannon Farley for her generous hospitality; Steven Caron of RYHT, Svetlana Podberezhnykh, Marina Yermolova and the staff of the HI St Petersburg Hostel and Helsinki's Eurohostel for all their assistance.

Thank you Marc Decker, Pyotr Rasha, Nancy Renner and Dima Deryabachev. At home, thanks to Corinna, and to Butch, Olivia, and Spike. And thanks to all the Saras and Sarahs in Lonely Planet's UK office.

This Book

FROM THE PUBLISHER

This book was edited at Lonely Planet's Melbourne office by Carolyn Bain, with help from Ron Gallagher and Elizabeth Swan, and proofed by Wendy Owen, Chris Wyness and Janet Austin. Piotr Czajkowski drew the maps, with help from Tamsin Wilson. Piotr also laid out the book. Maria Vallianos designed the cover. Illustrations were done by Trudi Canavan, Piotr Czajkowski, Margaret Jung, Jacqui Saunders and Tamsin Wilson. Thanks to Quentin Frayne for laying out the language section, Dan Levin for assistance with the Cyrillic font, Tim Uden for layout assistance, and to Mark Griffiths, Liz Filleul and Anthony Phelan for checking the artwork.

Acknowledgements

Many thanks to following travellers who used the last edition and wrote to us with helpful hints, useful advice and interesting anecdotes.

Nieka Apell, Lloyd Baugh Sj, Michael Beam, Oliver F Bischof, Soren Bjelke, Rachel Bowes, Tessa Chao, Megan Corrigan, Bob Cromwell, W F Dymond, Glenn Gourley, Yana Itskovich, Peter Jenkins, Eric Johnson, Galen Kaufman, Maureen Keogh, Marco Lambruschi, Maeve McPhillips, Sandra L Monyneaux, Debbie Morgan, Simeon Nichter, Magnus Norstrom, M W Pollock, Lindsay Rex, Matteo Terzi, Olga Toliarenko, Mark Waldon, Rasa Zdanius.

Foreword

ABOUT LONELY PLANET GUIDEBOOKS

The story begins with a classic travel adventure: Tony and Maureen Wheeler's 1972 journey across Europe and Asia to Australia. Useful information about the overland trail did not exist at that time, so Tony and Maureen published the first Lonely Planet guidebook to meet a growing need.

From a kitchen table, then from a tiny office in Melbourne (Australia), Lonely Planet has become the largest independent travel publisher in the world, an international company with offices in Melbourne, Oakland (USA), London (UK) and Paris (France).

Today Lonely Planet guidebooks cover the globe. There is an ever-growing list of books and there's information in a variety of forms and media. Some things haven't changed. The main aim is still to help make it possible for adventurous travellers to get out there – to explore and better understand the world.

At Lonely Planet we believe travellers can make a positive contribution to the countries they visit – if they respect their host communities and spend their money wisely. Since 1986 a percentage of the income from each book has been donated to aid projects and human rights campaigns.

Updates Lonely Planet thoroughly updates each guidebook as often as possible. This usually means there are around two years between editions, although for more unusual or more stable destinations the gap can be longer. Check the imprint page (following the colour map at the beginning of the book) for publication dates.

Between editions up-to-date information is available in two free newsletters – the paper *Planet Talk* and email *Comet* (to subscribe, contact any Lonely Planet office) – and on our Web site at www.lonelyplanet.com. The *Upgrades* section of the Web site covers a number of important and volatile destinations and is regularly updated by Lonely Planet authors. *Scoop* covers news and current affairs relevant to travellers. And, lastly, the *Thorn Tree* bulletin board, and *Postcards* section of the site carry unverified, but fascinating, reports from travellers.

Correspondence The process of creating new editions begins with the letters, postcards and emails received from travellers. This correspondence often includes suggestions, criticisms and comments about the current editions. Interesting excerpts are immediately passed on via newsletters and the Web site, and everything goes to our authors to be verified when they're researching on the road. We're keen to get more feedback from organisations or individuals who represent communities visited by travellers.

> **Lonely Planet gathers information for everyone who's curious about the planet – and especially for those who explore it first-hand. Through guidebooks, phrasebooks, activity guides, maps, literature, newsletters, image library, TV series and web site we act as an information exchange for a worldwide community of travellers.**

Research Authors aim to gather sufficient practical information to enable travellers to make informed choices and to make the mechanics of a journey run smoothly. They also research historical and cultural background to help enrich the travel experience and allow travellers to understand and respond appropriately to cultural and environmental issues.

Authors don't stay in every hotel because that would mean spending a couple of months in each medium-sized city and, no, they don't eat at every restaurant because that would mean stretching belts beyond capacity. They do visit hotels and restaurants to check standards and prices, but feedback based on readers' direct experiences can be very helpful.

Many of our authors work undercover, others aren't so secretive. None of them accept freebies in exchange for positive write-ups. And none of our guidebooks contain any advertising.

Production Authors submit their raw manuscripts and maps to offices in Australia, USA, UK or France. Editors and cartographers – all experienced travellers themselves – then begin the process of assembling the pieces. When the book finally hits the shops some things are already out of date, we start getting feedback from readers, and the process begins again....

WARNING & REQUEST

Things change – prices go up, schedules change, good places go bad and bad places go bankrupt – nothing stays the same. So, if you find things better or worse, recently opened or long since closed, please tell us and help make the next edition even more accurate and useful. We genuinely value all the feedback we receive. Julie Young coordinates a well-travelled team that reads and acknowledges every letter, postcard and email and ensures that every morsel of information finds its way to the appropriate authors, editors and cartographers for verification.

Everyone who writes to us will find their name in the next edition of the appropriate guidebook. They will also receive the latest issue of *Planet Talk*, our quarterly printed newsletter, or *Comet*, our monthly email newsletter. Subscriptions to both newsletters are free. The very best contributions will be rewarded with a free guidebook.

Excerpts from your correspondence may appear in new editions of Lonely Planet guidebooks, the Lonely Planet Web site, *Planet Talk* or *Comet*, so please let us know if you *don't* want your letter published or your name acknowledged.

Send all correspondence to the Lonely Planet office closest to you:

Australia: PO Box 617, Hawthorn, Victoria 3122
UK: 10A Spring Place, London NW5 3BH
USA: 150 Linden St, Oakland CA 94607
France: 1 rue du Dahomey, Paris 75011

Or email us at: talk2us@lonelyplanet.com.au

For news, views and updates see our web site: www.lonelyplanet.com

HOW TO USE A LONELY PLANET GUIDEBOOK

The best way to use a Lonely Planet guidebook is any way you choose. At Lonely Planet we believe the most memorable travel experiences are often those that are unexpected, and the finest discoveries are those you make yourself. Guidebooks are not intended to be used as if they provide a detailed set of infallible instructions!

Contents All Lonely Planet guidebooks follow the same format. The Facts about the Country chapters or sections give background information ranging from history to weather. Facts for the Visitor gives practical information on issues like visas and health. Getting There & Away gives a brief starting point for researching travel to and from the destination. Getting Around gives an overview of the transport options when you arrive.

The peculiar demands of each destination determine how subsequent chapters are broken up, but some things remain constant. We always start with background, then proceed to sights, places to stay, places to eat, entertainment, getting there and away, and getting around information – in that order.

Heading Hierarchy Lonely Planet headings are used in a strict hierarchical structure that can be visualised as a set of Russian dolls. Each heading (and its following text) is encompassed by any preceding heading that is higher on the hierarchical ladder.

Entry Points We do not assume guidebooks will be read from beginning to end, but that people will dip into them. The traditional entry points are the list of contents and the index. In addition, however, there is a complete list of maps and an index map illustrating map coverage.

There's also a colour map that shows highlights. These highlights are dealt with in greater detail in the Facts for the Visitor chapter, along with planning questions and suggested itineraries. Each chapter covering a geographical region begins with a locator map and another list of highlights. Once you find something of interest in a list of highlights, turn to the index.

Maps Maps play a crucial role in Lonely Planet guidebooks and include a huge amount of information. A legend is printed on the back page. We seek to have complete consistency between maps and text, and to have every important place in the text captured on a map. Map key numbers usually start in the top left corner.

Although inclusion in a guidebook usually implies a recommendation we cannot list every good place. Exclusion does not necessarily imply criticism. In fact there are a number of reasons why we might exclude a place – sometimes it is simply inappropriate to encourage an influx of travellers.

Introduction

If Moscow is Europe's most Asiatic capital, then St Petersburg is Russia's most European city. Created by Peter the Great as his 'window on the West' at the only point where traditional Russian territory meets a seaway to Northern Europe, it was built with 18th and 19th century European pomp and orderliness by mainly European architects. The result is a city that remains one of Europe's most beautiful; where Moscow intimidates, St Petersburg enchants.

The vistas of elegant buildings across the wide Neva River and along the canals and avenues recall Paris, Amsterdam and Venice. But St Petersburg's beauty, happily little harmed by Stalinist reconstruction, is of a brand all its own.

The onion domes of Moscow seem almost passé here, where a more Western outlook was taken at every stage of planning and construction. Even the colours of the city's buildings – the green and gold of the Winter Palace; the red beside the Anichkov Bridge; the blue of Smolny Cathedral – reflect a stylistic allegiance more to the courts of Europe than to the Kremlin. The buildings' baroque façades exude the riotous opulence of tsarist Russia. Today, despite their problems, residents feel enough affection for their city to call it simply 'Piter' and visitors' taste buds are now receiving a much improved welcome from new private and foreign restaurant ventures. Reform and transformation is giving the city a facelift that's almost 80 years overdue.

The new Russia is here in spades: local businesses are popping up everywhere, Western businesses are following suit, and even the city itself is getting in on the money train by (get this) accepting corporate sponsorship of street signs. It's not your imagination, that street sign does say 'USA Today'. And the deification process has turned 180 degrees: the Order of Lenin plaque at Ploshchad Vosstania metro station was replaced with a Marlboro cigarette ad.

St Petersburg is chock-full of history: from here, two centuries of autocratic tsars ruled Russia with the splendour and stubbornness that led to their downfall at the hands of the city's workers and soldiers in March 1917. Here, that same year, Lenin came back from exile to lead his Bolshevik Party to power.

The city's two centuries as Russia's capital bequeathed it an artistic and entertainment tradition which enables it to remain at the forefront of the Russian cultural scene. Russian ballet was born here and the 19th century flowering of Russian music was centred here. Nijinsky, Tchaikovsky and Rimsky-Korsakov, to name but a few, spent important periods here. Pushkin was educated in, exiled from, re-admitted to and killed in St Petersburg; Dostoevsky set *Crime and Punishment* here; and Akhmatova penned her moving poetry about life in what was then Leningrad.

At one end of the cultural spectrum today are the Hermitage, one of the world's great art museums, housed in the superb Winter Palace, and the Kirov Ballet, which has recently overshadowed Moscow's Bolshoy. At the other end, St Petersburg has produced many of Russia's top rock bands; wealthy young Russians spend sultry summer evenings partying in dozens of Western-style nightclubs, or at rave parties that run all night long, with laser shows, top dance hits and DJs imported from Europe or Africa.

St Petersburg's latitude gives it nearly 24-hour daylight in midsummer but long, grey winters. From June to August, when temperatures usually reach 20°C, the city is absolutely packed with foreign and Russian tourists. From December to March, when the Neva is iced over and temperatures rarely exceed freezing, the long nights have a twinkling magic; the sun lazily lobs itself skyward at around 10 am and decides to call it a day around 3 pm.

Facts about St Petersburg

HISTORY

Alexandr of Novgorod defeated the Swedes near the mouth of the Neva River in 1240, earning him the title Nevsky (literally, 'of the Neva'). Sweden took control of the region in the 17th century and it was the desire of Peter I (the Great) to crush this rival and make Russia a European power that led to the founding of the city. At the start of the Great Northern War (1700-21) he captured the Swedish outposts on the Neva, and in 1703 he founded the Peter & Paul Fortress on the river a few kilometres in from the sea. After Peter trounced the Swedes at Poltava in 1709 the city he named Sankt Pieter Burkh (in Dutch style) really began to grow.

Peter the Great

Those Swedes weren't exactly pushovers; Peter's victory was the result of no small measure of ruthlessness. And as one might suspect, the rapid growth of St Petersburg from a muddy mess to a lavishly constructed world capital was not accomplished through the Russian peasantry's eleemosynary views towards their tsar.

Peasants were drafted as forced labour, many dying as a result. To raise money to construct the city, Peter taxed everything he could think of – including beards and coffins – and imposed the infamous 'Soul Tax' (essentially a death duty) on all lower-class adult males. Architects and artisans were brought from all over Europe; canals were dug to drain the marshy south bank, and in 1712 Peter made the place his capital, forcing administrators, nobles and merchants to move here from Moscow and build new homes. What's more, anyone entering the city had to bring building supplies with them – wagons were checked at the city line.

The upper classes were also thrown into a tizz by Peter's edicts on their performance: aristocrats could either serve in the army or the civil service, or lose their titles and land. Previously-bequeathed birth status counted for little, as state servants were subject to Peter's new Table of Ranks, a performance-based ladder of promotion with the upper grades conferring hereditary nobility. Some aristocrats lost all they had, while capable state employees of humble origin and even foreigners became Russian nobles.

Peter mobilised Russian resources to compete on equal terms with the West, eclipsing all but the most powerful nations of the day – a startling achievement. His territorial gains were small, but the strategic Baltic territories added ethnic variety, including a new class of German traders and administrators

Peter I – known as 'the Great' because of his 2.24m frame and his equally commanding victory over the Swedes.

which formed the backbone of Russia's commercial and military expansion.

Peter was also to have the last word on the authority of the Church. When it resisted his reforms he simply blocked the appointment of a new patriarch, put bishops under a government department and, in effect, made himself the head of the Church.

By the time of his death in 1725, Peter's city on the Neva had a population of 40,000 and 90% of Russia's foreign trade passed through it. The south bank around the Admiralty had become the centre of the now-bustling town.

Peter died without naming a successor. Had it not been for a government structure built on the Table of Ranks and a professional bureaucracy with a vested interest in its preservation, Peter's reforms might well have died with him.

After Peter

Peter's immediate successors moved the capital back to Moscow but Empress Anna Ioannovna (1730-40) returned to St Petersburg. Between 1741 and 1825 under Empress Elizabeth, Catherine the Great and Alexander I, it became a cosmopolitan city with a royal court of famous splendour. These monarchs commissioned great series of palaces, government buildings and churches, which turned the city into one of Europe's grandest capitals.

Catherine II (the Great)

Of Russia's female leaders, none is more famous, and infamous, than Catherine II. Born Sophie Fredericke Augusta in what is now Szczecin, Poland, on 2 May 1729, Catherine was the daughter of the German prince of Anhalt-Zerbst. At 15, young Sophie went to Russia to marry Peter, Empress Elizabeth's nephew and heir to the Russian throne (later, Catherine said of Peter: 'I believe the Crown of Russia attracted me more than his person'). On Elizabeth's death, Christmas Day 1761, Peter became Peter III.

Peter III was not only widely disliked, he was widely disliked by powerful members of his military who soon felt that perhaps his wife should take over (she was in full agreement). This was accomplished in June 1762 when a party of officers (led by the brother of one of Catherine's lovers) arrested and subsequently killed Peter, and Catherine became ruler of Russia.

While many claim that Catherine was something of a sex fiend (rumours persist that she 'had more lovers than a serf had hot dinners' and that she got a 'charge' from bestiality), it would seem that she was the target of some deft propaganda by jealous male members of the court. Her diaries are said to list fewer than 10 lovers, though some do run concurrently, which seems to put her somewhere to the more conservative side of ... well, Madonna, anyway.

Catherine as Leader Catherine's legacy stems from her constant self-education and love of culture. She was a big fan of the Enlightenment and brought Russia forward by leaps and bounds in terms of Westernisation. In 1767 she established an Assembly of Deputies to draft new laws, and wrote the *Nakaz* – instructions or guidelines. She instituted wide-scale reforms in the military as well as for the peasantry, and encouraged industrial and agricultural growth and trade.

This is not to say that Catherine was a bleeding heart. Her reign saw expansion through naval victory at the Black Sea coast, control over what is now roughly present-day Lithuania, Belarus and western Ukraine through the adroit appointment of a former lover as king in Poland, and ruthless suppression of the Cossack rebellion of 1773-74. But Catherine was benevolent, or at least pragmatic, by the standards of the time. To boost the efficiency of local government, Catherine replaced Peter's 12 provinces with 50 of roughly equal size, each with a governor. The lowest district administrative level was formed by landholders, newly freed from Peter's compulsory state service.

Catherine's most visible bequest was to bring Russia on to the world stage of arts and letters. She freed up regulations and restrictions on publishing and increased the number of schools and colleges. Her vast collection of paintings forms the core of the present-day Hermitage museum collection. And Catherine went on an architectural commissioning spree, inviting dozens of Western European architects to change the face of St Petersburg.

Her palaces are to this day reminders of the wealth, power and opulence enjoyed by the Russian nobility, and Catherine had them built almost as quickly as postwar Soviet engineers slapped together the hideous prefabricated buildings that mar the landscape of so many Russian and Eastern European cities.

Alexander I

When Catherine died in 1796 the throne passed to her son, Paul I. An old-school autocrat, he antagonised the gentry with attempts to reimpose compulsory state service and was killed in a coup in 1801. So much for Paul I.

Catherine II, known as 'the Great' for – amongst other things – her intelligence, her liberal reforms and her high number of lovers.

Paul's son, Alexander I (who had been Catherine's favourite grandson), had been trained by the best European tutors. He kicked off his reign with several reforms, including an expansion of the school system that brought education within reach of the lower-middle classes. But he was soon preoccupied with wars against Napoleon which were to dominate his career.

After being defeated by Napoleon at Austerlitz, north of Vienna, in 1805 and then at Friedland, near modern Kaliningrad, Alexander began to negotiate. The Treaty of Tilsit (1807) left Napoleon in charge as Emperor of the West and Alexander as Emperor of the East, both of them (in theory) united against England.

1812

The alliance between Napoleon and Alexander lasted only until 1810, when Russia resumed trade with England. A hopping-mad little Napoleon decided to crush the tsar with a Grand Army of 700,000, the largest force the world had ever seen for a single military operation.

Rather than meet the Grand Army in Prussia or Poland, Alexander shrewdly drew it into the vast Russian countryside in the summer of 1812, scorching the earth to deny sustenance to the French. Napoleon set his sights on Moscow, the symbolic heart of Russia. A bloody but inconclusive battle was fought at Borodino, 130km west of Moscow, with the Russians withdrawing in good order.

In September, Napoleon entered a deserted Moscow; a few days later the city was burnt down around him. Feeling awfully silly standing there amidst the ashes of a city that isn't so hot even when it's built up, and with winter coming and his supply lines overstretched, Napoleon ordered a retreat – he was unable to do anything else. His troops, harassed by Russian Partisans, froze and starved. Only one in 20 made it back to the relative safety of Poland, and the Russians pursued them all the way to Paris.

The Decembrists

Alexander's death without a clear heir in 1825 sparked the usual crisis. His reform-minded brother Constantine, married to a Pole and living happily in Warsaw thank you very much, had no interest in the throne. Officers who had brought back liberal ideas from Paris in 1815 preferred Constantine to Alexander's youngest brother, the militaristic Nicholas, who was due to be crowned on 26 December 1825. Their rally in St Petersburg was quashed by troops loyal to Nicholas, who threw those who weren't killed into the Peter & Paul Fortress. Nicholas demanded to look each so-called Decembrist traitor in the face before pronouncing sentence, psychologically terrorising many (executing some, while subjecting many others to mock executions, complete with blindfolds and macabre pronouncements, then telling them at the very last second that their sentences had been 'commuted'; after which they were exiled). More than 100 were sent into Siberian exile.

The remainder of Nicholas I's reign was as inauspicious as the beginning; though he granted title to peasants on state land (effectively freeing them) and restored trade with England, his foreign policy accomplished little else than to annoy everyone in the Balkans, most of the rest of Europe, and to start the Crimean War in which England and France sided against Russia. Inept command on both sides resulted in a bloody, stalemated war.

Alexander II & the 'Great Reforms'

Nicholas died in 1855. His son, Alexander II, saw the Crimean War stirring up discontent within Russia and accepted peace on unfavourable terms. The war had revealed the backwardness behind the post-1812 imperial glory and the time for reform had come.

The serfs were freed in 1861. Of the land they had worked, roughly a third was kept by established land-holders. The rest went to village communes which assigned it to individuals in return for 'redemption payments' to compensate former land-holders – a system that pleased no-one.

But the abolition of serfdom opened the way for a market economy, capitalism and an industrial revolution. Railroads and factories were built and cities expanded as peasants left the land. Nothing, though, was done to modernise farming and the peasants found their lot had not improved in half a century.

During the reign of Alexander II (1855-81) and his son, Alexander III (1881-94), Central Asia came under Russian control. In the east, Russia acquired a long strip of Pacific coast from China and built the port of Vladivostok, but sold the 'worthless' Alaskan territories to the US in 1867 for just US$7.2 million (the US was said to be also in the market for a slice of mainland Siberia but the Russians apparently asked too high a price for it).

The loosening of restrictions and rapid change in the make-up of Russian society took its toll, however. Industrialisation and the emancipation of the serfs brought a flood of poor workers into St Petersburg, leading to overcrowding, poor sanitation, epidemics and festering discontent. Revolutionary sentiment was rife and radicals were plotting the overthrow of the tsarist government as early as the second half of the 19th century. Alexander II was assassinated in St Petersburg by a terrorist bomb in 1881.

Most of the more reactionary members of society (that is, those expressing dissent of any sort) were rounded up and either executed or exiled, and the reign of Alexander III was marked by repression of revolutionaries and liberals alike.

The Russo-Japanese War

It's hard to imagine this today, but at the turn of the century, St Petersburg's dabbling in Asian affairs created problems. Port Arthur, home of the Russian Fleet during China's Boxer Uprising, was attacked by Japanese forces on 8 February 1904, after Russia refused to withdraw its troops from the region. The Russo-Japanese war which followed was quick, devastating and humiliating to the tsar's forces.

The tsar's strategy (as has always been the case in Russian military affairs) was to throw as many men (meaning hastily, in many cases violently, drafted peasants) as he could at the Japanese. The subsequent butchering of young Russians caused a huge political backlash and the series of defeats took their toll in the form of ever increasing civil unrest in St Petersburg. Under the terms of the peace treaty signed on 5 September 1905, Russia not only gave up Port Arthur, the larger half of Sakhalin Island and other properties, but also recognised Japanese predominance in Korea.

The 1905 Revolution

St Petersburg became a hotbed of strikes and political violence and the hub of the 1905 revolution, sparked by the 'Bloody Sunday' of 9 January 1905 when a strikers' march to petition the tsar in the Winter Palace was fired on by troops. The group was made up of about 150,000 workers who were staging what many say was a peaceful protest (it was being led by Father Georgy Gapon, a priest). It's unclear how many of the demonstrators were killed (most estimates say several hundred, but some say as many as 1000), but what is certain is that the incident served to solidify ties between squabbling opposition factions by giving them a much better idea of who was the common enemy.

In the months to follow, peasant uprisings, mutinies (most famously that aboard the Battleship Potyomkin) and other protests abounded. Soviets, or 'workers' councils', were formed by social democrat activists in St Petersburg and Moscow. The St Petersburg Soviet, led by Mensheviks (Minority People, who in fact outnumbered the Bolshevik, or Majority People's, party) under Leon Trotsky, called for a massive general strike in October, which brought the country to a standstill.

These protests resulted in Tsar Nicholas II's grudgingly issued 'October Manifesto' which, along with granting hitherto unheard of civil rights, laid the basis for the Duma, Russia's elected legislature. The Manifesto calmed an angry populace for the time being. By 1914, when in a wave of patriotism (or at least anti-German sentiment) at the start of WWI, the city's name was changed to the Russian-style Petrograd, it had a population of 2.1 million people. As early as 1917, Petrograd would again be the cradle of revolution.

WWI

Nicholas II' ham-fisted leadership during the formative years of WWI (by most accounts Nicholas was both a perfectly likeable fellow and an execrable leader) and a collapsing domestic policy were the straws that eventually broke the camel's back. After heavy losses in the first year of war, the second year saw disasters at every turn, with Russian troops bogged down and suffering badly. While the brilliantly executed Brusilov Offensive, embarked upon after Austro-German forces mounted a spring offensive against Italy, was a military success, it produced an additional one million Russian casualties. Facing total losses of almost two million people, and German incursions deep into the Russian homeland, the folks at home were not amused.

The 1917 Revolution

Actually, there were two. With all the confusion caused by the war, along with a breakdown in the chain of command and the increasing influence of the spooky Grigory Rasputin on the tsar's wife, Alexandra, morale was very low. People were blaming Nicholas for failures of the Russian armies (which is what rightly happens if one insists on leading troops into slaughter). Political fragmentation had resulted in a powerful reincarnation of the Petrograd Soviet of Workers & Soldiers Deputies, based on the 1905 model. Workers' protests turned into a general strike and troops mutinied, forcing the end of the monarchy. On 1 March Nicholas abdicated about 38 seconds after he was 'asked to' by the Duma. Nick's brother Mikhail (probably shrewdly) declined to take the reigns of power, and the Romanov dynasty of over 300 years officially came to an end. A short time later, Nicholas and his entire family were dragged out to Yekaterinberg, just east of the Ural mountains. They were later murdered and buried in a mass grave, though some of their bodies have been exhumed and re-buried at the Peter & Paul Fortress (see the boxed aside 'Reburying the Past').

A provisional government announced that general elections would be held in November. The Petrograd Soviet started meeting in the city's Tauride Palace alongside the country's reformist Provisional Government. It was to Petrograd's Finland Station that Vladimir Lenin travelled in April to organise the Bolshevik Party, and against Petrograd that the loyalist General Kornilov marched his troops in August, only to be headed off by rebel soldiers and armed workers from the city. The Smolny Institute, a former girls' college in the city,

Young Lenin after being arrested as a subversive and serving a term of exile in Siberia.

became the focus as the Bolsheviks took control of the Petrograd Soviet which had installed itself there.

During the summer, tensions were raised considerably by the co-existence of two power bases: the Provisional Government and the Petrograd Soviet. The Bolsheviks' propaganda campaign was winning over a substantial number of people who, understandably, thought that the slogan 'Peace, Land and Bread' was a good maxim by which to live (though the Soviets never quite got the knack of that last part). Tensions were high; Lenin thought that it was now the time for a Soviet coup. But a series of violent mass demonstrations in July, inspired by the Bolsheviks but in the end not fully backed by them, was quelled. Lenin fled to Finland, and Alexandr Kerensky, a moderate Social Revolutionary, became prime minister.

In September, the Russian military Chief-of-Staff, General Kornilov, sent cavalry to Petrograd to crush the soviets. Kerensky's government turned to the left for support against this insubordination, even courting the Bolsheviks, and the counter-revolution

Reburying the Past

On 17 July 1998, in a controversial ceremony snubbed by both the Church and the State, the remains of Tsar Nicholas II, his wife and three of his five children were buried in the Romanov family crypt at the SS Peter & Paul Cathedral within the fortress of the same name. The ceremony was controversial for many reasons – political, religious, scientific, and financial.

In the beginning, over 200 royals, the head of the Russian Orthodox Church and President Boris Yeltsin were scheduled to attend. Yeltsin did attend (after repeatedly threatening not to do so), along with St Petersburg's Governor (mayor), but the US and Swiss ambassadors skipped the ceremony altogether – as did the head of the Church and prominent surviving members of the Romanov family.

At the heart of the discord are the remains themselves, because the story of the execution, as told and retold by Soviet historians and experts, remains murky.

After the execution of the Romanovs in Yekaterinburg (Western Siberia) in July 1918, by a firing squad estimated at 11 men, the bodies were allegedly dropped down a mine shaft. An attempt was made to destroy the bodies and the shaft by hand grenades. Later the story emerged that, after the mine shaft had failed to collapse, the bodies had been dragged out, sprinkled haphazardly with acid and buried in a swamp. The lorry carrying their bodies had become bogged in the swamp and Yakov Sverdlov, the henchman in charge of the operation, said, 'Ahh the heck with it, let's just bury them here'. During the Soviet era, the town of Yekaterinburg was renamed Sverdlovsk in a bow to the death squad henchman's cunning

The Ipatiev House on Voznesensky prospekt, in which the Romanovs had been held and killed, was destroyed in 1977 by the then head of the Sverdlovsk Communist Party, Boris Yeltsin, on, he says, orders from the Politburo.

But the mystery of the whereabouts of the Romanov remains still excited archaeologists and, in 1991, a team opened a shallow pit near the now re-named Yekaterinburg and found the remains of nine bodies. These were tentatively identified as Nicholas II, Tsarina Alexandra, three of their four daughters, the royal doctor and three servants.

In 1993 a commission was established to identify the remains. With the help of DNA taken from other family members, the remains were identified in 1995 as almost certainly those of the Romanov family. The findings are, however, still in dispute. The Russian Orthodox Church has never fully believed the story. The Russian government, while stating that the remains are those of the Romanovs 'beyond any reasonable doubt', is simultaneously sanctioning and distancing itself from the burial. Russian citizens feel, understandably, that Soviet-era handling of the situation renders all evidence suspect.

According to the *St Petersburg Times*, Romanov descendant Grand Duchess Leonida Georgyevna, speaking from her home (in Paris, no less), stated the US$833,000 spent by the city (in a time of economic desperation) was a mere bag of shells or, as she put it, 'not ... organised in a way that befits an emperor'.

And not to be left out, some ultra-right wing Russian Orthodox idiots claim the findings do nothing to dissuade them from believing that the assassination was a ritualistic slaying carried out by Jews. The Russian Orthodox Church – and the Russian government itself – denies this.

Even the Church's role in the burial smacked of cautious participation: contrary to Orthodox tenets, the Romanovs' names were not spoken as the coffins were lowered into the vault.

After the brouhaha of the ceremony, St Petersburg is left with a partial closure to the years of Russian imperial rule from the city on the Neva. Maybe.

was defeated. After this, public opinion massively favoured the Bolsheviks, who quickly took control of the Petrograd Soviet (chaired by Trotsky, who had joined them) and, by extension, all the soviets in the land. Lenin (you'll remember he had been cowering in Finland through all this) decided it was time to seize power and returned from Finland in October.

The actual 'Great October Soviet etc etc' revolution came after Bolsheviks occupied key positions in Petrograd on 24 October. Next day, the All-Russian Congress of Soviets, meeting in the Smolny, appointed a Bolshevik government. That night, after some exchanges of gunfire and a blank shot fired from the cruiser *Aurora* on the Neva (which served to show the navy's allegiance to the uprising), the Provisional Government in the Winter Palace surrendered to the Bolsheviks.

Armistice was signed with the Germans in December 1917, followed by the Treaty of Brest-Litovsk in March 1918 that surrendered Poland, the Baltic provinces, Ukraine, Finland and Transcaucasia to the Germans. This negotiation for a separate peace with Germany enraged (but probably didn't shock) the Allied forces, who would later back anti-Bolshevik fighters in a nose-thumbing effort to punish the revolutionaries for taking their ball and going home. Germany, with its eastern boundaries out of harm's way, could turn its attentions towards Western European annoyances (not that it ended up helping much).

The Civil War

There was wide dissent after the revolution, and a number of political parties sprang up almost immediately to challenge the Bolsheviks' power. And the Bolsheviks found themselves the proud new owners of all the same problems that had plagued governments before them. The power struggle began peacefully in the November elections for the Constituent Assembly; the Socialist Revolutionaries won a sweeping victory, only to have the assembly shut down by a very mad Vlad. But before long, a multi-

sided civil war would erupt. Trotsky founded the Red Army in January 1918 and the Cheka, Russia's secret police force designed to fight opposition, was established.

The new government operated from the Smolny until March 1918, when it moved to Moscow, fearing attacks on Petrograd from within and without. Civil war raged until 1921, by which time the Communist Party had firmly established one-party rule thanks to the Red Army and the Cheka, which continued to eliminate opponents. Some escaped, joining an estimated 1.5 million citizens in exile.

The privations of the civil war caused Petrograd's population to drop to about 700,000, and in 1921 strikes in the city and a revolt by the sailors of nearby Kronstadt helped bring about Lenin's more liberal New Economic Policy (NEP).

Petrograd was renamed Leningrad after Lenin's death in 1924. It was a hub of Stalin's 1930s industrialisation program and by 1939 had a population of 3.1 million people and produced 11% of Soviet industrial output. But Stalin (probably rightly) feared the city as a rival power base and the 1934 assassination of the local Communist chief Sergey Kirov at Smolny was the start of Stalin's 1930s Party purge.

WWII

When the Germans attacked the USSR in June 1941, officially beginning what the Russians refer to as the Great Patriotic War, it took them only 2½ months to reach Leningrad. Hitler hated the place as the birthplace of Bolshevism, and he swore to wipe it from the face of the earth – but vowed to punish the city by slowly starving it to death as opposed to bombing it into oblivion. Nazi troops besieged Leningrad from 8 September 1941 until 27 January 1944. Over two million people (and three-quarters of the industrial plant) had been evacuated. Nevertheless, between 500,000 and a million people died from shelling, starvation and disease in what's called the '900 Days' (actually 872). By comparison, the US and the UK suffered about 700,000 combined deaths in all of WWII.

During the siege, Leningraders were forced to eat cats or rats and when none of these were left they ate glue off the back of wallpaper. Thousands of people dropped dead from hunger or the cold. The city was saved from an even worse fate, however, by the winter 'Road of Life' across frozen Lake Ladoga to the north-east, a thin supply line which remained in Soviet hands. The route across the lake was enormously dangerous, and because the lake wasn't entirely frozen, the city's potential saviours were forced to carry supplies in sub-zero temperatures while wading through the icy water.

The siege showed Leningraders at their toughest. Though some reports of cannibalism circulate, the populace is better remembered for its stubborn refusal to die or even to give up hope. One of the most famous examples was an evening concert of Shostakovich's 7th Symphony by the Leningrad Philharmonic which continued through a shelling attack.

Those who survived the siege were granted (and retain to this day) a hero's status and privileges, including access to special ticket queues and free public transport. Fresh flowers still adorn both the mass graves at Piskaryovka Cemetery, where a majority of the siege's dead were buried, and you can still see a warning at Nevsky prospekt 14 advising pedestrians that the north side of the street is more dangerous during artillery bombardment. (See the Things to See & Do chapter for more information on both of these.)

Finland Finland got a very shabby deal out of WWII. Invaded and conquered by the Soviets in 1939-40, and again in 1944, she was forced to give up almost 15% of her territory in the Karelia region and, to add insult to injury, pay the Soviets war reparations of over US$200 million. Over 400,000 Finns were displaced by the Soviet takeover of Karelia.

The Postwar Period

After the war, Leningrad was reconstructed and reborn, though it took until 1960 for the population to exceed pre-war levels. The centre and most of the inner surrounding areas have been reconstructed, though the outlying areas (as is the case practically everywhere in Russia) are lined with horrific, cookie-cutter cities of prefabricated apartment blocks that go on forever. Throughout the Khrushchev and Brezhnev years (when you could 'still get bread in the shops'), Leningrad confined its revolutionary activities to the worlds of arts, letters and music, at which it excelled: it was indisputably the Soviet Union's cultural and artistic centre. Many of the period's more innovative artistic contributions, such as rock music, came to the Soviet world via Leningrad.

The 1980s & Gorbachev

After Brezhnev's death in 1982 (it was only noticed in 1984), he was replaced by former KGB director Yuri Andropov, who shortly thereafter also dropped dead. The Supreme Soviet (still staffed by many hard-line Brezhnev supporters) then appointed Constantin Chernyenko, who after just 13 months in office dropped dead.

Seeing the need for some new, or at least circulating, blood, Mikhail Sergeyevich Gorbachev was installed in 1985 amid much unintentionally ironic talk of 'getting things moving again'.

Gorbachev launched an immediate turnover in the politburo, the bureaucracy and the military, replacing many of the Brezhnevite 'old guard' with his own, predominantly younger supporters. He clamped down on alcohol sales in an attempt to address alcoholism, a problem that was costing the Russian economy dearly. He also attempted to accelerate the economy and, most importantly, he announced a policy of *glasnost* (openness). The hope was that he could spur the economy by encouraging some management initiative, rewarding efficiency and allowing bad practices to be criticised.

Gorby, as he came to be known in the American and British tabloid press, stunned the world by adopting an extremely conciliatory attitude towards the West, and in his first summit meeting with US President Ronald Reagan in 1985, Gorbachev unilaterally suggested a 50% cut in long-range nuclear weapons. By 1987 the two superpowers had co-operatively agreed to remove all medium-range nuclear missiles from Europe; other significant cuts in arms and troop numbers followed. The 'new thinking' put an end to the Soviet Union's 'Vietnam', the unpopular Afghanistan war. Relations with China improved as well; in 1989 Gorbachev went to Beijing for the first Sino-Soviet summit in 30 years.

Chernobyl & Perestroika

The shock of the Chernobyl nuclear disaster in April 1986 fuelled the drive towards political restructure. Gorbachev announced that there would be greater openness in reporting things like disasters. It had taken a very un-glastnost-like 18 days to admit the (underplayed) extent of the Chernobyl disaster to the West, and even longer to inform the other socialist countries in the Warsaw Pact – and that was after prodding from Scandinavian and European observers who noted huge levels of radiation emanating from the region. It is worth noting that a now unclassified KGB document, commissioned and signed by Yuri Andropov, predicted the disaster on 21 February 1979, more than seven years before it occurred.

Gorbachev's anti-alcohol campaign brought him nothing but unpopularity and caused huge growth in illegal distilling. Before long it was abandoned. But above all it was becoming clear that no leader who relied on the Party could survive as a reformer. *Perestroika*, or 'restructuring', became the new cry. This meant limited private enterprise and private property, not unlike Lenin's New Economic Policy, and further efforts to push for grass-roots decision making, away from the central bureaucracy. New laws were enacted in both these fields in 1988.

The 'Sinatra Doctrine'

The forces unleashed by Gorbachev's laudable reforms precipitated the fall of the Soviet Union. The reduced threat of repression spurred a growing clamour for independence: first in the Soviet satellite states of Eastern Europe, followed by the Baltic republics, then in Moldavia, then in the Transcaucasian republics. The Eastern European countries threw off their puppet Soviet regimes one by one in the 'domino' autumn of 1989. The Berlin Wall fell on 9 November, sparking an international market for chunks of asbestos-laden cement. The Brezhnev Doctrine, Gorbachev's spokesperson said, had given way to the 'Sinatra Doctrine': let them do it their way. Over the next two years, the Soviet Union's leaders were engaged in maintaining control of Soviet republics and borders, sometimes through the use of the army, but they were never able to close the floodgates.

In what was a minor annoyance to Party leaders at the time, residents of the city of Leningrad voted to rename the city St Petersburg in a June 1991 referendum. They passed the referendum (though it's interesting that the region around the city refused to join in the fun and to this day calls itself the Leningradsky oblast), but the measure was stopped by Gorbachev and only ratified after the events of August 1991. In presidential elections, also held in June 1991, Boris Yeltsin won the title of President of the Russian Republic by a good majority.

1991 Coup

On 19 August 1991, a group of hardline communists staged what was perhaps the most inept coup of the 20th century. While Gorbachev was on holiday at his Crimean *dacha*, it was announced in Moscow that a 'state of emergency' was in effect; that Gorbachev was feeling quite poorly and would be unable to continue as leader. A self-appointed Committee of the State Emergency announced that it was in power.

Tanks and armed soldiers appeared on the streets of Moscow and Boris Yeltsin joined a group of protesters at the Russian Parliament's headquarters, the White House. When tanks approached, Yeltsin, in full view of CNN and other television cameras, leapt aboard one and implored the tank crew to use their heads and hold their fire. The crowds of protesters grew and grew and the disorganised plotters gradually fell apart, drank a lot of vodka, lost control and eventually gave up.

Showing an astounding ignorance of coup etiquette, the plotters neglected to turn off several avenues of communication with the West. From the 'what on earth were they thinking' department: Western news cameras and reporters were allowed to report from Moscow almost unhindered and cellular telecommunications and electronic mail were left intact, while an order from the government early in the coup placed a ban on, among other and of all things, home video recorders.

When Leningrad residents turned on their televisions and radios and saw and heard *Swan Lake* they took to the streets in protest. (For some reason *Swan Lake* is the program of choice during governmental upheaval in Russia.) Anatoly Sobchak, a reformer who had been elected in 1989 to the St Petersburg city council and became mayor in 1990, achieved a new height in obfuscatory oratory when he stormed into the regional military headquarters and talked the soldiers out of obeying their Moscow-issued orders to arrest him.

As hundreds of thousands of Leningrad protesters filled Palace Square, Sobchak appeared on local television denouncing the coup and asking local residents to do the same. Fearful but determined residents spent a jittery evening awaiting the tanks that Moscow had threatened to send in, but they never appeared.

After the Coup

A rather sheepish but healthy-looking Gorbachev returned to Moscow and announced that he was back in power. Yeltsin had been so public a rallying figure that it would have been foolish in the extreme to try and deny his importance, which is precisely what Gorbachev did by acting as if all was fine and everyone could go home now. Soon after, Yeltsin appeared on television proclaiming the Communist Party an illegal organisation, and what fragile threads remained of a Soviet Union were ripped apart. On 25 December 1991, Gorbachev resigned and the Soviet Union was officially pronounced dead. Next day, the Russian Federation's flag of red, white and blue flew over the Kremlin.

The 1990s

St Petersburg and Moscow immediately set about attracting foreign business. Unfortunately, the 74 years of Soviet rule had created a deeply entrenched bureaucracy that believed firmly that the way to attract foreigners was to intimidate and humiliate them, change regulations regularly, and to increase taxes, in some cases over 100%, in an effort to reach prosperity through taxation. The foreigners, in search of quick profits, proved them right and came in droves.

But hard-liners in the Russian Parliament were regularly wrangling with President Yeltsin, whose hard-drinking exploits and unpredictable behaviour had begun to cost him some of his popularity. In elections in the early 1990s, Communists and nationalists gained political power. By 1993, house speaker Ruslan Khasbulatov led a movement which eventually declared Yeltsin fired. Yeltsin, demonstrating that the military was on his side, fired right back at Congress, with tanks: the Russian White House was shelled mercilessly on 4 October, effectively securing Yeltsin's power.

Meanwhile, St Petersburg got rich. Plans for making it a tax-free port went the way of the dodo, but foreign business in the city is booming. Corny and over-used as the term may be, St Petersburg has in fact re-established itself as Russia's window on the West.

In 1994, the Goodwill Games were (as perhaps all Goodwill Games are) a disappointment in terms of turnout, but the preparations for them were a huge shot in the arm for the city, which invested millions of dollars in repairs and generally sprucing up the place. Roads were patched, stadiums renovated, buildings painted, parks manicured and replanted, and English-language signs began sprouting up everywhere.

Since the last edition of this book, the streets have become safer, more colourful and far, far prettier. Today, St Petersburg is truly an international city, with fine restaurants, chic clubs and every consumer product you could want. For the first time in almost a century, St Petersburg residents live in a city that's both stunningly beautiful *and* well stocked.

With all Moscow's in-fighting, dirty politics and entrenched lobbyist sub-culture, more than a few people are thinking that maybe Peter the Great had the right idea in moving a tumultuous country's capital northward, to the city on the Neva.

GEOGRAPHY

St Petersburg straddles the Neva River delta and is made up of almost 50 islands, connected by over 310 bridges. Branches of the Neva River divide the city's busiest areas – Petrograd Side, Vasilevsky Side, Vyborg Side and the historical heart. The city's main boulevard, Nevsky prospekt, runs directly through the historical heart of the city and connects the city's busiest train station, Moscow Station, with the Hermitage (2km west) and the Alexandr Nevsky Monastery (1km east). See the Orientation section in the Facts for the Visitor chapter for a complete rundown.

CLIMATE

St Petersburg's climate is maritime and much milder than its extreme northern latitude would suggest. January temperatures average –8°C ; a really cold day will get down to –15°C. It's a windy city though and in some areas (near the Pribaltiyskaya Hotel springs to mind) the wind chill is quite fierce, so bring a good warm hat and scarf.

Summer is cool and takes a while to get going: snow in late April is not uncommon

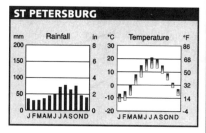

and the warm weather doesn't really start until the period between June and August, when temperatures usually reach 20°C. Winter usually sees the Neva freeze over, though the past few years have been unusually mild. Despite its Baltic location and profusion of canals, rivers and waterways, humidity is not a problem.

The city's northern latitude means long days in summer and long nights in winter. During the summer White Nights festival, around the time of the summer solstice, night is reduced to a brief dimming of the lights at around 1 am, only to turn to dawn a couple of hours later. And in winter the city seems to be in constant dusk.

ECOLOGY & ENVIRONMENT
Pollution

Air Thanks to St Petersburg's wide streets and prevalent winds, the place is relatively smog-free, but that's not for lack of trying. Cars roam free without the encumbrance of catalytic converters or pollution control devices and trucks and buses emit unbelievable clouds of soot-filled exhaust – and that's only part of the story. St Petersburg's industrial plant is a major air and water polluter and the situation is not getting any better, despite attempts at clean-up by Scandinavian and other Western observers and firms. But at the end of the day, the air quality here is about on a par with that of other developing cities.

Radiation St Petersburg's semi-infamous Sosnovy Bor nuclear power plant, about 70km west of the city, threatened to blow its stack in 1992 (it didn't). It's an RBMK-style reactor, the same model as the doomed Chernobyl reactor, except this one's older. It's also highly maintained and continually prodded by foreign experts (it's close enough to Scandinavian countries to make them take active interest). Radiation levels in the city are said to be consistent with the international norms.

GOVERNMENT & POLITICS

The city is managed by Governor Vladimir Anatolovich Yakovlev, whose first act after defeating Mayor Anatoly Sobchak in June 1996 was to change the title from mayor to governor. Not to be outdone in the grandiosity department, Sobchak, who calmed the crowds and essentially talked the army out of imposing martial law on St Petersburg during the 1991 coup, compared himself to Winston Churchill *and* Jesus Christ in his farewell press conference. Oh yeah, he said Yakovlev, his former lieutenant, was a 'Judas'.

Sobchak was accused of unbelievable levels of corruption and on 7 November 1996 – the 80th anniversary of the date Provisional Government chief Alexandr Kerensky fled the Bolsheviks – he fled the country for what amounted to a grand European tour.

Yakovlev's entire administration, it seems, is dedicated to a power struggle with the 50-man Legislative Assembly over a City Charter that would grant more power to, conveniently, the Legislative Assembly. Yakovlev is against this, along with the sweeping (and actually rather sensible) governmental reforms the charter proposes. The political stalemate surrounding this issue rages on as I write.

ECONOMY

The city and regional economies are doing far better than those in the rest of the country; St Petersburg's GDP fell only 0.3% in 1997 and growth was expected in 1998. Foreign investment in St Petersburg was expected to grow 20% from its 1997 levels of US$200 million.

The city's economy is undergoing rapid change as state industries are privatised. Though the city's privatisation director Mikhail Manevich was assassinated on the corner of ulitsa Rubinshteyna and Nevsky prospekt by a sniper one sunny morning in 1997, the level of privatisation of formerly state-run companies is well over 90%. The city is a high-tech centre – one in 10 Russian scientists work here – and is the country's largest commercial seaport.

The region's natural resources include timber and bauxite, an element used in aluminium production.

Despite the city government's unbelievably callous attitude towards it, tourism is a huge breadwinner, with well over a million tourists traipsing through every year. And there's *still* not a city-run tourist information office.

Almost every major multinational corporation has a presence in town. For more information, contact the St Petersburg International Business Association on ☎ 325 90 91 (spiba@online.ru).

POPULATION & PEOPLE

The number of residents in the city of St Petersburg in 1995 was estimated to be 4,829,000, or just over 5.5 million including the outer suburbs. As in much of the Russian Federation, the make-up of St Petersburg's population is almost entirely composed of ethnic Russians. Minorities include Jews (still considered to be a nationality in Russia), Ukrainians, Belarusians and other nationalities from within the former Soviet Union. The expatriate community of Western businesspeople and students is continually growing; in 1998 there were an estimated 15,000 such residents, among them almost 5000 Americans and a greater number of Germans. There are also significant numbers of students from African nations studying in the city.

ARTS
Architecture

Unrestricted by winding old streets or buildings from the past, the early European and European-trained designers of St Petersburg created a unique waterside city of straight avenues, wide plazas and grand edifices in the baroque, rococo and classical styles of the 18th and early 19th centuries.

Few major buildings had reached their final form by the time of Peter the Great's death in 1725, though his version of Petergof Palace was complete and the SS Peter & Paul Cathedral and the Twelve Colleges were well under way. Empress Elizabeth (1741-61) commissioned the first grand wave of buildings from Bartolomeo Rastrelli, an Italian who engraved her love of fun on the city's profile. His inspired creations, like the Winter Palace, Smolny Cathedral and the Great Palace at Pushkin, playful in their rococo detail yet majestic in form, mirrored the empress's glittering court, which drew European diplomats, artists and travellers.

Catherine the Great and Alexander I launched hosts of projects to make St Petersburg Europe's most imposing capital, employing an international array of designers to beat the West at its own architectural games. Both monarchs rode the new wave of classical taste, whose increasing severity can be traced through some of their chief buildings. The Academy of Arts by JBM Vallin de la Mothe (France), Pavlovsk Palace by Charles Cameron (England) and the Hermitage Theatre by Giacomo Quarenghi (Italy) display the simpler, earlier classicism of Catherine's reign. Quarenghi's Smolny Institute for Alexander was halfway towards the later, heavier works of another Italian, Carlo Rossi, who created the Mikhail Palace (now the Russian Museum), the General Staff building and ploshchad (square) Ostrovskogo.

The more grandiose branch of later classicism known as Russian Empire style is typified by the Kazan Cathedral and the Admiralty, both built by Russian designers for Alexander. The huge-domed St Isaac's Cathedral by Frenchman Ricard de Montferrand, mostly built under the reign of Nicholas I (1825-55), was the city's last major classical building.

Painting & Sculpture

St Petersburg was the birthplace of Russian futurism and neo-primitivism, and today the city is leading the Russian art scene with neo-academism, the most important Russian artistic movement of the late 20th century. The Russian Museum and Moscow's famous Tretyakov Gallery have the country's chief collections of Russian art, while the Hermitage has world-famous Western European collections. All major museums in St Petersburg have frequent temporary exhibitions, from within Russia and from overseas.

Peredvizhniki In the 18th century, when Peter the Great encouraged Western trends in Russian art, Dmitry Levitsky's portraits were outstanding. The major artistic force of the 19th century was the Peredvizhniki (Wanderers) movement, which saw art as a force for national awareness and social change. Its members included Vasily Surikov, who painted vivid Russian historical scenes, Nikolay Ge (biblical and historical scenes), and Ilya Repin, perhaps the best loved of all Russian artists, whose works ranged from social criticism *(Barge Haulers on the Volga)* through history *(Zaporozhie Cossacks Writing a Letter to the Turkish Sultan)* to portraits of the famous.

Isaak Levitan, who revealed the beauty of the Russian landscape, was one of many others associated with the Peredvizhniki. The end-of-century genius Mikhail Vrubel, inspired by sparkling Byzantine and Venetian mosaics, showed early traces of Western influence.

Futurism Around the turn of the 20th century the Mir Iskusstva (World of Art) movement in St Petersburg, led by Alexandr Benois and Sergey Diaghilev under the motto 'art pure and unfettered', opened Russia up to Western innovations like Impressionism, Art Nouveau and Symbolism. From about 1905 Russian art became a maelstrom of groups, styles and -isms as it absorbed decades of European change in a few years before giving birth to its own avant-garde futurist movements, which in turn helped Western art go head over heels.

Natalya Goncharova and Mikhail Larionov were at the centre of the Knave of Diamonds group (a Cézanne-influenced group with which Vasily Kandinsky was associated) before developing neo-primitivism, based on popular arts and primitive icons.

In 1915 Kazimir Malevich announced the arrival of suprematism, declaring that his utterly abstract geometrical shapes, with the black square representing the ultimate 'zero form', finally freed art from having to depict the material world and made it a doorway to higher realities. Another famed futurist, who managed to escape subordinate -isms, was acclaimed poet Vladimir Mayakovsky.

The Soviet Era Futurists enthusiastically supplied the revolution with posters, banners and education. They now had a chance to act on their theories of how art shapes society. But at the end of the 1920s, formalist (abstract) art fell out of favour. The Party wanted Socialist Realism. Striving workers, heroic soldiers and inspiring leaders took over; Malevich ended up painting penetrating portraits and doing designs for Red Square parades; Mayakovsky committed suicide.

After Stalin, an avant-garde 'conceptualist' underground was allowed to surface. Ilya Kabakov painted, or sometimes just arranged, the debris of everyday life to show the gap between the promises and realities of Soviet existence. Erik Bulatov's 'Sotsart' pointed to the devaluation of language by ironically reproducing Soviet slogans or depicting words disappearing over the horizon. In 1962 the authorities set up a show of such 'unofficial' art at the Moscow Manezh; Khrushchev called it 'dog shit' and sent it back underground.

Eventually a thaw set in and the avant-garde became international big business. In 1988, *A Fundamental Lexicon* by Grisha Bruskin, a multi-panelled iconostasis-like work satirising both Soviet propaganda and

the Church, sold for £242,000 at a Sotheby's sale in Moscow.

Neo-Academism The most exciting news in Russian art since the turn of the century is undoubtedly neo-academism, founded by St Petersburg artist Timur Novikov in the early 1990s as an antidote to 'the barbarism of modernism'. Novikov has been a leader of the St Petersburg and Russian arts scenes for over a decade. In 1982 his theory of 'Zero Object' acted as one of the foundations of Russian conceptual art, and his work with some of Russia's best artists and musicians in the 1980s and 90s culminated in his Museum of the New Academy of Fine Arts (☎ 315 28 32), ulitsa Pushkinskaya 10, established in 1993. Neo-academic artists, including co-founder Bella Matveeva, digital artist Olga Tobreluts and Oleg Maslov and Viktor Kuznetzov, pride themselves on – and even advertise – their propensity towards drugs, tobacco and alcohol while turning out works that pay homage to classicism though maintaining a thoroughly modern twist. Their works have been shown throughout the world.

Icons Icons – images intended to aid the veneration of the holy subjects they depict, and sometimes believed to be able to grant luck, wishes or even miracles – were the key art form up to the time of Peter the Great, though only in the 20th century did they really come to be seen as 'works of art'. They're most commonly found on the iconostasis of a church, the large screen in front of the east end sanctuary.

Literature

St Petersburg's status as artistic and cultural centre of Russia has much to do with the writers and poets associated with the city. The list is a veritable *Who's Who* of literary figures: Pushkin, Dostoevsky, Lermontov (whose *Death of a Poet* accused the government of plotting Pushkin's death), Blok, Akhmatova ...

Alexandr Pushkin, Russia's best-loved poet, was born in 1799. After his graduation in 1817, Pushkin started living it up in St Petersburg and committed many of his liberal ideas to paper. These papers eventually made their way to the police, who were not amused; Pushkin was exiled from St Petersburg in 1820, which probably is the only reason he wasn't standing with the Decembrists in 1825 (he said so himself, later, to Nicholas I).

In the 1830s Pushkin had lost popularity with the general Russian reading public and had married Natalya Goncharova with whom, some say, he was obsessed. He set up *The Contemporary*, a literary magazine, which was doomed to failure from the start despite Pushkin's tireless efforts to see it through. On 27 January 1837, Pushkin challenged Baron Georges D'Anths, a French nobleman who had been openly courting Natalya, to a duel. Pushkin was shot and died two days later. His last place of residence is now a museum (see the Things to See & Do chapter).

Pushkin's most famous work, published posthumously in 1841, is *The Bronze Horseman*, depicting the great flood of 1824. In it, the hopes and wishes of the people – represented here by the lowly clerk Yevgeni, who has lost his beloved in the flood – take on the conquering, empire-building spirit of Peter the Great, represented by the animation of the bronze statue of him installed by Catherine the Great.

Fyodor Dostoevsky's (1821-81) descriptions of St Petersburg's slums are legendary, and he was the first major writer to show fully the seedy, dangerous and filthy side of life in the grand Russian capital. For a walk through his *Crime and Punishment* and information on his last residence, now a museum, see the Things to See & Do chapter.

Alexandr Blok (1880-1921) took over where Dostoevsky left off, writing of prostitutes, drunks, Gypsies and other assorted 'rabble'. Blok's sympathies with the revolutions of 1905 and 1917 were held up by the Bolsheviks – as was the work of Mayakovsky – as an example of an established writer who had seen the light; Blok's *The Twelve*, published in 1918, is pretty much a love-letter to Lenin. The flat where Blok spent the last eight years of his life is now a museum (see the section on Teatralnaya ploshchad in the Things to See & Do chapter).

No literary figure, though, is as inextricably linked to the fate of St Petersburg-Petrograd-Leningrad as Anna Akhmatova (1889-1966), the long-suffering poet whose work contains bittersweet depictions of the city she so loved. Akhmatova's life was filled with sorrow and loss – her family was imprisoned and killed, her friends exiled, tortured and arrested, her colleagues were constantly hounded – but she refused to leave her beloved city, except for brief periods, and died there in 1966. Her work depicts the city with both realism and monumentalism, painted with Russian as well as personal history. While the characterisation of her (by the Communist Party in the 1940s) as a mixture of 'a nun and a whore' may not have been fair, her love for her city was unconditional but unblinking: 'The capital on the Neva, Having forgotten its greatness, Like a drunken whore, Did not know who was taking her.'

Akhmatova's flat is now a quiet little museum where you can see English translations of her work and hear recordings of her voice. There's a second, private Akhmatova museum in a flat in Pushkin (see South of the Summer Garden in the Things to See & Do chapter and the Pushkin section in the Excursions chapter).

Theatre

Theatre in Russia has its roots in religious battles between Western Christian and Russian Orthodox churches, which were vying for members as early as the 16th century. As Jesuits used dramatic scenes to propagandise and spread their message, the Russian Orthodox Church found it had to do likewise to stop an exodus to Catholicism. Over the next few centuries, drama was almost exclusively used in a similar fashion by schools and the Church, until

FACTS ABOUT ST PETERSBURG

tsars and nobility began importing tragedy and comedy from the West.

The galvanising force in Russian theatre was the defeat of Napoleon in 1812, after which nationalistic sentiment led writers to shun French as the language of drama in favour of Russian. There was also a return to Russian values in theatre which led to the ousting of French theatre companies from the country. Vaudeville – biting, satirical one-act comedies that had been created on the streets of Paris and which poked fun at the rich and powerful – had found its way into Russia and the practice of using theatre to put forth the party or church line on social issues came under attack by playwrights like Pushkin and Lermontov. Other writers, such as Gogol, Griboedov and Ostrovsky, wrote plays that attacked not just the aristocracy but the bourgeoisie as well.

Anton Chekhov's earlier one-act works were true to vaudeville, but his full-length plays, especially *Uncle Vanya* and *The Seagull*, are his legacy – though they took a while to catch on: the opening night of *The Seagull* at the Alexandrinsky Theatre was a disaster. Towards the end of the 19th century, Maxim Gorky's *The Stormy Petrel*, which raised workers to a level superior to that of the intellectual, earned him reverence by the Soviets as the initiator of Socialist Realism.

Nicholas I had set up an incredibly complex system to manage theatre, going so far as to put the secret police in charge of repertory (and he himself often acted as casting director) in order to protect the 'message' being put forth through drama – and Soviets always were good at picking up on efficient ways of managing information. The Soviet period saw drama used almost exclusively as a propaganda tool and when foreign plays were performed it was usually for a reason – hence the popularity in Russia of *Death of a Salesman*, which showed just what Western (US) greed and decadence will lead to.

Cinema

While producing greats like Sergey Eisenstein (*The Battleship Potyomkin*) and Andrey Tarkovsky (*Solaris*, *Andrey Rublev*), the Soviet film industry struggled to find a role for itself from the moment it was nationalised in August 1919 until the collapse of the Soviet Union. The battle between ideology and box-office success, between art and the need to provide inexpensive entertainment for the seething masses, resulted in a system that alternately produced touching human drama, blatant propaganda and sensationalist crap.

Some Soviet film makers, limited in their scope, range and budget by the powers that were, managed to create memorable films, pushing – often at great personal risk – the limits of the censorship to which they were subjected. Soviet comedies were amusing but not outstanding and, let's face it, a chase scene featuring two Ladas doesn't exactly hold up against the offerings of the West – even against stinkers like *To Live and Die in LA*.

The themes of many of the Soviet Union's films in the 1960s and 70s were less overtly political than one would imagine – they weren't about a bunch of happy workers harvesting wheat. Rather this was a time of cautious introspection. And, of course, cheap thrills: along with the favourite topics of the period like WWII, there was a lot of CIA/KGB intrigue ('Freeze, KGB!!') and 'hit-em-over-the-head' propaganda such as *The Nineteenth Committee*, which forecast the imminent use of bacteriological weapons by the West against the USSR.

With the fall of the Soviet Union the Russian film-making infrastructure was sent into a tailspin. A brain drain is in progress, with many talented Russians heading to more artistically generous countries like Italy, Norway, Sweden and the UK. Russian production is down from its height of over 400 films in 1991, to fewer than 100 in 1997 – many of which have never seen the light of a projector.

Many of the big-budget films in production today are being made with foreign money and, usually, lots of foreign intervention too. Generally speaking, many productions of note today consist of

Russian story, director, tech crew and cast ... and English, French or Italian producers.

The most notable Russian films to have emerged since the fall of the Soviet Union are Nikita Mikhalkov's *Burnt by the Sun*, which won the 1994 Academy Award for Best Foreign-Language Film, and *The Thief*, a 1997 entry. Both are set in Stalin-era Russia. *Burnt by the Sun* tells the story of Sergey Kotov, a war veteran living quietly in the Russian countryside until the appearance of his wife's former lover, now a member of the Secret Police. The main characters in *The Thief* are a starving single mother and her young son (representing the Russian people) who find refuge with a rogue army officer (representing Stalin). They are at first seduced, then shocked, then terrified by the soldier, whom they end up loathing.

There's no denying that at the end of the day, Russians would rather sit down and watch some good old Western-made schlock than any high-fallutin' Russian intellectual stuff. Necrophilia, sex, mysticism and violence fare far better, and make a lot more money, here. Yuri Gladilshchikov, writing in *Nezavisimaya Gazeta*, summed things up quite accurately: 'The most important of the arts for us continues to be movies ... bloody and immoral ones.'

Music

Classical The roots of Russian music lie in folk song and dance and Orthodox Church chants. Epic folk songs of Russia's peasantry, *byliny*, preserved folk culture and lore through celebration of particular events such as great battles or harvests. More formal music slowly reached acceptance in Russian society; first as a religious aid, then for military and other ceremonial use, and eventually for entertainment.

The defining period of Russian music was from the 1860s to 1900. As Russian composers (and painters and writers) struggled to find a national identity, several influential schools formed, from which some of Russia's most famous composers and finest music emerged. The Group of

Five – Mussorgsky, Rimsky-Korsakov, Borodin, Kui and Balakirev – believed that a radical departure was necessary, and they looked to byliny and folk music for themes. Their main opponent was the Russian Musical Society, and especially Anton Rubinshteyn, who felt that Russian classical music should be firmly based in the traditions of master composers like Schubert, Mendelssohn and Chopin.

The middle ground was, it seems, discovered by Pyotr Tchaikovsky (1840-93), a student of the St Petersburg Conservatory, who embraced Russian folklore and music as well as the disciplines of the Western European composers. Tchaikovsky is widely regarded as the father of Russian national composers.

Far from the middle ground was Dmitri Dmitrievich Shostakovich (1906-75), who wrote alternately brooding, bizarrely dissonant works, and accessible traditional classical works. His belief that music and

Mystery surrounded Tchaikovsky's death – it was rumoured that he committed suicide after his homosexuality was discovered.

ideology went hand in hand meant that his career would be alternately praised and condemned by the Soviet government; after official condemnation by Stalin, Shostakovich's 7th Symphony – the Leningrad – brought him honour and standing when it was performed by the Leningrad Philharmonic during the Siege of Leningrad. He was on the outer again in 1948 and then 'rehabilitated' after Stalin's death.

Opera When Peter the Great began throwing Western culture at his fledgling capital, the music of Western European composers was one of the chief weapons in his arsenal. He held weekly concerts of music by composers from the West – Vivaldi was a favourite. Catherine the Great further encouraged Western music and it gained popularity. St Petersburg was the birthplace of Russian opera when Mikhail Glinka's *A Life For The Tsar*, which merged traditional and Western influence, was performed on 9 December 1836. Russian opera borrowed heavily from other European operas, and many of the most popular works are translations. Opera continues to be one of St Petersburg's most popular entertainment forms and it's enjoying a surge in popularity thanks to a rejuvenation of the Kirov Opera Company at the Mariinsky Theatre (see the Entertainment chapter).

Rock Russian rock was born in the 1960s when the 'bourgeois' Beatles filtered through, despite official disapproval. Rock developed underground, starved of decent equipment and the chance to record or perform to big audiences, but it gathered a huge following among the disaffected, distrustful youth of the 1970s (the Soviet hippy era) and 1980s.

Bands in the 1970s started by imitating Western counterparts but eventually homegrown music emerged. Some artists, like Boris Grebenshikov and his band Akvarium (Aquarium), became household names but still needed other jobs to get by. Music was circulated by illegal tapes known as *magizdat*, passed from listener to listener;

concerts were held, if at all, in remote halls in city suburbs, and even to attend them could be risky.

Punk and heavy metal came into fashion in the early 1980s. Under glasnost, the authorities eventually allowed the true voices of youth to be heard, and the state record company, Melodia, started to produce albums by previously unacceptable groups. Rock flowered and New Wave music, fashionable from about the mid-1980s, appealed to a Russian taste for theatricality. Bands which started in the 1980s are still leaders in the field today, among them Akvarium; Va Bank from Moscow and DDT from St Petersburg, both punk-influenced; and Orkestr Populyarnaya Mekhanika (Popular Mechanics Orchestra), a St Petersburg 'performance rock' outfit.

Russian pop is as popular as ever. Top acts to look out for are Mumiy Troll, an Oasis-like acid-trip; the ever-popular Alla Pugachyova, a female solo singer who puts tons of energy into her shows, and Boyz-II-Men rip-offs like Ivanushki International.

Dance

First brought to Russia under Tsar Alexis Mikhailovich in the 17th century, Russian ballet evolved as an offshoot of French dance combined with Russian folk and peasant dance techniques. It stunned Western Europeans when it was first taken on tour in the 19th century.

The 'official' beginnings of Russian ballet date to 1738 and the establishment by French dance master Jean Baptiste Lande of a school of dance in the Winter Palace, the precursor to the famed Vaganova School of Choreography (see the Things to See & Do chapter). Catherine the Great created the Bolshoy Theatre to develop opera and ballet in 1765 and imported foreign composers and teachers.

Charles Louis Didelot (1767-1836) was a Swedish dancer and teacher who returned to Russia in 1816 (having spent 10 years here earlier) and revolutionised Russian ballet by cultivating an almost entirely Russian ensemble. But Marius Petipa (1819-1910) is considered to be the father of Russian ballet. The French dancer and choreographer acted first as principal dancer, then Premier Ballet Master of the Imperial Theatre. All told he produced more than 60 full ballets (including Tchaikovsky's *Sleeping Beauty* and *Swan Lake*).

At the turn of the 20th century, the heyday of Russian ballet, St Petersburg's Imperial School of Ballet rose to world prominence, cranking out superstar after superstar, including Vaslaw Nijinsky, Anna Pavlova and Olga Spessivtzeva – the *Ballets Russes* took Europe by storm. The stage décor was unlike anything seen before. Painted by artists (like Alexandr Benois) and not stagehands, it suspended disbelief and shattered the audience's sense of illusion.

Under the Soviets, ballet was treated as a natural resource – a nose-thumbing at the West. It enjoyed highly privileged status, which allowed schools like the Vaganova and companies like the Kirov to maintain a level of lavish production and no-expense-spared star-searches. And despite collapse of the economy and other hardships, and defections to the West (political and financial) by a number of stars, the Russian ballet and the Kirov company are still world renowned. In 1998 they broke their tradition of steadfast adherence to classical works and staged two works choreographed in the 1940s by French ballet master Roland Petit.

SOCIETY & CONDUCT

The key to harmonious interaction with Russians depends not just on you behaving inoffensively, but also in your reaction to what you may consider to be highly offensive behaviour. Blowing your top in reaction to a surly waiter, irascible ticket clerk or cheeky coat-check babushka is (a) unlikely to remedy the situation, (b) asking for further trouble and (c) offensive to those around you, who will look upon you as being 'uncultured'. Patience, here more than anywhere, is a virtue, and a smile goes

further than everything up to and perhaps including a revolver.

In Russian Orthodox religious services, hands in pockets attract frowns. Women visitors can often get away with not covering their heads, but miniskirts are most unwelcome and even trousers sometimes attract disapproval. Men in shorts are also frowned upon. Photography at services is generally not welcome, though you might get a yes if you ask. Always feel out the situation first, and ask if in doubt.

In everyday life, the role of men and women is still rather old-worldly by Western standards; men are expected to be gentlemanly by holding open doors, lighting cigarettes, pulling out chairs etc for women.

When visiting someone's house, always remove your shoes before entering – you'll be given slippers *(tapochki)* to wear inside.

Avoid nationalistic sentiment ('Boy, you Russians sure got whupped in the Cold War!') in conversation. Swearing is frowned upon and considered vulgar.

Superstition plays a large part in many customs, sometimes overtly (like never shaking hands across the threshold of a doorway) and sometimes covertly (like never shaking hands with gloves on). Big no-nos are returning home to get something you forgot, leaving empty bottles on the table during dinner parties and stepping on someone's foot without giving them the chance to do the same to you.

RELIGION
Russian Orthodox Church

After decades of closures and confiscation of property, and victimisation, deportation and execution of believers under the Soviet regime, the Russian Orthodox Church (Russkaya Pravoslavnaya Tserkov) is enjoying a big revival. By 1991 it already had an estimated 50 million members. Numbers have grown, thanks not only to the new religious freedom initiated by Mikhail Gorbachev and enshrined in Russia's 1993 constitution but also because of the growth of Russian nationalism. The Church is an intimate part of many Russians' notions of Russia and 'Russianness', despite recriminations over its infiltration by the KGB during the Soviet era – three metropolitans (senior bishops) were accused in 1992 of having been KGB agents.

History & Hierarchy Prince Vladimir of Kiev effectively founded the Russian Orthodox Church in 988 by adopting Christianity from Constantinople. The church's headquarters stayed in Kiev until 1300, when it moved north to Vladimir and then in the 1320s to Moscow.

Patriarch Alexy of Moscow & All Russia is head of the Church; Metropolitan (Senior Bishop) Vladimir is St Petersburg's spiritual leader and has a residence in the Alexandr Nevsky Lavra (monastery). The Russian Orthodox Church is one of the main fellowship of 15 autocephalous ('self-headed') orthodox churches, in which Constantinople is a kind of first among equals.

Beliefs & Practice Russian Orthodoxy is highly traditional and the atmosphere inside a church is formal and solemn. Priests dress imposingly, the smell of candles and incense permeates the air, old women bustle about sweeping and polishing. Churches have no seats, no music (only chanting), and no statues. They do, however, have many icons (see the earlier Arts section in this chapter) with people often praying – even kissing the ground – before them. Men bare their heads and women usually cover theirs.

As a rule, working churches are open to one and all but, as a visitor, take care not to disturb any devotions or offend sensibilities (see Society & Conduct).

The Virgin Mary (*Bogomater*, Mother of God) is greatly honoured. The language of the liturgy is 'Church Slavonic', the old Bulgarian dialect into which the Bible was first translated for Slavs. Easter (*Paskha*) is the focus of the Church year, with festive midnight services to launch Easter Day. Christmas (*Rozhdestvo*) falls on 7 January because the Church still uses the Julian calendar that the Soviet state abandoned in 1918.

In most churches, Divine Liturgy (*Bozhestvennaya Liturgia*), lasting about two hours, is at 8, 9 or 10 am Monday to Saturday, and usually at 7 and 10 am on Sunday and festival days. Most churches also hold services at 5 or 6 pm daily. Some of these include an akathistos (*akafist*), a series of chants to the Virgin or saints.

Church Names In Russian, *sobor* means cathedral; *tserkov* and *khram* mean church. Common church names include:

- Blagoveshchenskaya (Annunciation)
- Borisoglebskaya (SS Boris & Gleb)
- Nikolskaya (St Nicholas)
- Petropavlovskaya (SS Peter & Paul)
- Pokrovskaya (Intercession of the Virgin)
- Preobrazhenskaya (Transfiguration)
- Rizopolozhenskaya (Deposition of the Holy Robe)
- Rozhdestvenskaya (Nativity)
- Troitskaya (Trinity)
- Uspenskaya (Assumption or Dormition)
- Vladimirskaya (St Vladimir)
- Voskresenskaya (Resurrection)
- Voznesenskaya (Ascension)
- Znamenskaya (Holy Sign)

Old Believers The Russian Church was split in 1653 by the reforms of Patriarch Nikon, who thought it had departed from its roots. He insisted, among other things, that the translation of the Bible be altered to conform with the Greek original, and that the sign of the cross be made with three fingers, not two. Those who couldn't accept these changes became known as Old Believers (*Starovery*) and came in for persecution. Some fled to the Siberian forests or remote parts of Central Asia where one group which had never heard of Lenin, electricity or the revolution was found in the 1980s. Only in 1771-1827, 1905-18 and again recently have Old Believers had real freedom of worship. They probably number over a million but in 1917 there were as many as 20 million. Old Believers have two churches in St Petersburg, returned to them in 1988 (see Religious Services at the end of this section).

Other Christian Churches

Russia has small numbers of Roman Catholics and Lutheran and Baptist Protestants, mostly among the German and other non-Russian ethnic groups. Other groups such as the Mormons, Seventh Day Adventists and the Salvation Army are sending missionaries into the potentially fertile ground of a country where God officially didn't exist for 70 years.

Islam

Islam has, like Christianity, enjoyed growth since the mid-1980s. Though it has been some Muslim peoples – notably the Chechens and Tatars among Russian minorities – who have most resisted being brought within the Russian national fold since the fall of the Soviet Union in 1991, nationalism has played at least as big a part as religion in this. Militant Islam has as yet barely raised its head in Russia.

Islam in Russia is fairly secularised – eg women are not veiled, the Friday sabbath is not a commercial holiday. St Petersburg's working Sunni-Muslim mosque is closed to women and often to non-Muslim men, though men may occasionally be invited in.

Judaism

Many of Russia's 700,000 or so Jews have been assimilated into Russian culture and do not seriously practise Judaism. However there were approximately 30 synagogues in Russia by 1991. Jews have long been the target of prejudice and even pogroms – ethnic cleansing – in Russia. Since glasnost, hundreds of thousands of Jews have emigrated to Israel and other countries to escape the state-sponsored anti-Semitism that existed under the former government.

Buddhism

The members of St Petersburg's Buddhist *datsan* (monastery) belong to the Gelugpa or 'Yellow-Hat' sect of Tibetan Buddhism, whose spiritual leader is the Dalai Lama. Buddhism was tolerated by the Soviet state until Stalin nearly wiped it out in the 1930s.

Religious Services

There are a number of English and other Western-language services in town; check the *St Petersburg Times* for current information during your stay. Places of worship, and information on some services in English (E), German (G), Hebrew (H), Russian (R) and Latin (L), follow:

Anglican/Episcopalian Open Christianity Centre (☎ 277 87 50), Slavanskaya ulitsa 13; services Thursday, Saturday and Sunday (E)

Armenian Church of St Catherine (☎ 219 41 08), Nevsky prospekt 40/42

Buddhist Datsan (☎ 239 03 41), Primorsky prospekt 91, services daily (R)

Choral Synagogue (☎ 114 11 53), Lermontovsky prospekt 2; Shabbas services Friday at sundown, daily services at 9.30 am etc (H)

Church of Jesus Christ of Latter Day Saints (☎ 325 61 48), naberezhnaya reki Moyki 11; services daily (E, R)

Evangelical Lutheran Church (☎ 311 24 23), Nevsky prospekt 22 and St Anne's Church (Spartak Cinema), Saltikova-Shchedrina ulitsa 8; service at 10.30 am Sunday (G)

Mosque of the Congregation of Muslims (☎ 233 98 19), Kronverksky prospekt 7; services daily from 10 am to 7 pm (R, E)

Old Believers, Yunnatov ulitsa 32 (no telephone number), and Aleksandrovskoy Fermy prospekt 20 (☎ 262 25 87) (R)

Our Lady of Lourdes (Roman Catholic; ☎ 242 04 42), Kovensky pereulok 7 (near ulitsa Mayakovskaya); Sunday Mass 11.30 am (L, R), 1.30 pm (E), 5 pm (G)

Russian Orthodox services are available at several locations throughout the city. Check the *St Petersburg Times*, *Luchshee V Sankt Peterburge* or *The Traveller's Yellow Pages* for listings.

Facts for the Visitor

WARNING

Regulations and exchange rates change in any country, but due to the nature of Russian politics, the information contained in this chapter is subject to change at any second. At the time of writing, the Russian government was reeling from cabinet-level changes, high profile attacks from the national parliament and the Communist Party, and a currency crisis that saw the rouble lose 68.4% of its value against the US dollar (from 6.2 to 19 roubles to the US dollar) in just three months.

Anything major – for example, the death of a charismatic leader, organised worker uprisings or international pressures – could send the country and its markets into a tailspin. Despite almost a decade of laudable and successful commitment to sometimes painful reforms, Russian politics is still about as volatile as a nitroglycerin cocktail on a long-distance bus in Sumatra.

So while the guidelines, regulations and exchange rates listed herein were the case at the time of going to print, you can expect further currency valuation shifts and minor (or even major) changes in the visa regime. Sources for further information are listed as often as possible; check them for regulation changes before your visit.

WHEN TO GO

When to go depends on what you're visiting for: St Petersburg is a year-round destination (see the Things to See & Do chapter for ideas). In winter, hotels and tourist attractions are less crowded and, while some describe the weather merely as 'dark', there's a twinkling magic about the winter sky that others find very romantic. And while white nights in mid-summer are undeniably beautiful, some people find it rather disconcerting to look out of a hotel window and think it's about 8 pm when it's really 3 am! Practically speaking, most attractions other than the statuary in the Summer Garden and the like are open year round. If you do go in winter, remember that it gets very slushy, so bring along good waterproof boots. In summer, dive-bombing mosquitoes are rife (St Petersburg was built on a swamp), so bring mosquito repellent (see the Dangers & Annoyances section later in this chapter).

ORIENTATION

St Petersburg sprawls across and around the delta of the Neva River, at the end of the easternmost arm of the Baltic Sea, known as the Gulf of Finland. Entering St Petersburg at the city's south-eastern corner, the Neva first flows north and then turns west across the middle of the city; from here it divides into several branches and forms the islands of the delta. The two biggest branches, diverging in front of the Winter Palace on the south bank, are the Bolshaya (Big) and Malaya (Small) Neva, which flow into the sea either side of Vasilevsky Island.

The heart of St Petersburg is the area spreading back from the Winter Palace and the Admiralty on the south bank, its skyline dominated by the golden dome of St Isaac's Cathedral. Nevsky prospekt, stretching east-south-east from the Admiralty, is the main street, with many of the city's sights, shops and restaurants. Nevsky prospekt crosses three waterways cutting across from the Neva to the sea, the biggest being the Fontanka River.

The north side of the city has three main areas. The westernmost is Vasilevsky Island at the eastern end of which – the Strelka – stand many of the city's fine early buildings. The middle area is Petrograd Side, a cluster of delta islands whose southern end is marked by the tall gold spire of the SS Peter & Paul Cathedral. This is where the city began. These two islands, or 'sides', are

Bronze Horseman statue

NICK SELBY

Peter & Paul Fortress

GEORGI SHABLOVSKY

The multi-domed Church of the Resurrection of Christ

NICK SELBY

Open bridge during white nights in St Petersburg

GEORGI SHABLOVSKY

Beloselsky-Belozersky Palace

JOHN NOBLE

NICK SELBY

St Isaac's Cathedral

ROGER HAYNE

Interior of St Isaac's Cathedral, main dome

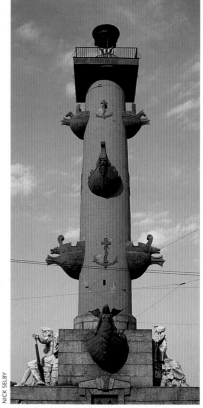

NICK SELBY

Rostral Column on the Strelka (Vasilevsky Island)

NICK SELBY

Bankovsky most (Bank Bridge) over the Griboedova Canal

often abbreviated on local maps and written directions appear as 'VS' (Vasilevsky Side) and 'PS' (Petrograd Side).

The third, eastern, area is Vyborg Side, divided from Petrograd Side by the Bolshaya Nevka channel (not to be confused with the Bolshaya Neva) and stretching east along the north bank of the Neva.

MAPS

Hotels and restaurants hand out decent walking maps of the city as a matter of routine and city, regional and even country maps are readily available at bookshops and kiosks. Metro maps are handed out free at most metro stations.

The *Marshruty Gorodskogo Transporta (Municipal Transit Routes)* map published by St Petersburg's now defunct Culture and Tourism Office is very useful and is available at kiosks throughout the city. Kiosks also sell an astounding variety of other good city street maps, including Polyplan's *Plan Goroda Sankt-Peterburga*, Russian Publishing's *Sankt Peterburge*, part of their Russian Cities series, and the comprehensive *Sankt Peterburg I Prigorody*, by Atlas Maps, a complete atlas covering the city and suburbs, including Petrodvorets.

Interesting for the central areas – and useful now that many streets are reverting to pre-communist names – is *Peterburg Leningrad Starye i Novye Grodskie Nazvania (Peterburg Leningrad Old and New City Names)*, which gives the 1989 and 1878 names of most streets. I found it on sale at the Russian Museum and you could also try in antiquarian bookshops on Nevsky prospekt and Liteyny prospekt.

Street Name Changes

In the early to mid-1990s, St Petersburg went on a rampage, changing the names of most of its streets. In many cases this simply meant restoring the pre-communist names. There have already been such fundamental changes to the names of the city's streets that any map more than five years old is useless. More infuriating, residents sometimes refer to renamed streets, even

major ones, by their old name. The table on page 192 shows street (and other) name changes that were in place in July 1998; more recent changes may be found in publications such as the *St Petersburg Times*, the Russian-language and English-indexed yellow pages *Luchshee V Sankt Peterburge* and *The Traveller's Yellow Pages*. In this book the new street names are used, with the exceptions of ulitsa Plekhanova and naberezhnaya Kanala Griboedova (names no-one will stop using despite their new names – which most don't even know).

St Petersburg has two streets called Bolshoy prospekt: one on Petrograd Side, one on Vasilevsky Island. The two sides of some Vasilevsky Island streets are known as lines *(linii)* and opposite sides of these streets have different names – thus 4-ya linia (4th line) and 5-ya linia (5th line) are the east and west sides of the same street – which collectively is called 4-ya i 5-ya linii (4th and 5th lines).

TOURIST OFFICES & INFORMATION

It's amazing, but as I write there's still no official city-run tourist information office in St Petersburg. The city keeps threatening to open one in the Oktyabrskaya Hotel and claims it will be open by the time you read this, but I don't believe it. The best sources of information in the city are unofficial.

HI St Petersburg Hostel

The registration desk at the HI St Petersburg Hostel (Map 8, ☎ 329 80 18), 3-ya Sovetskaya ulitsa 28, is staffed by very helpful English-speaking people who are experienced in getting around the city cheaply. They'll book most of the things that can be booked by other agencies and hotels, but they'll give you more of an idea of what's really available. Sindbad Travel also has an office here (see the Travel Agencies section in the Getting There & Away chapter), and sells domestically and internationally published guidebooks (including Lonely Planet).

St Petersburg Travel Company

The St Petersburg Travel Company (formerly Intourist) (Map 6, ☎ 315 51 29) has its main office at naberezhnaya reki Moyki 60B, but the most commonly visited office is its excursions office (Map 8, ☎ 312 12 42), at Nevsky prospekt 16. Here you can get tourist information and book tours.

Hotels

Concierge desks in the top-end hotels have extremely knowledgeable and helpful staff, and they'll usually help you even if you don't look like a millionaire (but it's a good idea to dress neatly when you approach them). They can arrange everything that you'd expect a city travel desk to arrange: tours, excursions, car rentals, theatre tickets etc. These services cost a lot in the form of marked-up prices, though the staff will also dish out a good deal of free advice.

Other Information Sources

Newspapers The *St Petersburg Times* is a high quality weekly English-language newspaper, available free throughout town and online at www.sptimes.ru. It's well worth checking out.

Pulse is a slick colour monthly with tons of club, pub, nightlife and other information about the city, written with a very young and fresh outlook. It's available free all over the city.

The city's other English-language offering, the *Neva News*, has somehow managed to cling to life. It's less slick than the *Times* but occasionally has good features. It's also free.

Expatriate Organisations If you're staying in town for business, you may want to attend a monthly meeting of the St Petersburg International Business Association, a group of Western businesspeople which addresses problems and concerns of expatriate residents. For more information contact Anna Kassner, SPIBA's Executive Director on ☎ 325 90 91 (spiba@online.ru).

Notice Boards There's a board inside the US Consulate that sometimes has notices advertising accommodation, translators, language tutors etc. There's also a board at the HI St Petersburg Hostel where travellers post notices and restaurant reviews, tips etc, but it's under-used.

VISAS & DOCUMENTS

All foreigners visiting Russia need visas. To get one you must technically have confirmed accommodation for every night you'll be in the country, though in practice there are countless ways around this.

At the time of writing, a Russian visa is a passport-sized paper document; but nothing goes into your passport. The visa lists entry/exit dates, your passport number, any children travelling with you, and visa type (see Types of Visa later). It's an exit permit too, so if you lose it (or overstay), leaving the country can be harder than getting in.

The following sections give general information about visa procedures – before you go to Russia and once you're there. Despite changes in details here and there, these guidelines have remained essentially static since the fall of the Soviet Union.

Processing Fees

Each Russian consulate charges as much as it can, so rates fluctuate depending on where and when you apply. Note, too, that US citizens pay more than anyone else for their visas – a retaliatory measure imposed by Russians who have been shamefully treated when applying for US visas. The US State Department continually announces it will streamline procedures and give clerks sensitivity training, but until that actually happens, Russians are trying, with some success, to treat Americans as poorly as Americans treat Russians. When you get upset about it, consider this: despite any poor treatment you receive, the Russians are no doubt far nicer to you than the US consulate is to them.

Registration

When you check in to a hotel, camping ground or hostel, you must surrender your

Changing Times

Visa regulations change constantly in Russia, though usually in little smidgens as opposed to full-scale overhauls of the regime. (It's significant that whenever Russian visas are discussed, the word 'regime' comes up.) Try Lonely Planet Online (www .lonelyplanet.com), the Russian Embassy in Washington DC (www.russianembassy .org), or www.russia.net/travel/visas.html – the best places to get the latest, up-to-date information.

passport and visa so the hotel can register you with OVIR *(Otdel Viz i Registratsii)*, the Department of Visas & Registration. You'll get your documents back the next morning – you'll usually need to ask, as nobody seems to remember to return them to you.

All Russian visas must be registered with OVIR within three business days of your arrival in Russia. No ifs or buts about it. Some travel agencies claim that their 'visas needn't be registered'. Buffalo bagels: *all* Russian visas – whether issued by the HI St Petersburg Hostel or the office of the Russian President – need to be registered with the nearest office of OVIR within three working days of arrival in the country. Be highly suspicious of any company that tells you otherwise. Sometimes you have to pay a registration fee of US$5 to US$10.

Extending a visa that's not registered can be impossible, and getting out of the country with an unregistered visa could be a very expensive proposition. On the other hand, you may waltz out with just a lecture or even unhindered. But travellers have reported that fines of up to US$500 have been levied at the Finnish and Norwegian borders, and St Petersburg and Moscow airport officials aren't about to let a juicy penalty walk past them. It's not worth the risk.

Visa Registration Offices The main office of OVIR (Map 8, ☎ 278 24 81), Saltykova-Shchedrina ulitsa 4, is open Monday to Friday from 9 am to 1 pm and 2 to 5 pm. Each district in the city has its own OVIR branch office (a complete list, with opening hours, is available in *Luchshee V Sankt Peterburge*), but most visa inquiries can be handled at the main branch.

Registration Problems The company or organisation that invited you to Russia is responsible for your registration, and no other company can support your visa. You can't take a visa that was issued on the invitation of, say, the HI Hostel in St Petersburg and have it registered in Moscow by the Travellers Guest House.

If you're not sure which organisation invited you (if the sponsorship line – on tourist visas this begins with the words *V uchrezhdenie* – has a name you've never heard of), the simplest option is to spend a night at one of the major (expensive) hotels, which will register your visa for you right at the front desk. There may be a fee involved, but usually the cost of the room will suffice. If for some reason you can't do this, inquire at the HI St Petersburg Hostel – they're the most experienced and competent in dealing with visa problems and can give you the best advice.

HIV/AIDS Testing

At the time of writing, HIV/AIDS testing is required for foreigners staying in the Russian Federation longer than three months. By definition, this does *not* affect tourist visas, which are only issued for shorter stays. The medical certificate must be in English and in Russian. Consult the company sponsoring your business visa for the latest regulations.

Types of Visa

Six types of visas are available to foreign visitors and are listed below.

For all visas you'll need:

- a passport valid for at least a month beyond your return date. A UK Visitor's passport or other temporary papers won't do. You may be able to get away with giving the embassy or consulate only photocopies of the data pages of

your passport, though some consulates, notably Munich, charge you for this 'service';
- three passport-size (4x4.5cm), full-face photos, not more than a year old. Vending-machine photos with white background are fine if they're essentially identical;
- a completed application form, including entry/exit dates;
- a handling fee (an amount that varies from country to country and depending on your citizenship).

Tourist Visa A tourist visa is issued to, well, tourists: those who have booked hotel or hostel beds and are in Russia for purposes other than business. These are the most straightforward and inflexible visas available. In theory you're supposed to have booked accommodation for every night you'll be in the country, but in practice you can often get away with only booking a few, even just one – ask the travel agent, hotel or hostel you're booking through.

Extending a tourist visa is hugely difficult and the extension, if granted, will usually be only for a short time. Tourist visas are best for trips when you know exactly what you're doing, when and where and for how long you'll be doing it. To obtain a tourist visa, you will need, in addition to the above:

- confirmation of hotel reservations, which can be a faxed copy on hotel letterhead signed and stamped by the hotel; or confirmation of bookings from a travel agent; or
- a visa-support letter from a youth hostel/guesthouse. (See the business visa section for tourist visa support fees charged by some hostels and guesthouses.)

Business Visa Far more flexible and desirable for the independent traveller is a business (or commercial) visa supported by a Russian company. The invitation eliminates the need for pre-arranged hotel confirmations because the company inviting you ostensibly puts you up for the duration of your stay. While a visa to Russia supposedly allows you to travel anywhere, holders of tourist visas may have a harder time getting accommodation in smaller regional cities that are not listed on their visas

than will holders of business visas doing the same thing.

To obtain a business visa you must have a letter of invitation from a registered Russian company guaranteeing to provide accommodation during the entire length of your stay, and a cover letter from your company (or you) stating the purpose of your trip.

There are many organisations that will send you a business invitation for a fee, usually not an outrageous amount. The fastest and most reliable way to get a business invitation is through hostels: the HI St Petersburg Hostel issues business invitations and is extremely reliable. You will need to send them a fax or email containing your name as it appears in your passport, date and place of birth, nationality, passport number and expiry date, dates of entry to and exit from Russia (these can be approximate) and the consulate at which you intend to apply for your visa. Sample fees for visa-support services include:

HI St Petersburg Hostel (☎ 812-329 80 18; fax 812-329 80 19, ryh@ryh.ru), 3-ya Sovetskaya ulitsa 28, St Petersburg. Organised through the hostel, a tourist visa (with reservation for accommodation booked, plus two weeks of added time in country) costs US$25 including registration, plus $10 for the fax. The hostel will require credit card (Visa/MasterCard) or other payment in advance.

RTT Matkapalvelut Travel Agency (☎ 09-659 052), Laivasillankatu 14, Helsinki, near the Russian embassy. This agency charges Americans US$86 for an invitation and all visa processing at the Helsinki consulate for five-day service, and US$190 for same-day service. Other nationalities pay less. Note that their prices include the Russian consulate's visa fees in addition to RTT's invitation fees.

IRO Travel (095-234 65 53), Bolshoy Pereyaslav-skaya ulitsa 50, Moscow, at the Travellers Guest House. This organisation charges US$48.50 for a tourist invitation for up to 25 days maximum, US$88 for a one month business visa invitation, and US$201 for three-month multiple-entry business visa support (21-day processing time required).

There are scores of companies in Russia willing to issue commercial visa invitations, some cheaper, some more expensive. I'm listing the above because I know them to be reliable and experienced, and because they follow through with registration.

Student Visa Student visas can be wonderful things; flexible, extendable and they even entitle you to pay Russian prices for airfares, train fares and other items affected under the country's dual-pricing system (see the boxed aside later in this chapter). You'll need proof of enrolment at an accredited Russian school or university, which usually requires prepayment.

'Private' Visa This is what you get for a visit by personal invitation, and it's also referred to as an 'ordinary' visa by some authorities. The visa itself is as easy to get as a tourist visa but getting the invitation is complex.

The person who is inviting you must go to their local office of OVIR and fill out an invitation form for approval of the invitation. Approval, which takes several weeks, comes in the form of a notice of permission *(izveshchenie)*, good for one year, which the person inviting must send to you. You will need this invitation approval notice together with the standard application form to apply for the visa, which is valid for as many as 60 days in your host's town.

'On-the-Spot' Visa These are fast-track business visas, freed from the requirement for advance invitations. Individuals arriving at Moscow's Sheremetevo-2 or St Petersburg's Pulkovo-2 airports can get short-term visas at a special consular office before going through passport control. To get one of these visas, you'll have to have a copy of an MID (Ministry of Foreign Affairs) invitation and have a representative of your inviting company meet you at the airport. Note, however, that airlines may not necessarily let you board your flight to Russia, because if you're turned down for the fast-track visa the airline is responsible for bringing you out again – so check with the airlines in advance.

This kind of visa is good for up to a month and attracts fees from about US$150 to US$250. Though expensive and problematic, it may be one way around the paperchase.

Transit Visa This is for 'passing through', which is loosely interpreted. For transit by air it's usually good for 48 hours. For a nonstop trans-Siberian railway journey it's valid for 10 days, giving westbound passengers a few days in Moscow without the obligatory hotel prebooking (those heading east can't linger in Moscow). Under certain circumstances, travellers transiting through Russia and holding valid entry/exit visas to Armenia, Belarus, Kazakhstan, Kyrgyzstan, Tajikistan or Uzbekistan need not apply for a Russian transit visa. The requirements on this are sketchy, and while a Russian consulate may say it's unnecessary, the odds of being allowed into or out of Russia on the premise that you're holding a Tajik visa are slim. Many border guards are not familiar with the latest regulations handed down in Moscow, so it's always best to play it safe, especially when travelling to border crossings in remote areas.

When to Apply

Apply as soon as you have all the documents you need (but not more than two months ahead). Business, tourist, private and student visas all take the same amount of time to process once you have the paperwork – be it invitation, confirmation or izveshchenie. This ought to be 10 working days, but at busy embassies (such as San Francisco's), bureaucratically annoying ones (such as London's) or hateful ones (such as Munich's) it may be longer.

You can pay a higher fee for quicker service at most embassies; for example, in 1998 I received a visa in just over one hour from the embassy in Helsinki for about US$120.

Transit visas normally take seven working days but may take as little as a few hours at the Russian embassy in Beijing.

How to Apply

Individuals can arrange their own visas, though long queues at embassies and consulates are common in the high season and Russian consular officials are sometimes somewhat less than bright and perky – and they rarely answer the telephone. If you're booking your flight or accommodation through a travel agency, they'll get your visa too for an extra fee, usually between US$5 and US$30 (agencies in Hong Kong, which must go through the embassy in Bangkok for visas, charge you more). For group tours, the agency does the work.

Visa Agencies Certain agencies specialise in getting visas: in the US, Visa Services, Inc (☎ 202-387 0300), 1519 Connecticut Ave NW, Washington DC 20036, and Travel Document Systems (☎ 202-638 3800, toll-free within the US ☎ 800-874-5100, info@traveldocs.com), 734 15th Street NW, Suite 400, Washington DC 20005; in the UK, Worldwide Visas (☎ 0181-995 2492), 9 Adelaide St, Charing Cross, London WC2 N4HZ. An agency will put your paperwork together and forward it to the embassy for you – for a fee of up to US$65. Unless you're really pressed for time or especially badly affected by impersonal bureaucracies, it seems a bit lavish really.

In Person To apply for a visa yourself, go to the nearest Russian embassy or consulate (see the following By Mail section if you're not near one). Bring your passport or photocopies of the pages covering your personal information and passport validity, your photographs and your hotel confirmation, hostel or business invitation, proof of enrolment, izveshchenie or transit tickets. Ask for, and complete, the visa application, and then wait.

How long you wait depends on how much you're willing to pay. Rush fees vary not just by country but by individual consulate, but, as an example, the Russian consulate in Seattle charges US$20 for service in 10 working days, US$40 for five-day service, US$60 for three-day service and US$100 for same or next-day service. A visa issued within half an hour or a multi-entry visa costs US$120.

While Russian consular officials in some locations are friendly and even smile once in a while, those at others are often not. Unfortunately there's not much you can do except be very polite and get out of there as quickly as you can. You *do* have the right to shop around: nothing is stopping you from taking care of your visa by mail at a known friendly consular office (in our experience) such as Helsinki, Warsaw or San Francisco.

By Mail It's possible to do it all by mail, with stamped, self-addressed envelopes or, if you have them, FedEx, Airborne, DHL or TNT airbills, complete with your account number for all requested forms and completed documents. When you receive the visa, check it carefully – especially the expiry, entry and exit dates and any restrictions on entry or exit points.

Fax-Back Service For callers in the UK, the Russian embassy's consular section in London offers an interactive recorded message about visas (☎ 0891-171 271). This is a premium-rate number which costs UK£0.49 per minute peak, UK£0.38 per minute cheap rate, but it tells you most of what you'll need to know in five to 10 minutes. You then have to visit or write to the consulate to get the relevant forms. Even if (by some administrative oversight) you were so lucky as to get through on the main consulate number, you'd be referred to this recording anyway.

Internet Resources Those crazy, hacking diplomats in the American Russian diplomatic corps have come up with a couple of web resources; for the embassy, try the superb www.russianembassy.org, with good up-to-date information, and www.russia.net/travel/visas.html, an informative visa regulations section produced by the Russian consulate in Seattle. If you have further questions you can email the above two organisations at webmaster@russianembassy .org, or consul@seanet.com. Though after receiving replies from the latter I was more confused than when I began ...

Visa Extensions & Changes

Extensions have become time-consuming, if not downright difficult. A tourist visa can now only be extended through official hotels (not hostels) and with a great deal of advance notice (and perhaps of money).

Where Can You Go?

Some cities in Russia are still off-limits to foreigners but these are few and far between. Technically, any visa is valid for all of Russia except these closed cities. Practically speaking, no-one cares where you go.

You may have trouble with a tourist visa in a hotel in a strange city (ie a city not listed on the visa), though this can usually be talked around. If you will be venturing off the beaten path, it's best to play it safe and get a business visa, the authoritative appearance of which effectively grants you the run of the country.

Lost or Stolen Documents

In order to facilitate replacement of your documents it is imperative that you make and carry photocopies of them, especially your Russian visa. Without this photocopy, replacing a lost or stolen visa can be a nightmare, sometimes you'll even have to contact the issuing embassy and ask it to track down your visa number – after I stop laughing we'll continue.

Your embassy or consulate in Russia can replace a lost or stolen passport, but if you lose your visa you must go to the local visa office, OVIR. A Russian travel agent, Sindbad Travel, your hotel service bureau or the youth hostels can help with this, including reporting the loss to the police. Again, both procedures are much easier if you've stashed away a few passport-size photos, your visa number and photocopies of your visa and your passport's personal information and validity pages.

Youth, Student & Senior Cards

Full-time students and people aged under 26 or over 59 tend to get a substantial discount on admissions, transport and perhaps even hotels in St Petersburg. The Hermitage swears to me that students with an ISIC (see below) gain free entry. Always try flashing your ID before paying in order to obtain any possible discount.

For about US$6, full-time students can get an International Student Identification Card (ISIC) from student agencies worldwide and at Sindbad Travel (in the HI St Petersburg Hostel). If you're not a student but you are under 26, ask a student agency at home for an ISIC Youth Card. The HI St Petersburg Hostel has an up-to-date list of where ISICs will get you a discount while you're in St Petersburg.

British Railways and the American Association for Retired People both issue identification cards for senior travellers, and similar organisations exist in other Western countries.

EMBASSIES & CONSULATES
Russian Embassies Abroad

Australia
  Embassy:
  (☎ 02-6295 9033 or 6295 9474, fax 6295 1847)
  78 Canberra Ave, Griffith, ACT 2603
  Consulate:
  (☎ 02-9326 1866)
  7 Fullerton St, Woollahra, NSW 2025
Azerbaijan
  Embassy:
  (☎ 8922-98 60 16, fax 9822-98 60 83)
  Hotel Azerbaijan, 370133 Baku
Belarus
  Embassy:
  (☎ 0172-345 497, fax 503 664)
  vulitsa Staravilenskaya 48, 220002 Minsk
Canada
  Embassy:
  (☎ 613-235 4341, fax 236 6342)
  285 Charlotte St, Ottawa, Canada
  Visa Department:
  (☎ 613-236 7220 or 236 6215, fax 238 6158)
  Consulate:
  (☎ 514-843 5901 or 842 5343, fax 842 2012)
  3655 Ave Du Musee, Montreal, Quebec, H3G 2EI

China
  Embassy:
  (☎ 10-532 2051, visa section ☎ 532 1267)
  4 Baizhongjie, Beijing 100600
  Consulate:
  (☎ 21-324 2682)
  20 Huangpu Lu, Shanghai 200080
Estonia
  Embassy:
  (☎ 22-44 30 14, fax 44 37 73)
  Pikk 19, EE-0200 Tallinn
  Consulate:
  (☎/fax 235-3 13 67)
  Vilde 8, EE-2020 Narva
Finland
  Embassy:
  (☎ 09-66 14 49, 66 18 76/77 or 60 70 50,
  fax 66 10 06)
  Tehtaankatu 1B, FIN-00140 Helsinki
France
  Embassy:
  (☎ 1-45 04 05 50 or 45 04 71 71,
  fax 45 04 17 65)
  40-50 Boulevard Lannes, F-75116 Paris
  Consulate:
  (☎ 91-77 15 25, fax 77 34 54)
  8 Rue Ambrois Pare, F-13008 Marseille
Germany
  Embassy:
  (☎ 0228-312 08 5/6/7 or 312 52 9,
  fax 311 56 3)
  Waldstrasse 42, 53177 Bonn
  Consular affairs:
  (☎ 0228-312 08 3, fax 384 56 1)
  Consulates:
  (☎ 030 229 14 20, fax 2299 397)
  Unter den Linden 63-65, 10117 Berlin
  (☎ 040-229 52 01, fax 229 77 27)
  Am Feenteich 20, 22085 Hamburg
  (☎ 0341-518 76, fax 585 24 04)
  Kickerlingsberg 18, 04105 Leipzig
  (☎ 089-592 50 3, fax 550 38 28)
  Seidelstrasse 8, 80335 Munich
  (☎ 0381-226 42, fax 227 43)
  Tuhnenstrasse 3, 18057 Rostock
Ireland
  Embassy:
  (☎ 01-494 3525 or 492 2048, fax 492 3525)
  186 Orwell Rd, Rathgar, Dublin 6
Kazakhstan
  Embassy:
  (☎ 3272-44 83 32, ☎ 44 66 44)
  ulitsa Dzhandosova 4, Almaty
Kyrgyzstan
  Embassy:
  (☎ 3312-22 16 91, fax 22 18 23, 22 17 10)
  ulitsa Pervomayskaya 17, Bishkek

Latvia
  Embassy:
  (☎ 2-33 21 51 or 22 06 93, fax 21 25 79)
  Paeglesiela 2, LV-1397 Riga
Lithuania
  Embassy:
  (☎ 22-35 17 63, fax 35 38 77)
  Juozapaviciaus gatve 11, LT-2000 Vilnius
Moldova
  Embassy:
  (☎/fax 2-23 26 00)
  bulvar Stefan del Mare 151, 277019 Chisinau
Mongolia
  Embassy:
  (☎ 1-7 28 51 or 2 68 36, ☎ 2 75 06)
  Friendship St A 6, Ulan Bator
Netherlands
  Embassy:
  (☎ 070-345 13 00/01, 346 88 88 or 34 10 75 06,
  fax 361 7960)
  Andries Bickerweg 2, NL-2517 JP The Hague
New Zealand
  Embassy:
  (☎ 04-476 6113)
  57 Messines Rd, Karori, Wellington
Poland
  Embassy:
  (☎ 022-621 55 75)
  ulica Belwederska 49, PL-00-761 Warsaw
  Consulates:
  (☎ 058-41 42 00 or 41 96 39)
  ulica Batorego 15, PL-80-251 Gdansk-
  Wrzeszcz
  (☎ 012-22 26 47, 22 92 33 or 22 83 88)
  ulica Westerplatte 11, PL-31-033 Kraków
  (☎ 061-41 75 23, ☎ 4! 77 40)
  ulica Dukowska 53A, PL-60-567 Poznan
  (☎ 091-22 22 45, 22 48 77, 22 21 19 or
  22 03 33)
  ulica P. Skargi 14, PL-71-422 Szczecin
Turkmenistan
  Embassy:
  (☎ 3632-25 39 57 or 29 84 66, fax 29 84 66)
  11 Turkmenbashy Shaely, 744004 Ashkhabad
Ukraine
  Embassy:
  (☎ 044-294 79 36, fax 292 66 31)
  vulitsya Kutuzova 8, UKR-252000 Kiev
UK
  Embassy:
  (☎ 0171-229 3628/29, fax 727 8624/25 or
  299 5804)
  13 Kensington Palace Gardens, London W8
  4QX
  Consular Section:
  (☎ 0171-229 8027, visa information message
  ☎ 0891-171 271, fax 0171-229 3215)

5 Kensington Palace Gardens, London W8
4QS
Consulate:
(☎ 0131-225 7098, fax 225 9587)
9 Coates Crescent, Edinburgh E13 7RL
USA
Embassy:
(☎ 202-298 5700 or 298 5772, fax 298 5749)
2650 Wisconsin Ave, NW, Washington DC
20007
Visa Department:
(☎ 202-939 8907, fax 939 8909)
1825 Phelps Place NW, Washington DC
20008
Consulates:
(☎ 212-348 0926, fax 831 9162)
9 East 91 St, New York, NY 10128
(☎ 415-928 6878, fax 929 0306)
2790 Green St, San Francisco, CA 94123
(☎ 206-728 1910, fax 728 1871)
2323 Westin Building, 2001 Sixth Avenue,
Seattle, WA 98121-2617
Uzbekistan
Embassy:
(☎ 3712-54 36 41, 55 92 18 or 55 91 57, fax
55 87 74)
ulitsa Nukusskaya (formerly ulitsa Proletarskaya) 83, 750015 Tashkent

Foreign Consulates in St Petersburg
Canada
(☎ 325 84 48 or 316 72 22)
Malodetskoselsky prospekt 32
China
(☎ 114 62 30)
naberezhnaya Kanala Griboedova 134
Estonia
(☎ 238 18 04)
Bolshaya Monetnaya ulitsa 14
Finland
(☎ 273 73 21)
ulitsa Chaykovskogo 71
France
(☎ 312 11 30 or 311 85 11)
naberezhnaya reki Moyki 15
Germany
(☎ 327 31 11)
ulitsa Furshtadtskaya 39
Latvia
(☎ 327 60 53)
10-ya Linia 11 (Vasilevsky Side)
Netherlands
(☎ 315 01 97)
naberezhnaya reki Moyki 11

Poland
(☎ 274 41 70)
5-ya Sovetskaya ulitsa 12
UK
(☎ 325 60 36 or 325 61 66)
ploshchad Proletarskoy Diktatury 5
USA
(☎ 275 17 01)
ulitsa Furshtadtskaya 15

Australian and New Zealand citizens must contact their embassy in Moscow, though in emergencies you can seek help at the British, Canadian and US consulates.

CUSTOMS
Customs agents seem as little interested in hassles as you and rarely seem to make wilful trouble, though a 1998 clampdown made customs a bit more stringent than in the past. The most important rule is that you are no longer allowed to bring in over 50kg of baggage with you (35kg on trains). If you do, you'll be charged a fee, allegedly a uniform tariff of 30% of the cost of the goods with a minimum of 4 euros (about US$5 as I write) per kilogram over the limit. But in practice the fee seems to range from whatever the agent feels like to however much they can get. My friend discovered this in June 1998 when he was charged US$150 for bringing in just over 50kg of personal belongings.

On arrival, fill out a customs declaration *(deklaratsia)*, listing on the back of the form all your money and valuables, including jewellery, cameras, portable electronics etc. There is no 'Green' (ie nothing to declare) line through customs – everyone's checked except diplomats.

The deklaratsia is duly stamped and returned to you. When you leave Russia you give it to customs, as well as another declaration of what you're taking out.

What You Can Bring In
You may bring in modest amounts of anything for personal use except, obviously, illegal drugs and weapons. Cameras, notebook computers, video cameras, radios and Walkmans, and video and audio tapes

are OK. If you're bringing in hypodermic needles, make sure you bring in a prescription for them and declare them under the line 'Narcotics and appliances for use thereof'.

A few pairs of jeans and up to 250 cigarettes are fine but large amounts of anything saleable are suspect. Food is allowed (except for some fresh fruit and vegetables) and a litre of hard liquor or wine.

You can get a receipt *(kvitantsia)* for any confiscated item and you might succeed in reclaiming the item when you leave.

What You Can Take Out

Anything bought from a legitimate shop or department store can go out, but save your receipts. You technically can't take Russian currency with you, though officials won't usually check your pockets or wallet. The money statement on your declaration is designed to prevent you from taking more money *out* of the country than you brought *in*. If you're bringing in a large amount, declare it; when you bring in amounts over US$1000 in cash you will probably be asked to show the cash to the customs agent when you arrive – this is to prevent you from inflating your claim on the way in to cover an amount you plan to take out.

Anything vaguely 'arty', such as manuscripts, instruments, coins, jewellery, antiques or antiquarian books (meaning those published before 1975), must be assessed by the Ministry of Culture (Map 6, ☎ 314 82 34), naberezhnaya Kanala Griboedova 107. There, bean-counting bureaucrats will issue a receipt for tax paid (usually 100% of the purchase price – bring your sales receipt) which you show to customs on your way out of the country. If you buy something large, a photograph will usually be fine for assessment purposes.

If you're counting on a benevolent customs agent on the way out, I've got some first-rate Chernobyl beachfront property to sell you; uncleared art commands punitive taxation in excess of 600% at customs, when you're trying to get on that plane and you're in a hurry ...

A painting bought at tourist art markets, in a department store or from a commercial gallery should be declared and receipts should be kept. Generally speaking, customs in airports is much more strict and thorough than at any border crossing.

Since 1990, the removal from the country of certain consumer goods – including furs, caviar, tea, fabrics, some clothing, carpets, leather, photography equipment, electrical appliances and precious metal and stones (but not fine art) has been prohibited. Customs agents at Pulkovo-2 airport seem to have magic noses capable of sniffing caviar at 100 metres. They'll happily rip through bags to find it, and when they do they'll confiscate it.

MONEY

The Russian unit of currency is the rouble *(ROO-bl)*, whose name is its most consistent property. Governmental mucking about aside, it's been a relatively free-floating currency since 1991. The rouble was one of the world's most pathetic currencies in the early 1990s, but from 1995 to 1998 it remained surprisingly stable on international exchanges, due in no small part to government intervention and austerity measures. While from 1993 to 1995 the rouble lost 80% of its value against the US dollar, it only lost 17% of its value against the dollar from 1995 to early 1998, or an average (issues of compounding notwithstanding) of less than 6% per year.

All that ended in 1998 when the Russian economy teetered on the edge of collapse (see the boxed text). At first glance this would seem to be good news for travellers, who will enjoy reduced prices on many goods and services. But there is a very real danger of complete economic and governmental collapse that could have very serious repercussions for both Russians and foreigners. For up-to-date information check Lonely Planet's website at www.lonelyplanet.com.

Despite the rouble's exciting movements from shimmering highs to earth shattering lows, in the past, prices have stayed relatively stable when looked at in US$ equivalents,

Economic Crisis

The Russian economic crisis that existed as we went to press had been caused by myriad reasons, including economic policies dating from the time of the Soviet Union. As the country grappled with economic reform, a sort of netherworld of semi-private enterprises developed. Government-owned industries ran incredibly short of cash, as the money supply was tightened to reduce inflation. Many industries, notably manufacturing and coal mining, resorted to extraordinary means to pay workers who, on average, were owed six months worth of wages. Some companies paid workers with goods which the workers could then try to sell for cash. A system of barter between companies developed a 'company store' economy, where workers could 'buy' goods against their owed earnings (company managers often did nothing all day but contact other factories in similar financial difficulties to trade output).

President Boris Yeltsin came under increasing pressure to speed up reforms and to pay workers their back-wages. His response was typically Yeltsonian – in March 1998 he fired his entire government and appointed a complete unknown, Sergey Kiriyenko, as prime minister. It took a threat from Yeltsin to dissolve parliament to have his decision ratified.

For several months it seemed that the reforms put in place by Kiriyenko, the boyish former bank manager, made sense: austerity, conservative reform goals and steady-as-she-goes policies.

But the Communists had smelled blood and were gaining public support for their cries that International Monetary Fund (IMF) bailouts were homogenising Russia, and that only Russians could plan the future of the country. The ripple effects of US political scandals added to the turmoil (the Russian markets felt that US President Bill Clinton's support of Yeltsin simply wasn't enough to guarantee reforms and continuing profits), as did pressure from currency traders, hard currency flight, a lack of confidence in the government, continuing strikes, the collapse of the Asian financial markets and a failure to carry out enough reforms to guarantee further IMF bailouts.

In late August 1998 as political heat increased, Yeltsin once again fired his entire government and tried to replace Kiriyenko with the very man the young banker had earlier replaced, 60 year old Viktor Chernomyrdin.

It was a complete disaster. The move signalled panic from every corner. A run against the rouble made the currency impossible to support and its value began to spiral downward on the Moscow stock exchange. After being rejected as prime minister by parliament, Chernomyrdin backed down as prime ministerial candidate and was replaced by Yeltsin's then foreign minister, Yevgeny Primakov.

At the time of writing, the business of Russian government goes on, and plans to pay workers by printing more roubles seems to be going forward. The downward spiral of the rouble seems likely to continue.

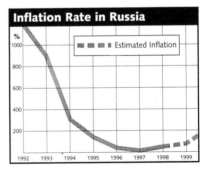

Inflation Rate in Russia

%
1000 ■ ■ ■ ■ Estimated Inflation
800
600
400
200

1992 1993 1994 1995 1996 1997 1998 1999

And it was going so well ... The Russian economy collapsed in 1998, bringing hardship (again) to millions of Russian citizens.

which is what we use in this book (we also round up to the nearest US$0.10 or US$1, depending on the value of the particular listing).

From January 1999, all banknotes issued before 1997 are worthless. Don't accept any R5000 or R10,000 notes, or any note bearing a picture of Lenin, unless you're looking for souvenirs – in which case negotiate knowing that their true value is nothing (coin collectors: Soviet boxed coin sets are not good value; the coins often tarnish and rust within their plastic protective cases!).

At the time of writing, all transactions must be made in roubles – hard-currency bars or shops are no more. Prices may be listed in dollars (or the latest euphemism, 'Units'), but barring a major change (and they're always possible here), you pay in roubles. Credit card transactions are charged in roubles at the central bank rate for the day, as published in newspapers.

Foreign Currency

US dollars are the most widely accepted foreign currency, followed by Deutschmarks and Finnish markka. It's best to carry one of these because other currencies, no matter what they're worth on the international marketplace, are difficult to change into roubles.

Whatever currency you're taking into Russia, make certain that all the notes are in pristine condition. Worn, damaged, faded or written-on notes will be refused. Larger notes are more readily accepted than smaller notes, but you should always also have at least US$100 in small denominations for times when you're stuck changing money at an awful rate.

If you're taking US dollars, make sure all your US$20s were minted after 1991. Your US$100s must have been produced after 1995 and US$50s after 1997. These bear the new design – a slightly different green colour, larger portraits than before (placed slightly off-centre), and other new features. Older US$100s are very difficult to change in Russia.

Exchange Rates

Again, these were valid at the time of writing and are likely to change:

country	unit		rouble
Australia	A$1	=	R10.53
Canada	C$1	=	R11.02
euro	1€	=	R19.09
Finland	FIM1	=	R3.42
France	FF1	=	R3.10
Germany	DM1	=	R10.38
Ireland	IR£1	=	R25.94
Japan	¥100	=	R14.41
New Zealand	NZ$1	=	R9.00
Netherlands	fl	=	R9.20
UK	UK£1	=	R28.73
USA	US$1	=	R17.01

Exchanging Money

Banks & Exchange Offices There are legal exchange offices practically everywhere in St Petersburg – in hotels, restaurants, boutiques, back alleys etc.

Promstroy (Industry & Construction) Bank and Saint Petersburg Savings Bank are two prominent banks. Both have a head office located at Nevsky prospekt 38 (Map 8, entrance in Mikhailovskaya ulitsa across from the Grand Hotel Europe). Both banks offer cash advances on Visa/MasterCard/ Eurocard; Promstroy has ATMs and Saint Petersburg Savings Bank buys and sells travellers cheques. Astrobank is at Nevsky prospekt 58 and is a money-changing office.

Of the hotel exchange offices, the Astoria, Grand Hotel Europe, Sheraton Nevskij Palace, Oktyabrskaya, Moskva, St Petersburg, Pribaltiyskaya, Hotelship Peterhof, Helen, Pulkovskaya and others offer cash advances on Visa/MasterCard/Eurocard. The Grand Hotel Europe and Sheraton Nevskij Palace Hotel can organise travellers cheques as well.

Banks and exchange offices are competitive; representative rates are printed in the *St Petersburg Times*, so comparison shopping is quite easy.

Whether you change money in a bank or an exchange office, they will fill out an official receipt showing your name, the date and the currency and exchange rate. This is for your records only; practically speaking, you don't need this receipt to reconvert roubles and you needn't show it to customs on the way out to justify expenditure of money along the way.

Technically, you must show your passport whenever you change money in the Russian Federation, whether at a private exchange office or a bank. This may or may not be current practice when you visit – I used my driving licence on several occasions.

Whenever you change money, your cash will be subjected to some of the most ridiculous counterfeit detection methods you'll ever see. Try not to get insulted, and if there is a question about your note, point out watermarks and other counterfeit prevention features. If you're turned away, hit the next exchange office.

Black Market At the time of writing there are banks and ATMs everywhere, and the black marketeers are as quaint as the dictatorship of the proletariat. This should continue, but should a complete currency collapse occur, these resilient folk might return: see the anti-crime tips under Dangers & Annoyances later in this chapter for advice on how to safely change money on the street.

Travellers Cheques, Cash or Credit Cards? Yes. Take all three if you can. Cash is always the preferred method of payment, though credit cards are making big inroads, at least in the city itself, where Visa, MasterCard/Eurocard and American Express are widely accepted. Banks in Australia, New Zealand and the UK are now selling Visa Travel Money, a pre-paid Visa card: your credit limit is the amount you buy the card with, and while it's not rechargeable, it's accepted like a regular Visa card. They charge a fee (2% of the purchase price of the card), so it's more expensive than travellers cheques, but more accessible.

The fact that travellers cheques are refundable makes them the safest way to carry your money, and you can also use them to pay directly for many goods and services. But outside St Petersburg (and Moscow), cheques can be more difficult to cash, and as difficult as cash to replace. Americans: make certain you fill in dates on travellers cheques in the format everyone else on the planet uses (day, month, year); doing it the US way (month, day, year) probably will result in your cheque being refused!

US dollar travellers cheques are probably your best bet. Take both small denominations (for buying roubles when the rate is awful) and big ones (to minimise commission, which is charged per cheque, for when you need to cash a lot of money). American Express is the most widely recognised brand in Russia, and its full service office (☎ 329 60 60) at the Grand Hotel Europe (Map 8), Mikhailovskaya ulitsa 1/7, is open from 9 am to 5 pm daily except Sunday.

Thomas Cook is another widely recognised international brand of travellers cheques, though every time I've called them their telephone representatives have been cagey to the point of hostility about refund procedures. What I know is that if your cheques are lost or stolen you are required to call their world headquarters in the UK (☎ 44-1733-502 995), which will prudently, patiently and thoroughly assess your claim and, if they're very happy about everything and you don't sound dodgy, they'll authorise a refund through agents in St Petersburg (whose address and contact information the aforementioned telephone representatives won't tell me). Sounds as if Amex is the better bet.

Visa travellers cheques can be exchanged for cash in St Petersburg and Moscow relatively easily.

Credit cards are accepted at many of the better restaurants, hotels and shops, and cash advances against Visa and MasterCard are a simple matter in St Petersburg. Generally, there's a 3% to 5% commission tacked onto the amount of the cash advance. Visa, MasterCard/Eurocard and

American Express/Optima are the most commonly accepted cards, while some places also accept Diners Club and JCB. The Discover card is not accepted in Russia. When paying by credit card, be very careful that you see how many slips are being made of your card, that you destroy all carbons, and that as few people as possible get hold of your card number and expiry date. The stolen credit card market in Russia is booming, so protect your card as much as possible.

ATMs There are reliable and safe-to-use ATMs throughout the city and their numbers are increasing. Currently there are ATMs in such convenient locations as the north-eastern corner of Nevsky prospekt and Mikhailovskaya ulitsa, and inside many metro stations, shops and department stores. They all accept Visa, MasterCard, Eurocard, Plus and Cirrus cards.

Wire Transfers Wire-transferring money to Russia is far easier than it used to be, though the price is high. The fastest way to transfer money from the US, Canada, UK, New Zealand, Australia, Germany, France and Finland, as well as the most expensive, is through Western Union, which has branch offices in St Petersburg in dozens of banks and at the Grand Hotel Europe. Western Union charges US$18 for a US$100 transfer and US$54 for a US$500 transfer.

Direct bank-to-bank wire transfer is also possible. You'll probably need to open an account at a local bank and pay fees and a percentage of the money wired into that account.

Depending on the bank, transferring money can take anything from one to five days. Ask at the hotels or the hostels or check *Luchshee V Sankt Peterburge* for a listing of banks in the city.

Dual-Pricing System

You can call it an outrage, you can call it unfair, the Russian courts have called it unconstitutional, but at the end of the day, you'll *still* call it 100% more for foreigners. You'll pay that much more than for Russians on entry fees to most museums and cultural events. Foreigners will also have to pay about twice the Russian rate for many hotels, about a third more for train travel and several times more for flights.

Ask Russians why this is so and they'll give you a variety of justifications. 'It is not so much for you, I think', 'You have more money than us', and 'This museum is here for Russians, not for foreigners' top the list of frequently heard responses (that last one came from the head curator of St Petersburg's Hermitage, who was justifying why foreigners pay 450% more than Russians for admission).

There's nothing you can do but try as often as you can to get the Russian rate. Speak Russian as best you can – try this: as gruffly as possible say 'Ah-DEEN bil-LET pa-ZHAL-stuh' and glower at the ticket seller who is looking monumentally bored and indifferent. Say 'Da' to whatever he or she says next, proffer the Russian ticket price and get the hell away from there as fast as possible.

Use student and senior citizen discount cards as often as possible and fight for the discount. Don't show your passport until the last possible second, never volunteer the foreigner rate unless you're feeling philanthropic, and have Russian friends buy train, bus and theatre tickets for you wherever possible (for more information see the Getting Around chapter). Note that it's difficult to get a Russian price on the train between St Petersburg and Moscow unless your Russian is quite good.

Emergency Cheque Cashing If you're an American Express or Optima card-holder you can use a personal cheque to buy travellers cheques from the American Express full-service office at the Grand Hotel Europe, Mikhailovskaya ulitsa 1/7. If you don't have a personal cheque, you can still get travellers cheques, but the limits are much lower. Laws on this were hazy at the time of writing; if the American Express office can't perform this service for some reason, it will refer you to a nearby bank that can. Limits depend on your card type and/or credit limit. Every 21 days you can get up to US$1000 on a green card, US$5000 on a gold card and US$10,000 on a platinum card (on Optima cards you're also limited by the amount of available credit).

Costs

All the following information is, of course, subject to change. St Petersburg is not as cheap as other Eastern European cities, nor even as cheap as the rest of Russia (outside of Moscow). But the good news is that since our last edition prices have remained fairly stable – and in some cases they've even come down a bit.

A major cost is accommodation: unless you're staying at one of the hostels or at a homestay, it's hard to get accommodation for less than US$20 to US$30 a day, even if a hotel's rack (standard, walk-in) rate is listed here as less. The reason is a serious demand-versus-supply situation and what amounts to one of the world's great seller's markets.

If you're careful – that is, you stay in a cheap B&B or hostel, stick to self-catering and inexpensive restaurants/cafés, and don't drink much beer, other alcohol or Western soft drinks – you may be able to squeak through on about US$25 to US$30 per day in summer (high season). Staying at a higher-end B&B or inexpensive hotel, and eating in inexpensive restaurants will cost US$35 to US$50. A double room in a hotel with a private bath, a television and a telephone will cost an average of US$60 with advance reservations or through a travel agent, much more without such reservations.

It's still worth checking out package tours as an option. While Lonely Planet readers need no introduction to the benefits of individual travel, Russia's tourism infrastructure, which was for so many years geared to moving in herds of tourists and shepherding them from site to site, still rewards group travellers with some pretty hard-to-beat bargains.

In 'pre-economic-crisis' 1998, a ride on a bus or the metro cost US$0.25. Taxis are more expensive (and slightly complicated; see the Getting Around chapter for more information) but are still priced far less than their Western equivalents.

Here are a few sample prices just to give you an idea:

- lunch or dinner with drinks (per person) in a hotel or inexpensive restaurant: US$5 to US$15; in a good restaurant: US$30 to US$100
- bus, tram, trolleybus or metro ride: about US$0.25
- taxi from the Admiralty to the airport: US$10 to US$15; taxi from the airport to the HI St Petersburg Hostel: US$20 to US$25 (unless your Russian's great); taxi from Petrogradskaya metro to the HI St Petersburg Hostel: US$4
- excursion from St Petersburg to Petrodvorets: US$15 per person in a group; US$100 for up to six people in St Petersburg Travel Company car with guide; US$8 unguided using public hydrofoil
- admission to the Hermitage: US$10 for foreigners, US$2.25 for Russians
- litre of milk: US$0.60
- loaf of bread: US$0.50
- copy of *Time*: US$3
- bottle of Russian/imported beer in a kiosk or shop: US$0.75/1.25

Tipping

A lasting bequest of communism in this place is that tipping is not as widespread as it could be. It's standard in the better restaurants (count on leaving 10%), whereas elsewhere 5% to 10% of the total is fine. Tipping your guide, if you have one, is an accepted practice. This is totally discretionary: I tend to tip more to guides from smaller companies than larger ones (Peter, though, from Peter's Tours, needs no tip – see the Getting Around chapter for information on his tours), but generally about US$5 to US$10 for a day would be a good tip. Small gifts, like a bottle of skin cream, a box of imported chocolates or a cassette or CD are appropriate if the service was great, but remember that the gifts of yore (packets of Marlboro, badges and pins etc) are no longer of value here.

Value Added Tax

The usurious 23% Value Added Tax (VAT, in Russian NDS) is usually included in the price listed for purchases, but ask just to make sure.

POST & COMMUNICATIONS
Post

St Petersburg's main international and domestic post and telegraph office (*glavpochtamt;* Map 6) is at ulitsa Pochtamtskaya 9, two blocks south-west of St Isaac's Cathedral. It is open seven days a week. There are also over 400 branch offices scattered throughout the city. The services provided by each branch is usually in proportion to its size – most can cope with international letters and postcards, some can even send international telegrams

Outward post is slow but fairly reliable. Air-mail letters take two to three weeks from St Petersburg to the Europe and the UK, and three to four weeks to the USA or Australasia. Inward post is decidedly unreliable, with delivery times ranging from three weeks to never.

An air-mail letter (up to 20g) or postcard to any foreign address costs US$0.30 (but see below for information on sending postcards). Registration *(zakaznoe)* – a good idea for anything of value – is another US$0.60.

Books and printed matter are cheaper to send by surface mail at small-packet *(melkiy paket)* rates; eg about US$5.80 (unregistered) as opposed to US$12 by air. An international parcel must go from the city's designated international post office; go to any window marked *posylki* (parcels).

In addition to selling stamps, envelopes and postcards, a few hotel post offices also provide registration and express services, and will wrap and post books and printed matter (only). They usually register these and fill out the required customs forms (they must be filled out in Russian).

Some 'postcards' on sale in souvenir kiosks are not meant to be posted as such. They have a message on the back like Отправлять По Почте Только В Конверте ('to be sent through the post only in an envelope'). If you send these as postcards they may not make it to their intended destination.

Visitors can usually find what they need – postcards, envelopes and stamps – at the small postal desks in tourist hotels. You can also post books and printed matter abroad from these desks. They tend to open from about 10 am to 3 pm.

Non-book parcels (clothing, for example) must go from the main post office. For the moment, Windows 27, 28 and 29 are for international mail, though this order keeps being shuffled – so just walk to the far left side of the counter at the opposite end of where you enter the hall and look for a sign. Window 38 is for fax, photocopying and domestic and international telegrams.

Express Services The term Express Mail Service (EMS), provided by EMS Garantpost (☎ 311 96 71 or 311 78 21), is a relative one: packages (a 500g package costs about US$46) take about a week to reach their destination, though they generally do get there. The packages must be taken to Garantpost (Map 6), bulvar Konnogvar- deysky 6, Dom 4.

US-managed Westpost (Map 8, ☎ 275 07 84, westpost@westpost.ru) is a privately run, international mail service for monthly and one-time clients. Mail is transported daily from St Petersburg to Lappeenranta, Finland (the Switzerland of matters postal around here), and mailed from there. Through Skynet they offer express international mail services: to the US, two to three-day service is US$2.20 per letter or

US$43 for a 500g package. They'll courier envelopes within town for US$2.50. And they offer Internet access (see later in this section), computer terminals, fax and copiers (see Doing Business later in this chapter), and video rental (see the Entertainment chapter). Westpost is located at Dom Aktyor, Nevsky prospekt 86 (through the main entrance and through the first door on the right hand side).

The three main Western express mail services in town offer two-day delivery to Europe and the USA/Canada, and three-day delivery to Australia/New Zealand, all with services starting at US$38 for letters. They are TNT Express Worldwide at the Grand Hotel Europe (☎ 122 96 70), DHL, with offices at Izmailovsky prospekt 4 (☎ 326 64 00) and at the Sheraton Nevskij Palace Hotel (☎ 325 61 00), and Federal Express, ulitsa Mayakovskogo 2 (☎ 279 12 87).

Sending Mail You can address outgoing international mail as you would from any country, in your own language, though it might help to *precede* it with the country name in Cyrillic. Some Cyrillic country names are:

- America (USA) – Америка (США)
- Australia – Австралия
- Canada – Канада
- France – Франция
- Germany – Германия
- Great Britain – Великобритания
- New Zealand – Новая Зеландия

Russian addresses are written in a reverse style to Western ones, starting with the country and ending with the addressee's name – eg Россия 103123, г. Москва, улица Островского, д. 32 кв. 14, ИВАНОВ А. В. (Russia 103123, g. Moskva, ulitsa Ostrovskogo, d. 32 kv. 14, Ivanov A V). The return address is written below the main address.

The six-digit number is the Russian postal code.

Receiving Mail The incoming state mail service is so flaky that it's rare for anyone on the move to find anything, but you can try. The most reliable option for those not staying in luxury hotels or the HI St Petersburg Hostel (which all provide mail service via Finland or other Scandinavian countries) is limited to American Express and Optima card-holders. The wonderful folk at American Express (☎ 329 60 09) will hold mail (letters only, no packages) and messages for card-holders and holders of travellers cheques for up to 30 days at the company's office in the Grand Hotel Europe; the mailing address is American Express, PO Box 87, SF-53501 Lappeenranta, Finland – mail is brought from Lappeenranta to the American Express office daily, at no charge. You'll need to bring your card or travellers cheques with you, along with your passport or other ID, to get your mail. Mail takes about a week to arrive from the USA, Canada and Western Europe.

Westpost (see Express Services earlier) offers post boxes in Lappeenranta, with daily pick up and delivery to the Westpost office, or, for corporate clients, to their address in St Petersburg. You can become a basic Westpost client for US$20 per month, and they also offer magazine subscription services. Nonclient visitors can have mail delivered for a US$1 fee to PL 8, SF-53501 Lappeenranta, Finland; you can pick it up at the Westpost office.

When sending mail from abroad to Russia, it's best to put Latin characters on top to get it to Russia, and Cyrillic on the bottom to get it to it's ultimate destination.

Embassies and consulates won't hold mail for transient visitors.

Telephone

Russia's country code is ☎ 7. The city code is ☎ 812.

The world of international and even domestic telecommunications has changed immensely since 1991; it's now possible to do all sorts of magical things like dial a number in another country and have it connect. But with the improvement in services there's been an explosion of providers that can get confusing and, if you're not careful, expensive.

Private Telephones From a private phone in St Petersburg, dialling outside Russia is very simple, but the prices keep rising and are now even higher than equivalent calls from the West to Russia. To call internationally dial ☎ 8, wait for the second tone, then dial 10 plus the country and city codes, then the number. Omit any noughts (zeroes) from the city code (eg to call Sydney the code would be 8 (tone) 10 61 2 and then the phone number).

At the time of writing, daytime telephone prices per minute were US$2.40 to the USA, Canada and Australasia; and US$1.10 to Continental Europe and the UK.

When calling abroad, some useful country codes are:

Australia	☎ 8 10 61
Canada	☎ 8 10 1
Denmark	☎ 8 10 45
Estonia	☎ 8 10 372
Finland	☎ 8 10 358
France	☎ 8 10 33
Germany	☎ 8 10 49
Latvia	☎ 8 10 371
Lithuania	☎ 8 10 370
New Zealand	☎ 8 10 64
Norway	☎ 8 10 47
Poland	☎ 8 10 48
Sweden	☎ 8 10 46
UK	☎ 8 10 44
USA	☎ 8 10 1

Payphones Payphones – Таксофон *(tak-sofon)* – are located throughout the city and are generally in working order. Most take prepaid telephone cards which are available from metro token booths or from kiosks. There are several types of card payphones, and not all cards are interchangeable. Card payphones can be used for local and domestic or international long distance calls.

Some older phone booths accept metro tokens *(zhetony)* as payment. Place the token in the slot on top of the phone and dial the number; when the party answers,

the token should drop. A series of beeps means you need to place another token in the slot or you could risk disconnection.

Domestic (which means within Russia or to any former Soviet republic) long-distance calls may be made from payphones marked Междугородный *(mezhdugorod-ny)*; using different, wrinkled-metal tokens available only in telephone offices. They work on a similar principle, but you need to push the Ответ *(otvet)* button on the phone's face when your party answers. Dial 8, wait for the second tone, then dial the city code (including noughts) and the number.

State/Central Telephone Office The state-run long-distance telephone office (Map 8) is at ulitsa Bolshaya Morskaya 3/5 (formerly ulitsa Gertsena and often still referred to as such). International phones (card-operated) are straight to the back of the office and to the left – you can buy cards from the kiosk in the centre of the hall. Alternatively, you can turn left as soon as you enter and head for the hexagonal kiosks where you can pre-pay and the operator will connect you immediately. Prices are identical to those of home (private) phones.

Country Direct This service allows you to dial a toll-free number in St Petersburg (or in Moscow) for connection with an operator from the USA who can put through collect or calling-card calls to the USA, though not yet to other countries. Country direct numbers include:

• MCI	☎ 8 10 800 497 7222
• AT&T	☎ 325 50 42
• Sprint	☎ 095-155 61 33

Calling from a Hotel The Grand Hotel Europe, Sheraton Nevskij Palace, Okhtinskaya, Astoria, Pribaltiyskaya and other hotels, as well as the HI St Petersburg Hostel, have satellite-linked, international direct-dial telephones with no waiting. They all charge varying outrageous fees; the HI St Petersburg Hostel has the lowest rates (US$4/minute to USA/Canada/Australia/

NZ, US$3.60 to UK/Europe, US$5.50 to other countries).

If you're staying at a hotel that doesn't offer satellite service, international and domestic long-distance calls may be booked with hotel reception. Most hotel-room telephones have a direct-dial number (on a card in the room, or ask reception) for incoming calls, which saves you having to be connected through the switchboard.

Local calls can usually be made free from your room (sometimes directly, sometimes with a prefix number).

Cellular Service Any Western European or Scandinavian (I distinguish the two because of differing cellular standards) cell phone can roam into St Petersburg, but the price for calls – incoming and outgoing – is very high. For incoming calls, you pay to get the call from your home country to Russia at a very high rate; for outgoing calls, prices vary depending on your service contract. In Helsinki and other Finnish cities, you can rent cell phones that work in Russia. Rentals are also available in St Petersburg, but the price is sky-high.

Fax
Faxes can be sent and received at the Central Telephone Office: the incoming fax number is 314 33 60. Generally speaking, faxes are sent out within 48 hours of your dropping them off, but you can request *srochny* (express) and have it sent out immediately for twice the price. Faxes can also be sent and received at all major hotels and at the two youth hostels (see listings for incoming fax numbers), at varying prices.

Faxes usually average US$5 per page to the US, Canada and Australia and about US$3 to Europe.

Telegram
Telegrams are another cheap and reliable way to reach the outside world and can take from three to five days to arrive at their destination. International telegrams can be sent from many of the larger post offices, as well as from Window 38 at the main post office;

Emergency Contact

In an emergency the most straightforward way for someone to reach you from outside Russia is by telephone to your hotel or hostel – language problems, bad connections, slack service and changeable numbers notwithstanding. Your itinerary will be of help in the hunt for you, so leave a copy with someone at home.

International calls to major cities in Russia can be dialled directly and operators can assist in reaching many of even the smallest towns. Next best is a fax or telegram care of your hotel, though the staff won't always chase you up if one arrives. A telegram takes one to two days to arrive.

As a last resort, most foreign affairs ministries maintain 24-hour emergency operators – eg the British Foreign Office (☎ 0171-270 3000), the US State Department (☎ 202-647 5225; or 647 4000 outside business hours), and the Australian Department of Foreign Affairs & Trade (☎ 06-6261 3305) – which can call your embassy in Russia. Embassies prefer that other means have been exhausted before they're contacted.

---

ask for a *blank mezhdunarodny telegramma* (international telegram form). A message in English is no problem if it's printed clearly. At the time of writing, approximate telegram rates per word were: to Europe US$0.35, to USA/Canada/Australasia US$0.45.

If you can get an English-speaking operator you can also arrange telegrams from a private telephone (☎ 066).

Email & Internet Access
Electronic mail is the most reliable and inexpensive method of communication between Russia and the rest of the world. The vast majority of foreign residents in Russia use email as one of their primary international communications methods, so service is readily available.

Sprint, Deutsche Telekom and France Telecom combined forces with GlobalOne, an Internet (and email) provider with a presence in several Russian cities including St Petersburg; contact them here on ☎ 325 12 00 for information if you're not already a member.

The HI St Petersburg Hostel will let you use the terminals in Sindbad Travel's office (which doubles as the hostel's common area) for US$3 per half hour for email and web access.

Westpost (see Post, above) has several terminals with fast Internet connections for US$2.50 per half hour. They'll also give you an email address (user@westpost.ru) if you'll be in town for a while.

Tetris (Map 5, ☎ 164 67 85) is the city's first proper Internet café, about 10 minutes from the HI St Petersburg Hostel at ulitsa Charnykhovskogo 33, right down the street from the Ligovsky Prospekt metro station. They charge US$4 an hour for access from 10 am to 1 pm, US$8 an hour from 1 to 9 pm.

Other Internet service providers in Russia include: Sovam Teleport (www.sovam.com; spbsales@sovam.com) and Glasnet (www.glas.apc.org; support@glas.apc.org).

INTERNET RESOURCES

Getting information, other than the bare basics, out of Russian government sources can be a frustrating and fruitless task. So it's good to know that St Pete – and Russia – has a huge presence on the Internet. There are Internet service providers and websites in almost every large Russian city offering information on hundreds of subjects: from club dates to KGB documents, guided photo tours of the Hermitage to gay and lesbian resources, to the nitty-gritty on registering a Russian company.

A good starting place for links about St Petersburg and Russia is Lonely Planet Online, www.lonelyplanet.com, our award-winning travel website which has destination profiles, feature stories, reports from travellers on the road, and much more. You can also visit Lonely Planet Online on America On Line (Keyword: lp), or on the French Minitel system at 3615 lonelyplanet.

The web addresses below are just a few of the better, more reliable links I've used in the past. For the non-English sections you run into, you'll need to get KOI8 or other Cyrillic fonts and install them, though if you don't speak Russian it won't matter if you go without.

- www.spb.ru – A great general starting point for St Petersburg information, including links to the St Petersburg Times.
- www.glas.apc.org – Glasnet, with connections to ecological resources and information from all over the world, Al-Anon, religious sights, helpful and educational resources and Russia Cams (cameras you can click on to get a live view of streets and sights around Russia.
- www.hermitage-museum.com – A beautiful site on the Hermitage, showing current exhibitions and press releases.
- www.odci.gov/cia/publications/factbook/rs.html – The CIA's home page, which has lists and lists of mind-numbing facts about Russia and the former Soviet Union.
- www.mid.ru/eng/bod.htm – Moscow's Ministry of Foreign Affairs website.

BOOKS
Lonely Planet

If you're travelling outside St Petersburg, Lonely Planet's *Russia, Ukraine & Belarus* is the most comprehensive practical guide available on those countries. Lonely Planet also has guides to many neighbouring countries including Finland, Scandinavian Europe, Estonia, Latvia & Lithuania, Poland, the Czech & Slovak Republics, Hungary and Central Asia.

Guidebooks

St Petersburg History, Art and Architecture by Kathleen Berton Murrell is a lovely book complete with colour photographs. It's published by the Russian Troika Publishing house, and it's available in many shops in St Petersburg and Moscow.

Travel

Much of *USSR: From an Original Idea by Karl Marx* by Marc Polonsky and Russell Taylor is still all too relevant. It's a 1980s streetwise look at the headaches of travel by authors who ran a company specialising in 'real life' Soviet tours. It's funny enough to keep you up when the trip gets you down. It's hard to find, but worth looking for.

History & Politics

For a quick coverage, *A Traveller's History of The USSR and Russia* by Peter Neville is quite a good read, and it's good on pre-Gorbachev Russia. An excellent history of the Soviet period from start to finish is in Robert Service's *A History of Twentieth-Century Russia*.

The 900 Days by Harrison E Salisbury (Pan Books, 1969) is out of print but a must if you can find it. It is a wonderfully written history of the Siege of Leningrad.

Robert K Massie's *Peter the Great: His Life and World* is an excellent read on the history of St Petersburg's founder. And a fascinating read, if not St Petersburg-centric, is Edvard Radzinsky's *Stalin*, a biography of the murderous leader compiled by the Russian playwright and based on his unprecedented access to KGB and government files.

Imperium by Ryszard Kapuscinski is a 1994 collection of essays, journalism and recollections of the Soviet empire by the Polish correspondent and travel writer. Kapuscinski's boyhood town, Pinsk, was in the area of Poland taken over by the USSR in 1939 (it's in Belarus today). His teacher and some classmates were deported at the time, and the experience left him with a loathing of the Soviet system which comes across strongly to the reader.

Between Heaven and Hell: The Story of a Thousand Years of Artistic Life in Russia by W Bruce Lincoln is a fascinating in-depth history of arts and artists in Russia, ranging from religious icons to Soviet film makers. Its author also wrote the eminently readable *Romanovs: Autocrats of All the Russias*, a complete history of the Romanov dynasty.

Robert Kaiser's *Russia: The People and The Power* is a wonderful account of Soviet life in the 1970s that gives terrific detail while escaping the trap of judging the place by Western standards. *The New Russians* by Hedrick Smith is this former *New York Times* correspondent's overview of Russian life – a 1990 update of the original version but still useful. The USSR, incidentally, produced its own equivalent of Hedrick Smith's book back in the 1960s in the shape of *Those Americans* by N Mikhailov and Z Kossenko, published in English by Henry Regnery (1962). The authors quote normal American men-on-the-street as remarking that 'Capitalism has degraded America to the point that ... the individual is on the verge of decay ...'

Women's Glasnost vs Naglost by Tatyana Mamonova (1994) combines essays by this leader of the Russian women's movement with interviews with a cross-section of women in a country where wife-beating and abortion reach horrific levels.

City Reference Books

The Russian language (and English indexed) *Luchshee V Sankt Peterburge*, and its English version, *The Traveller's Yellow Pages*, are comprehensive and accurate yellow-pages telephone books. They have good city maps that include helpful seating plans to major theatres, opera houses and stadiums. The companion pamphlet *The Traveller's Yellow Pages Essential St Petersburg* is a very brief English yellow pages and guidebook. It has good listings of most of what travellers are interested in, updated twice a year. It also has a good city centre map. All are available in St Petersburg or through the Telinfo website at www.infoservices.com.

The Fresh Guide, a locally-produced guide to the city from Fresh Air Publications, is sometimes available at the HI St Petersburg Hostel and Eurohostel in Helsinki. It's a hilarious read, and great on cultural attractions and off-beat tips.

General

If you're planning any trips to the former gulag camps in Russia's north-west, *The Gulag Archipelago* by Alexandr Solzhenitsyn is required reading. Through interviews with and testimony from hundreds of gulag prisoners, Solzhenitsyn brings to light some of the most heinous prison conditions the world has ever known in a style so familiar that you are enveloped in the stories before you're quite aware of it.

NEWSPAPERS & MAGAZINES

Russian print media has come an awfully long way. Scandals are sought and exposed, sometimes to the detriment of the reporter (several have been killed over the past years while investigating corruption and misman- agement of the military and intelligence organs). The free press in Russia has pro- duced some truly surprising scoops and hard-hitting investigative stories in papers such as *Izvestya* and *Moskovky Komsomo- lets*. It's also produced heaps of shite, which is much more fun to read.

Most of the dozens of Russian-language newspapers in St Petersburg are mouth- pieces for various political parties, or are involved in sensationalism in one way or another.

The weekly *Argumenty I Fakty* covers politics, economics and the occasional movie star interview. *Chas Pik (Rush Hour)* is a daily rag that's as serious as you'd want. There are several information and listings papers, like *Vsyo Dla Vas (Everything for You)* which is a free classified advert paper; *To Da Syo (This and That)* is a 'what's on' listings paper, and *Chto Pochyom (What Costs What)* has listings of prices around town for everything from construction ma- terials to tanning salons and everything in between.

The scandal rags are as sleazy as can be and make *The News of the World* appear to have journalistic integrity. Papers like *Pop- utchik* and *Slukhi & Fakty* have the usual sex, drugs and scandals along with horo- scopes and celebrity 'news'.

Finally, pick up a copy of one of the city's fringe rags; *Novy Svet (New Light)* is an occasionally published anarchist paper ('Free the Chechens! Bash the Govern- ment!'), and *Trudovaya Rossi (Labour Russia)*, espouses the usual stuff about the noble workers etc, etc.

English-Language Print Media

The undisputed king of the hill in locally published English-language news is the ex- cellent *St Petersburg Times*, which was begun by a Kiwi-led team in 1993, and grew so big it was bought by the *Moscow Times*. Today it's a reliable twice-weekly paper packed with practical information and list- ings of clubs, pubs, restaurants, museums, theatre etc. It's available at bookshops, hotels, restaurants and youth hostels.

Pulse is a slick colour monthly with English and Russian editions, both packed with tons of club, pub, nightlife and other information about the city, written with a very young and fresh outlook. It's available free from outlets all over the city.

Newsstands in the bigger hotels usually have a few good Western newspapers of the *International Herald-Tribune*, *Times*, *Guar- dian* variety, costing about 1½ times more than back home.

RADIO & TV

From the little *radio tochka* box in your hotel room you can usually get Radio Rossii – it consists of annoying programs and an offensive hourly rendition of *Moscow Nights* played on the boing-a-phone. The switch on that box will be set either to 'Off' or 'Loud'.

Private Russian-language radio has come a long way and it's worth listening to, though it's rare to hear any Russian bands other than oldies-but-goodies like Akvari- um, Kino and Time Machine. Radio in Russia is broken into three bands, AM, UKV (the lower band of FM from 66-77 mHz) and FM (100-107 mHz). A Western- made FM radio usually won't go lower than 85 mHz. Check the *St Petersburg Times* for radio listings.

On Russian television news programs, if it bleeds it leads: violence, sex and sensational- ism rule the day. Lots of émigrés have returned from America, bringing with them that stronghold of American culture, the shamelessly crude talk show. Athletic Elena Hanga hosts *Pro Eto*, on which guests bare their sexual souls ('I had sex with every man in Belomorsk') as well as the occasional show on abstinence (and, presumably, how to avoid it). On *Semya*, Russian celebrities give their advice to everyday mortals on how to handle their everyday problems ('I wouldn't take that, no sir. I'd send my personal assistant right over to complain'). And *Strip Show*, something like strip poker, has Russian women getting their kit off (well, most of it anyway) in front of a live audience.

It's not all scandal and sleaze, though: the well-respected Vladimir Posner's *My* ('we') is a consumer advocacy program pointing out newfangled rip-offs and scams.

English-Language Radio

The clearest BBC World Service shortwave (SW) frequencies in the morning, late evening and at night are near 9410, 12,095 (the most reliable) and 15,070 mHz. You can tune in to the BBC:

- from midnight to 2 am GMT/UTC at 6180 and 7325 mHz
- from 2 to 4 am at 6195 mHz
- from 2 to 7 am at 9410 mHz
- from 4 am to 8.30 pm at 12,095 mHz
- from 1 to 8 pm at 13,070 mHz
- from 8 pm to midnight at 5930, 6180 and 7325 mHz.

St Petersburg English-language radio also includes Radio Modern, 104 FM Saturday at 11.15 am and Tuesday at 6.15 pm; and the BBC World Service every day on 1260 AM.

Russian-Language TV

In St Petersburg you can see the two national channels plus two local ones; St Petersburg Television, with some pithy, unconventional current-affairs programs that have gained a wide audience, and Channel 4, educational evening TV.

English-Language TV

Most large hotels have satellite television, showing a wide variety of Western programming from CNN, CNBC, The Discovery Channel, MTV, BBC, TV 5 and Pro7.

PHOTOGRAPHY & VIDEO
Photography

Kodak Express has over a dozen drop-off locations and two full-service shops in town, providing fast developing and selling a range of film at European prices. Main branches are at ulitsa Bolshaya Morskaya 32 and ulitsa Malaya Konyushennaya 7.

Agfa does fast (if not one-hour) developing and sells film and camera supplies on the 3rd floor of Nevsky prospekt 20. Fuji's shop near the Anichkov Bridge does much the same; it's at naberezhnaya reki Fontanki 23.

You can get a great deal on Russian photographic equipment at Photo Shop No 76 (Map 4), Bolshoy prospekt (Petrograd Side) 63; it's open from 10 am to 7 pm.

For cheap passport photographs (US$3.25 for six) head for the photo studio at Nevsky prospekt 63 (follow the Срочное Фото signs through the tunnels).

Video

Properly used, a video camera can give a fascinating record of your holiday (and/or bore your friends back home). Remember, however, to follow the same rules regarding people's sensitivities as for a still photograph – having a video camera shoved in their face is probably even more annoying and offensive for locals than a still camera. Always ask permission first.

TIME

Russians use a 24-hour clock; midnight is 0000, 7 am is 0700, 1 pm is 1300, 9 pm is 2100.

From the early hours of the last Sunday in September to the early hours of the last Sunday in March, St Petersburg time is GMT/UTC plus three hours. From the last Sunday in March to the last Sunday in September, 'summer time' is in force and it's GMT/UTC plus four hours.

When it's noon in St Petersburg it's ...

- 1 am in San Francisco;
- 4 am in New York and Toronto;
- 9 am in London;
- 10 am in Paris, Warsaw, Prague, Budapest and Stockholm;

FACTS FOR THE VISITOR

FACTS FOR THE VISITOR

See Them While You Can

There are relatively few statues of good ol' Vladimir Ilyich Lenin left in St Petersburg; the ones not sold or removed are biding their time, though there is a nascent movement to preserve them as part of the city's history. But you never can tell – so if you're here, you should seek them out while you can. Something to tell the grandkids about or, at the least, a great photo opportunity.

The best statue of Lenin is at Moskovsky prospekt just north of ploshchad Pobedy (seen on the drive from the airport into the city), where Vlad definitely appears to be hailing a taxi. Others are in front of Warsaw Station (Map 6) and Finland Station (Map 5), along Bolshoy prospekt on Vasilevsky Island (Map 6), and in the Tauride Gardens (Map 5). And don't forget the plaques around town, wherever he spent a night, and the Order of Lenin plaques in some metro stations (commemorating one of the Soviet Union's highest honours).

There's a great statue of Kirov, one of Stalin's leading henchmen, just south of Narvskaya metro on prospekt Stachek, and one of Dzerzhinsky, founder of the Soviet secret police (the Cheka, forerunner to the KGB) right near the Smolny (Map 5).

NICK SELBY

Warsaw Station is home to one of the few remaining statues of Lenin.

- 11 am in Helsinki, Bucharest and Ankara;
- 5 pm in Ulan Bator and Beijing, 4 pm in summer Beijing;
- 8 pm in summer Sydney, 6 pm in winter Sydney;
- 10 pm in summer Auckland, 8 pm in winter Auckland.

ELECTRICITY

Electricity is 220 volts, 50Hz AC, and very reliable in St Petersburg. Sockets require a Continental or European plug adaptor with two round pins. American and Japanese appliances need a 220V to 110V/100V converter.

WEIGHTS & MEASURES

The metric system is in use. Drinks are served in measures of 50g or 100g, about 1.75 or 3.5 ounces (whoo). Russian restaurant menus list food and drink servings by weight; a glass of tea is about 200g.

The unit of items sold by the piece, such as eggs, is Штука (*shtuka*) or Шт. (*sht.*) which literally means 'thing' or 'piece'.

Numbers are written with the comma and decimal point reversed relative to US, Canadian, Australian and English standards (so, for example, $1,000.00 would appear written as $1.000,00 in Russia).

LAUNDRY

Unless you're staying at a hotel, the laundrette is as close as your bathroom. The HI St Petersburg Hostel has a washing machine (but no dryer) for the use of hostel guests for US$5 for up to 5kg. Hotels (even cheap ones) offer laundry services for various prices – these services usually take between one and three days. As yet there's no public laundry facilities to speak of in town.

TOILETS

Free or inexpensive toilets are scattered around town, marked with the Latin characters 'WC' or the Russian Платный туалет *(platny tualet;* pay toilet). There are also free or inexpensive toilets at bus and train stations. Many are even clean nowadays. In any toilet, Ж stands for *zhenskiy* (women's), and M for *muzhkoy* (men's). Walking into restaurants or hotels and asking usually results in permission to use the, er, facilities.

HEALTH
Predeparture Planning

Most visitors to St Petersburg don't experience any serious health problems providing they adhere to the golden rule regarding drinking the city's water, but comprehensive travel insurance (covering theft, loss and medical problems, as well as medical evacuation if necessary) is essential.

If you are visiting in winter, be prepared for cold conditions. Make sure childhood vaccinations, including polio, diphtheria and tetanus, are up to date. It's a good idea to travel with a basic medical kit (including aspirin or paracetamol, antiseptic, Band-aids etc) even though most medical supplies should be available in the larger pharmacies. Don't forget any medication you're already taking.

Under a 1995 Russian law, anyone applying for a visa for a stay of more than three months must provide a certificate showing HIV negative status. The certificate needs to have this information written in both English and Russian (see the Visas section earlier in this chapter).

Water

No matter how thirsty you are, avoid drinking the tap water in St Petersburg. It contains *Giardia lamblia*, a nasty parasite that causes unpleasant stomach cramps, nausea, bloated stomach, watery and foul-smelling diarrhoea and frequent gas. There is no preventative drug. Metronidazole (brand name Flagyl) or Tinidazole, known as Fasigyn, are the recommended treatments. Antibiotics are of no use. Symptoms may not appear for up to several weeks after infection.

To be absolutely safe, only drink water that has been boiled for 10 minutes or filtered through an antimicrobial water filter (PUR brand makes a good portable one; check with a sporting goods store before you leave). Treat ice with suspicion and avoid fruits and vegetables that may have been washed in the water – vegetables that peel are safest.

But even if you boil or filter away the Giardia, there are still very high levels of pollution and heavy metals present in the water here; it's best to stick to bottled water, even for brushing your teeth. Bathing, showering and shaving, though, should cause no problems.

Medical Services

Unless you're an uninsured US or South African resident and citizen, medical treatment in St Petersburg will be beneath the standards you're used to receiving at home. Nonetheless,within Russia St Petersburg is second only to Moscow in the area of medical services and offers adequate routine, and some emergency, treatment. More serious medical emergencies are best treated outside Russia; Finland is the best option (a good travel insurance policy should cover the costs involved in medical evacuation).

The best bet for Western-quality treatment in St Petersburg is the American Medical Center (AMC; Map 7, ☎ 326 17 30), Serpukhovskaya ulitsa 10, a US-run facility offering a range of medical services including prenatal, gynaecological and paediatric care, dentistry, 24-hour emergency care, on-site urgent care facilities, private ambulance services, house calls and 24-hour coordination of medical evacuations from the CIS. They also have a complete Western pharmacy. Of course it's going to cost you: prices are stellar, with a basic check-up clocking in at a robust US$100 for members and US$150 for non-members – and it's all uphill from there.

For routine matters, however, a Russian *poliklinika* is often able to provide perfectly adequate care. I asked AMC doctors where they'd send their family members if the AMC weren't an option: they all said Poliklinika No 2 (Map 7, ☎ 316 62 72), the former clinic of choice for diplomatic staff, at Moskovsky prospekt 22; or Gastello Hospital (Map 3, ☎ 291 79 60 or 293 70 10) at ulitsa Gastello 20. For more listings, check *Luchshee V Sankt Peterburge* or *The Traveller's Yellow Pages*.

Ambulance

The state-run ambulance service is still free; Russian speakers can get help by dialling ☎ 03. Saying it's for a foreigner may help you receive faster and better service. If you're trying to find out if someone's been in an accident and been picked up by ambulance (and where they were taken), dial ☎ 278 00 55. Private ambulance service is available through the AMC, and house calls are available 24 hours a day.

Pharmacies

Pharmacies (singular *apteka*, which is what you should ask for) are located all over the city. Generally, pharmacies in St Petersburg are almost well stocked, and many have Western medications and toiletries. The higher quality ones have everything you may need.

Apteka Petrofarm is an all-night pharmacy that's packed with Western everything. The entrance is at the corner of Nevsky and Bolshaya Konyushennaya. Apteka No 4 at Nevsky prospekt 5 is a good pharmacy with a large range of Western stuff. There's also a full Western pharmacy at the AMC.

Sexually Transmitted Diseases

Treatment of gonorrhoea or syphilis is by antibiotics, available from the AMC and at Skin and Venereal Dispensaries *(Kozhno-venerichskie Dispansery)* throughout the city, which offer diagnosis and treatment of sexually transmitted diseases (check *Luchshee V Sankt Peterburge* or *The Traveller's Yellow Pages* for listings of these clinics). The incidence of AIDS is on the rise in Russia, so the usual precautions need to be taken.

WOMEN TRAVELLERS

In general you're unlikely to experience sexual harassment on the streets, but sexual stereotyping remains strong (if you're with a man, finer restaurants will hand you a 'ladies' menu' without prices) and revealing clothing will probably attract unwanted attention. With lawlessness and crime on the rise, you need to be wary; a woman alone should certainly avoid private taxis at night.

Any young or youngish woman alone in or near flashy foreigner-haunt bars risks being mistaken for a prostitute.

Russian women dress up and wear lots of make-up on nights out. If you wear casual gear, you might feel uncomfortable at dinner in a restaurant, or at a theatre or the ballet. Consider packing something 'smart' to change into at the end of a day's travel or sightseeing.

You might be treated rudely or ignored by female service bureau staff while a man standing next to you is getting smiles and answers to his questions. Persevere to get the help you need. Even if your Russian isn't up to much, you can get by.

GAY & LESBIAN TRAVELLERS

Article 121.1 of the Russian Criminal Code, which banned homosexual sex, was repealed in May 1993. There is an active gay and lesbian scene in St Petersburg, but it's still in its infancy. To date there are only a couple of gay/lesbian clubs (see the Entertainment chapter). Organisations are cagey about contact details (understandably so, given the volatile political climate in the country), and there's not anything approaching the kind of community support infrastructure common in the West.

Key reading is *The Rights of Lesbians & Gay Men in the Russian Federation*, a 130-page, US$15 book in Russian and English published by the International Gay & Lesbian Human Rights Commission (☎ 415-255 8680, fax 415-255 8662), 1360 Mission St, Suite 200, San Francisco, CA 94103.

The *Spartacus guide* (readily available in the West) lists several organisations, clubs, cruising areas and health services, though its listings date quickly – some gay travellers have reported problems when relying on a dated listing, so be sure to confirm information.

KRILYA (wings) (☎ 312 31 80, krilija@ ilga.org), is the city's oldest gay and lesbian community organisation that can assist travellers with information (in English), accommodation suggestions and emergency assistance. Safo (☎/fax 528 18 30) is a new lesbian organisation in town that also collects clothes and books for the needy. They're on the lookout for donations to open a book and video library.

On the web, www.vmt.com/gayrussia has some good information on bars and clubs in St Petersburg and a list of links to gay Russia sites. Another site, at www.gayrussia.msk.ru is a Moscow-centric gay page, with heaps of listings for Moscow and basic information on St Petersburg.

DISABLED TRAVELLERS

Inaccessible transport, lack of ramps and lifts and no centralised policy for people with physical limitations make St Petersburg a challenging destination for wheelchair-bound visitors. More mobile travellers will have a relatively easier time, but keep in mind that there are obstacles along the way. Toilets are frequently accessed from stairs in restaurants and museums; distances are great and public transport extremely crowded. While disabled people are treated with respect and people do go out of their way to be helpful, the experience may be frustrating.

There are exceptions. The Grand Hotel Europe and the Sheraton Nevskij Palace Hotel are wheelchair accessible, as are their restaurants. While the HI St Petersburg Hostel has no lift, it has a good amount of experience with wheelchair-bound visitors. Other major hotels will all provide assistance and information. Patience and forward planning are required, however.

Organisations

There are a number of organisations and tour providers around the world that specialise in the needs of disabled travellers.

Australia
  Independent Travellers (☎ 08-232 2555, toll-free ☎ 008-811 355, fax 232 6877), 167 Gilles St, Adelaide SA 5000, is a travel agent that provides specialised advice for disabled travellers to a number of destinations.
Russia
  The All-Union Association for the Rehabilitation of the Disabled (☎ 095-298 87 37, fax 230 24 07) is at 1 Kuibyahera ploshchad, Moscow
UK
  RADAR (☎ 0171-250 3222), 250 City Rd London, is a good resource centre for travellers with disabilities.
USA
  Twin Peaks Press (☎ 202-694-2462, or toll free in the USA and Canada ☎ 800-637-2256) publishes several useful handbooks for disabled travellers, including *Travel for the Disabled* and the *Directory of Travel Agencies for the Disabled*. They can be contacted at PO Box 129, Vancouver, WA 98666
  Access, the Foundation for Accessibility by the Disabled (☎ 516-887-5798), can be contacted at PO Box 356, Malverne, NY 11565.
  The Information Center for Individuals with Disabilities (☎ 617-727 5540, TTY 345-9743 or toll-free ☎ 800-248-3737) is at Fort Point Place, 1st Floor, 27-43 Wormwood Street, Boston, MA 02210. Call or write for their listings and free advice.
  Mobility International USA (☎ TDD 503-343-1284, fax 343-6812; miusa@igc.apc.org), PO Box 3551, Eugene, OR 97403, advises disabled travellers on mobility issues. It also runs an exchange program, and has run several programs in Russia.
  SATH, Society for the Advancement of Travel for the Handicapped (☎ 212-447 7284), is at 347 Fifth Ave No 610, New York, NY 10016.

FACTS FOR THE VISITOR

Handicapped Travel Newsletter is a nonprofit, bimonthly publication with good information on travelling around the world. Subscriptions are US$10 annually. Its address is PO Drawer 269, Athens, TX 75751 (☎/fax 903-677 1260). Moss Rehabilitation Hospital's Travel Information Service (☎ 215-456 9600, TTY 456-9602) is at 1200 W Tabor Road, Philadelphia, PA 19141-3099.

Internet Resources

As you would imagine, the Internet is brimming with information on the subject of physical disabilities. EKA (Evan Kemp Associates), a company selling products for the disabled, runs a good site with lots of links. They're at www.eka.com. Disabled Peoples' International has a home page at www.dpi.org. It's a nonprofit and well-done website with tons of listings and great links; those behind it are based in Canada and seem to think truly globally.

SENIOR TRAVELLERS

Travellers over age 60 can expect senior citizen discounts and a good degree of respect from Russian ticket agents. Respect for the elderly is far more ingrained in the Russian mentality than in some countries, such as America. Organisations in your home country, like the American Association of Retired Persons (www.aarp.org), for which you don't need to be retired, or even a senior, to join, can assist with age-specific information before you leave.

ST PETERSBURG FOR CHILDREN

There's heaps to do with kids in St Petersburg; there are even museums your kids will like! For starters, the Kunstkammer in the Museum of Anthropology & Ethnography is an all-time favourite, as are most of the interesting cultural displays in the State Museum of Ethnography. If it's winter, head for the Flowers Exhibition hall just before you go to the Smolny and watch the little ones gawk at the tropical plants.

And then of course there's the zoo and circus, the Peter & Paul Fortress and the Planetarium, all of which hold special kids' programs.

The city's parks are first rate; there's a full-scale amusement park right behind the Peter & Paul Fortress, and a smaller one in the Tauride Gardens which has a small children's park. There's an awesome children's playground on the east side of ulitsa Bolshaya Pushkarskaya just north of ulitsa Lenina, Petrograd Side. And there are rowing boat rental outlets behind the Peter & Paul Fortress, on Yelagin Island and sometimes in other places around the city. Check the Things to See & Do chapter for more information, or ask at your hotel or hostel for kids' activities and babysitting services.

LIBRARIES

The enormous Mayakovskogo City Central Public Library (Map 8, ☎ 112 51 03), naberezhnaya reki Fontanki 44, is St Petersburg's biggest, with 1.5 million books in over 20 languages, including English.

There are other English libraries at the British Council and the American Center (see Cultural Centres later in this chapter). The Prince George Vladimirovich Golitsyna Memorial Library (Map 8, ☎ 311 13 33), naberezhnaya reki Fontanki 46, is a lovely reading room containing books in English and Russian pertaining to Russian culture and British-Russian links. They also have encyclopaedias and other reference books, and they allow you to photocopy sections free of charge.

The University Fundamental Library (☎ 552 75 59), Politekhnicheskaya ulitsa 29, has almost three million titles, mainly in Russian, but was the first Russian library to have a high-speed fibre-optic Internet connection.

UNIVERSITIES

St Petersburg has long been an academic centre and its numerous universities and trade schools have, since tsarist days, produced some of the country's leading scholars, engineers, scientists and professionals. For a complete list of the city's two dozen universities, check *Luchshee V Sankt Peterburge* or *The Traveller's Yellow Pages*.

St Petersburg State University (☎ 218 20 00), with its main campus on the Strelka, has over 20 schools including mathematics, languages, philosophy and geology. It is held to be the finest university in the country after the State University in Moscow. All students are on full scholarship. The campus is made up of some of the city's most beautiful buildings.

St Petersburg Technical University (☎ 552 78 82) produces some of the best engineers in Eastern Europe and some of Russia's best computer technicians. Its schools range from electronics and engineering to computers and network security to satellite communications. The campus is south of the centre, around metro Tekhnologichesky Institut.

CULTURAL CENTRES

There's a whole lot o' culture going on at naberezhnaya reki Fontanki 46 (Map 8). On the 3rd floor sits the British Council St Petersburg (☎ 325 60 74), which holds classical concerts, theatre and other performances and arranges for exchanges between Russia and the UK of students, professionals and (frighteningly) economists. It has a great resource centre for foreign teachers of English.

The Goethe Institute St Petersburg (☎ 311 21 00) is in the same building but is hard to find: walk into the lobby, straight to the back, turn right, follow the narrow hallway and go up the flight of stairs to find the German cultural centre.

The American Center (Map 5, ☎ 311 89 05) at the Marble Palace disseminates American culture (snigger) when they're not too busy doing very important things. It's open from 9 am to 5.30 pm at ulitsa Millionnaya 5.

DANGERS & ANNOYANCES
Street Crime

St Petersburg's streets are about as safe or dangerous as New York's, Mexico City's, London's or Amsterdam's. There's petty theft, pickpocketing, purse-snatching and other such crimes that are endemic in big-city life anywhere in the world. Travellers have reported muggings in broad daylight along Nevsky prospekt. Many travellers have reported problems with groups of Gypsies (Roma or Travellers), who surround foreigners, ostensibly to panhandle, but end up closing in, with dozens of hands probing your pockets.

The key here is to be neither paranoid nor insouciant. Common sense must be applied, and you'll need to be aware that it's pretty obvious you're a Westerner, but that doesn't automatically make you a target. Here are some anti-crime tips:

- Bum bags (fanny packs) are out; they're easily cut with a razor and hey, wasn't that your wallet? If you're going to use a pouch, use a strong leather one or, better yet, an under-the-clothes model so your money is next to your skin. Carry around enough cash so you won't have to pull your pants down to buy a can of drink.
- An exciting way to meet Russian photo enthusiasts is to walk down Nevsky prospekt with your Nikon slung carelessly over your shoulder. Bag it.
- Don't do anything you wouldn't normally do at home. Flashing jewellery, cash, or speaking on your cellular phone while walking down the street is inviting trouble.
- Keep your wallet in your front pants pocket, never in back or outside pockets, such as in your coat or jacket.
- Watch out when in crowds and on public transport. Assume any displays of anger or altercations in crowds to be diversionary tactics and act accordingly.
- Don't change money on the street unless it's absolutely necessary, and then take as much control as you can of the situation and stay alert. Keep your Western and Russian currencies in different pockets. Always pocket the roubles before handing over your Western currency. Isolate yourself, and never let yourself be the centre of a group – even a group of three including yourself. Or just go to a bank, for God's sake.

The 'Mafia'

The Western media has had a field day talking about the dangers of the Russian Mafia, painting a portrait of a country inundated with Al Capone types who race through the streets indiscriminately firing

Kalashnikov rifles at tourists. In fact, the organised crime problem in Russia is far more complex, and far less of a threat to visitors than one would guess after reading an issue of *Newsweek*.

In general, when people discuss the 'Mafia' they're speaking of the black marketeers and criminal gangs that blossomed with glasnost's removal of the state's channels of fear. It's a loosely applied term, ranging from any group making a few payoffs to hold down a little corner of the black market, to vicious gangsters who do indeed occasionally settle scores with Kalashnikovs.

Mafia fingers are in all sorts of pies, including currency speculation, extortion from businesses, drugs, transportation, staple goods distribution, bootlegging, gunrunning and prostitution.

Crime against foreigners has grown as well, but the Western press has completely gone over the top, making it sound as if the moment you leave the airport you're going to get shot by the 'Mafia'.

Assume for a moment that you're a Mafioso. You have at your disposal the criminal might to extort, say, a percentage of the profits of a multinational food and beverage corporation with a nationwide distribution network, *or*, alternatively, the contents of the handbag of Mrs J Whistlethwaite of Staines. What would you do? The same as Mafiosi do in Russia: unless you're involved in high-flying currency speculation, organised criminals aren't really going to waste their time with you. What you have to watch for is the very real threat of street crime carried out by drunken or angry punks and hoods.

Burglary

Break-ins to flats and cars are epidemic so don't leave anything of value in a car. Valuables left lying around hotel rooms are also tempting providence. If you'll be living in a flat, it's imperative that you invest in a steel door (see *Luchshee V Sankt Peterburge* for suppliers).

Reporting Theft & Loss

If you're here in a group, your tour guide or service bureau should be your first resort if you want to report a theft or loss. If not, speak to your hotel or hostel administrator for help. You may end up talking to the police *(militsia)*, whose telephone number is ☎ 02, and if you don't speak Russian you'll need a translator. *Vorovstvo* and *krazha* both mean theft in Russian. For lost passports or visas, see the Visas section earlier in this chapter.

Racism

Overt hostility is almost unheard of, though a high level of entrenched racism, or at least racist attitudes, exists in St Petersburg and indeed in Russia. What is most surprising is that racist attitudes or statements can come from otherwise highly educated Russian men and women. The word 'nigger' is not generally regarded here as anything other than racially descriptive, and the word is liberally used when speaking about (not to) anyone with dark skin, including Georgians or Chechens. Jews, targets of state-sponsored anti-Semitism during the communist reign, are more distrusted than hated, though the hatred certainly exists. Roma, also known as Gypsies or Travellers, however, are openly reviled.

The KGB

The *Komitet Gosudarstvennoy Bezopastnosti* (the Committee for State Security) is on the scrap-heap of Soviet history. Its successor, the *Federalnaya Sluzhba Kontrrazvedki* (the Federal Counter-Intelligence Service; ☎ 095-924 31 58) has far better things to do with its time than run around following a bunch of tourists.

Mosquitoes

St Petersburg's prime swamp-front location means that in summer, mossies are rife. Malaria isn't a problem, it's just that the damn things are so completely annoying you may wish to leap from the very window that let the bastards in in the first place. In St Petersburg or any point north of it (where they get huge and become *screaming* dive bombers), you will want to bring along industrial-strength mosquito repellent that's at least 95% DEET. This, or mosquito coils or a net, is essential. If you're dead against DEET, some say that taking regular doses of vitamin B complex for two weeks before your trip will help make you less attractive to mossies. You can also bring along some of the plug-in gizmos, commonly available throughout Europe, that slowly heat cardboard pads that have been saturated with repellent.

Holes

There are uncovered manholes and other subterranean access ports throughout the city: there are no signs, flags or other markers (except the occasional reverberating 'aaaaahhhhh' emanating from the deep). Watch your step.

General Annoyances

One thing you can't do anything about is the tangle of opening hours whereby every shop, museum and café seems to be having its lunch or afternoon break, or day off, or is *remont* (closed for repairs), or is simply closed full stop, just when you want to visit.

Other things you might find annoying are alcoholic late-night comings, goings and door banging in hotel corridors; engine-revving, car-alarm testing, tyre-screeching and more door-banging outside hotels after the restaurant closes; the brain-numbing volume of restaurant bands; the redolent clouds of cigarette smoke that billow from most gatherings of Russian citizens; and prostitutes who sometimes (still!) walk into or telephone your hotel room offering sex.

LEGAL MATTERS
Arrest

If you are arrested, the Russian authorities are obliged to inform your embassy or consulate immediately and allow you to communicate with it without delay. You can insist on seeing an official from your embassy or consulate straight away. Be polite and respectful and things will go far more smoothly for you. *'Pazhalsta, ya khatelbi pozvanit v posoltstvo moyay stroni'* means 'I'd like to call my embassy'.

BUSINESS HOURS

Government offices are open Monday to Friday from 9 or 10 am to 5 or 6 pm. Foreign exchange banks are usually open from 9 am to noon; those in major cities are also open from 1 to 8.30 pm.

Most shops are open Monday to Saturday. Food shops tend to open from 8 am to 8 pm except for a break *(pereryv)* from 1 to 2 pm or 2 to 3 pm; some close later, some open Sunday until 5 pm. Other shops operate from 10 or 11 am to 7 or 8 pm with a 2 to 3 pm break. Department stores may open from 8 am to 8 or 9 pm without a break. A few shops stay open through the weekend and close Monday.

Restaurants typically open from noon to midnight except for a break between afternoon and evening meals. Cafés may open and close earlier. Museum hours change like quicksilver, as do their weekly days off. Most shut entrance doors 30 minutes or an hour before closing time and may have shorter hours on the day before their day off. Some just seem to close without reason and a few stay that way for years.

Beware the *şanitarny den* (sanitary day). Once a month, usually near the end of the month (the last Tuesday, for example), nearly all establishments – shops, museums, restaurants, hotel dining rooms – shut down for cleaning, each on its own day and not always with much publicity.

PUBLIC HOLIDAYS & SPECIAL EVENTS

After more than seven decades of official atheism, religious holidays are once again kosher in Russia. During the last 10 days of June, when night never falls, many St Petersburgers stay out all night celebrating White Nights (particularly at weekends). There's a tourist-oriented White Nights Dance Festival with events ranging from folk to ballet, but the main Kirov company

Dance Festival with events ranging from folk to ballet, but the main Kirov company doesn't always take part – more often its students do. The Russian Winter (25 December to 5 January) and Goodbye Russian Winter (late February to early March) festivities centre outside the city, with *troyka* (horse-drawn sleigh) rides, folk shows and performing bears.

Less tourist-oriented are the Christmas Musical Meetings in Northern Palmyra, a classical music festival held since 1991 during the week before Christmas. The locations change; check the *St Petersburg Times* for details. The St Petersburg Music Spring is an international classical music festival held in April or May, and the mid-November International Jazz Festival, Osenie Ritmy (Autumn Rhythms), is centred around St Petersburg's jazz club.

Russian festivals have shaken off the Soviet-era image of joyous workers marching past decrepit Party leaders.

January
New Year's Day
    1 January
Russian Orthodox Christmas *(Rozhdestvo)*
    7 January. Begins with midnight church services.

February and March
Defenders of the Motherland Day
    23 February. A new holiday from 1996 to celebrate the anniversary of the founding of the Red Army.
Goodbye Russian Winter
    Late February – early March. Festivities centre outside the city, with troyka rides, folk shows etc.
International Women's Day
    8 March

April and May
International Labour Day/Spring Festival
    1–2 May
Easter *(Paskha)*
    The main festival of the Orthodox Church year. Easter Day begins with celebratory midnight services after which people eat special dome-shaped cakes called *kulichy* and curd-cakes called *paskha* and may exchange painted wooden Easter eggs. The devout deny themselves meat, milk, alcohol and sex in the 40-day pre-Easter fasting period of Lent. Palm Sunday in Russia is Pussy Willow Sunday, as palms don't exist this far north (honest!).
Victory (1945) Day
    9 May
St Petersburg Music Spring
    International classical music festival.

June and July
Russian Independence Day
    12 June
St Petersburg White Nights
    Last 10 days of June. General merrymaking and staying out late, plus dance festival.
Fishermen's Day *(Den Rybaka)*
    Second Sunday in July. Games, stalls, evening music and dance in fishing ports.

November
Great October Socialist Revolution Anniversary
    7 November. See the generals on TV staying heroically upright as they salute the tribal roars of their troops parading over the Red Square cobbles. Just kidding; it's actually not still celebrated as such, though it is still a holiday.
Autumn Rhythms *(Osenie Ritmy)*
    Mid-November Jazz festival.

December
Christmas Musical Meetings in Northern Palmyra
    20 December–8 January. A classical music festival held since 1991 in St Petersburg. Runs for three weeks, from the week before Western Christmas to Orthodox Christmas; hence exact dates may vary slightly.
Russian Winter Festival
    25 December–5 January. Tourist-oriented troyka rides, folklore shows, games, vodka. Still celebrated in St Petersburg (Olgino).
Sylvestr and New Year 31 December–1 January. The main winter and gift-giving festival. Gifts are put under the traditional fir tree *(yolka)*. See out the old year with vodka and welcome the new one with champagne while listening to the Kremlin chimes on radio and TV.

DOING BUSINESS
For computer time, copiers, fax and Internet access, Westpost (☎ 275 07 84; westpost@westpost.ru) at Nevsky prospekt 86 (see Post & Communications earlier) is the best deal.

Each of the major luxury hotels (and some of the cheesy ones) has a full-service

Winter Palace – residence of tsars until the revolution, now housing part of the Hermitage museum

Malachite vase, the Hermitage

Rembrandt Hall, the Hermitage

Queue to enter the Hermitage

Atlas statues, outside the New Hermitage

NICK SELBY

Siege warning from WWII, Nevsky prospekt 14

NICK SELBY

Mortar plaque, Resurrection Church

NICK SELBY

Mourners, Piskaryovka Cemetery

NICK SELBY

Mass grave, Piskaryovka Cemetery

NICK SELBY

Statue of Mother Russia, Piskaryovka Cemetery

business centre, each quite expensive for anything other than a one-time fax or photocopy, with rates at about US$0.50 per page for copies and outrageous international telephone and fax charges.

At Shvedsky Pereulok 2 is Ipris (Map 8, ☎ 210 76 69), a very friendly copy centre with Xerox brand copiers, which does photocopies for about US$0.15 each.

WORK

Relatively few people who come to Russia to get rich achieve this ambition. But working your way through Russia, especially if you've got some knowledge of the Russian language and a sophisticated sense of humour, is a great way to really get to know the country and its people.

Things have changed drastically since the early 1990s, when your CV was your Western passport and willingness to work in Russia. Today there's stiff competition for positions in Russia, which are seen as sidedoor entry ports to multinational corporations or, if you're already in the front door, a highly-paid hardship post to be followed by a cushy assignment at the end of your Russian tenure. These days, employment recruiters (and there are lots) use phrases like 'target career goals', 'personal success strategy' and 'pay cheque'.

While regulations on foreigners working in Russia are arcane and visa procedures Byzantine, getting permission to work here is, practically speaking, more a question of lining up a job than fumbling with paperwork. Once you have an employer, all the red tape seems to magically disappear and a multiple-entry business visa will be yours once your new company's facilitators are on the job. There are taxes and duties and residence problems to be coped with, but these change so quickly and so regularly that committing them to ink is folly (though we're a follyful lot; see the earlier Visas section for some key regulations).

If you can hold out financially, working for a Russian company (count on a salary of US$1000 a month) can be rewarding in non-financial ways, such as working on your language, learning the ropes from a truly Russian perspective, and has possibilities of pleasure and business trips with co-workers that will gain you entry to activities and places that would probably be closed to foreigners under normal circumstances. If you're looking to live like a Russian, you should probably start by being paid like one.

To work for a foreign company in St Petersburg, you'll almost always need a headhunter; there are several agencies, like Kelly Services (☎ 325 73 00, fax 325 73 01, resume@kellycis.spb.ru) Nevsky prospekt 11, office 6, that specialise in long and short-term placement of foreigners and Russians. The situation in Moscow is still such that you can just show up and start looking, but in St Pete, competition is simply too fierce for that – don't come here with the idea that you'll just score a top job.

Use resources overseas to get your search started. Operate on the theory that you won't get anything till you arrive, but you can make things much easier by making as many connections as you can beforehand. Check the *St Petersburg Times* and the *Moscow Times* classified sections on the Net for jobs postings as well as employment services at home. Use Internet connections to get in Russian business circles and establish a presence before you arrive.

The Expat Community

The expatriate community in St Petersburg is a close-knit one; the feeling of being ground-breakers in a hostile territory is still a factor, though it has diminished over the last few years. Foreign business associations are well established in St Petersburg. The network of expatriates looks after its own and, once you're accepted as a serious resident, it's as chummy as any old-boy network the West has to offer. The St Petersburg International Business Association (see Information, earlier) is a good place to start.

Getting There & Away

AIR

Pulkovo-1 and -2, respectively the domestic and international airports that serve St Petersburg, are 17km south of the city centre (Map 3), about a half-hour taxi ride and about an hour by public transport.

There are regular services to St Petersburg from many European capitals on carriers including British Airways, Lufthansa, Finnair, Delta, SAS, Swissair, Air France, Alitalia, and ANA (All Nippon Airways). Other carriers, notably CSA, LOT Polish, Balkan and Malév, offer services to St Petersburg several times a week. Many major airlines have offices in St Petersburg (see Leaving St Petersburg by Air).

Departure Tax

There is an air departure tax of US$11, payable when you buy your ticket.

Other Parts Of Russia

Transaero, a high-quality Russian airline offering Western-standard service aboard mostly Western-made aircraft (mainly Boeing 737s and 757s), and Pulkovo Airlines, the 'baby-flot' that previously had the route monopoly, fly between St Petersburg and Moscow. While air travel in Russia is generally not to be recommended, the route between these cities is the safest in the country.

Until recently, Pulkovo Airlines had held exclusive rights to the route since Soviet times, when it was the Leningrad division of Aeroflot. The result of the new arrangement is better service and – dare I say it – choice. Prices between the two carriers are competitive, with Transaero coming in a bit cheaper in economy class; airfares between the cities start at US$115 (economy class) and US$225 (business class) each way on Transaero and from as low as US$140 return on weekends on Pulkovo.

Tickets for both Pulkovo and Transaero can be purchased from travel agencies such as Sindbad Travel (☎ 327 8384) at the HI St Petersburg Hostel, 3-ya Sovetskaya ulitsa 28, and from IRO Travel (☎ 095-234 65 53) at the Travellers Guest House in Moscow, Bolshoy Pereyaslavskaya ulitsa 50, and through Transaero agents in both cities.

Other Countries

Bargain Tickets & Flights Airlines are not the place to buy cheap tickets, but their best deals, usually advance-purchase tickets, will give you a reference point. Cheaper and more convenient are agencies which specialise in finding low fares, like STA Travel and Trailfinders in the UK, Kilroy Travel in Finland, Travel Overland in Germany, Council Travel in the USA, Travel Cuts in Canada and the UK and STA Travel in Australia and New Zealand. See the sections following for more country-specific information.

Apex (Advance-Purchase Excursion) Fares You get sizeable discounts from some carriers by booking well ahead (eg a 28-day advance booking knocks 25% off the London-St Petersburg return fare). But Apex fares come with big penalties for changes or cancellations.

Charter Flights Group-tour charters can be as much as a third cheaper than scheduled flights in the low season. You may be able to arrange one of these in advance but normally it's a last-minute affair.

Discount Flights Some airlines drop prices as they get closer to the departure date. In many large cities, 'bucket shops' – discount clearing houses – offer some of the best bargains in the Western hemisphere, but some are just crooks in disguise. Check that they're licensed by the International Air Transport Association (IATA) or an equivalent national body and get the tickets before you pay.

In London, bucket shops advertise in Sunday-paper travel sections, the 'What's On' section of *Time Out* (the weekly entertainment guide) and in the free weekly *TNT* magazine. In the USA, major city newspapers often have classified ads in their Sunday travel sections. Bucket shops advertise in papers like the *Village Voice* (New York), the *San Francisco Examiner* and the *New Times* (Miami). In Germany, try *In (München)*, a free biweekly available in cafés and bars.

In Australia, the *Sydney Morning Herald* and the Melbourne *Age* weekend travel sections have advertisements for bucket shops and bargains. Good Asian bucket-shop cities are Bangkok, Hong Kong, Singapore and Delhi.

Nowadays, any travel agent in the world can assist you to get bookings, confirmations and domestic tickets for many areas of Russia – you needn't go through a Russia specialist or Intourist to book a trip. Obviously, if you're booking land packages in addition to flights, the more experience your agent has the better off you'll probably be. The exception to this is if you're just looking for a cheap ticket to the country, in which case you should go with whatever agency has the best deal at the time you're flying.

The following sections include travel agencies specialising in Russian or discount travel from abroad. See also Organised Tours later in this chapter.

The UK London is arguably the world headquarters for bucket shops, which are well advertised and can usually beat published airline fares.

Intourist UK (☎ 0171-538 8600, fax 538-5967, london@intourist.co.uk) may be the best of its ilk; its office is in the Docklands at 219 Marsh Wall, Isle of Dogs, London E14 9FJ. It offers budget trips including both Moscow and St Petersburg with prices in the UK£400 to UK£600 range.

Most British travel agents are registered with the ABTA (Association of British Travel Agents). If you have paid for your

flight to an ABTA-registered agent who then goes out of business, ABTA will guarantee a refund or an alternative. Unregistered bucket shops are riskier but sometimes cheaper.

Good, reliable agents for cheap tickets in the UK are Trailfinders (☎ 0171-937 5400), 194 Kensington High St, London W8 7RG; Council Travel (☎ 0171-437 7767) 28a Poland St, London W1, and STA Travel (☎ 0171-937 9971), 86 Old Brompton Rd, London SW7 3LQ. The Globetrotters Club (BCM Roving, London WC1N 3XX) publishes a newsletter called *Globe* that covers obscure destinations and can help you find travelling companions.

Continental Europe NBBS Travels (☎ 020-638 17 38), the Dutch Student Travel Service, is a reliable source of bargain air tickets from Amsterdam, though as a bargain ticket hub, Amsterdam isn't what it used to be. NBBS has offices throughout the Netherlands.

Because of restrictions, travel from Germany to Russia is quite expensive, with a Frankfurt-St Petersburg ticket costing about DM1000, or about DM600 from a discount travel agency. The best deal at the time of writing was from Munich and Frankfurt on Aeroflot; the round-trip ticket, valid for three months, was DM550 plus DM60 tax. The flight on Malév, via and including a stop in Budapest, was DM615 plus DM60 tax.

In Germany, an awesome travel discounter for students and non-students alike is Travel Overland, with offices in several cities; for the nearest one, contact their Munich office (☎ 089-272 76 30 0) Barerstrasse 73, 80799 München. In Berlin, try Die Neue Reisewelle (☎ 030-323 10 78).

From Warsaw, the terrific folk at LOT Polish Airlines and other carriers offer round trips to St Petersburg for under US$250. Expect similar fares from Prague and Budapest.

North America A heavily restricted discount flight from New York to St Petersburg was about US$600 at the time of writing (slightly more from Los Angeles).

STA Travel (☎ 212-627-3111), 10 Downing St, New York, NY 10014, is the US incarnation of the Australian student travel specialist. It doesn't offer tours but does offer cheap-as-possible bookings on all major airlines. It has offices throughout the USA and Canada; call ☎ 800-777-0112 for the nearest one.

CCTE Council Travel (☎ 212-661-1450, or toll-free from the USA and Canada ☎ 800-226-8624), at 205 East 42nd St, 16th Floor, New York, is the head office of a national chain of student travel offices, doing essentially the same thing as STA on a larger scale.

Australasia Flight Centres International (☎ 131600) and STA Travel (☎ 1300 360 960) are major dealers in cheap airfares, each with offices throughout Australia and New Zealand.

Flight Centre has offices at 19 Bourke St, Melbourne (☎ 03-9650 2899) and 83 Elizabeth St, Sydney (☎ 02-9235 3522), and also in Christchurch (☎ 03-366 1091), 118 Cashell Mall, PO Box 4627, Christchurch. STA has offices at 222 Faraday St, Carlton 3053 (☎ 03-9349 2411), 855 George St, Sydney (☎ 02-9212 1255 and 10 High St, Auckland (☎ 09-309 9995).

Passport Travel (☎ 03-9867-3888, fax 03-9867 1055), Suite 11a, 401 St Kilda Rd, Melbourne 3004, is the agent for Red Bear Tours (see Organised Tours later in this chapter).

Hong Kong & Beijing Monkey Business is a well-established specialist which books trans-Siberian trips (from US$390), flights and accommodation at the Moscow Travellers Guest House and the HI St Petersburg Hostel. It's at Chung King Mansions, E-block, 4th floor, flat 6, Nathan Road 36-44, Kowloon, Hong Kong (☎ 852-2723-1376); or Capital Forbidden City Hotel, 48 Guang An Men South Street, South Building, 3/F Xuan Wu District, 100054 Beijing (☎ 8610-

6356 2126). It can be contacted by email at monkeychina@compuserve.com.

Arriving in St Petersburg by Air

There is a currency exchange office inside the arrivals hall at Pulkovo-2 airport which has very odd hours of operation. It pays little attention to its posted opening hours, which are Monday to Friday from 9 am to 5 pm.

See the Getting Around chapter for information on transport to and from the airport.

Leaving St Petersburg by Air

All airlines accept credit cards and almost all offer same-day ticketing. Most are open from 9 am to 5 pm.

Aeroflot
  (☎ 123 83 12) Pulkovo-2 airport
Air France
  (☎ 325 82 52) ulitsa Bolshaya Morskaya 35
Austrian Airlines
  (☎ 325 32 60) Nevskij Palace Hotel, Nevsky prospekt 57
Balkan Bulgarian Airlines
  (☎ 315 50 30) ulitsa Bolshaya Morskaya 36
British Airways
  (☎ 329 25 65) Malaya Konyushennaya ulitsa 1/3
CSA Czech Airlines
  (☎ 315 52 59) ulitsa Bolshaya Morskaya 36
Delta Airlines (USA)
  (☎ 311 58 19) ulitsa Bolshaya Morskaya 36
Finnair
  (☎ 325 95 00) ulitsa Malaya Morskaya 19
KLM
  (☎ 325 89 89) Zagorodny prospekt 5
LOT Polish Airlines
  (☎ 273 57 21) Karavannaya ulitsa 1 at ploshchad Manezhnaya
Lufthansa
  (☎ 314 49 79) Voznesensky prospekt 7
Malév Hungarian Airlines
  (☎ 315 54 55) Voznesensky prospekt 7
Scandinavian Airlines System (SAS)
  (☎ 325 32 55) Nevskij Palace Hotel, Nevsky prospekt 57
Swissair
  (☎ 325 32 50) Nevskij Palace Hotel, Nevsky prospekt 57
Transaero
  (☎ 279 64 63) Liteyny prospekt 48

BUS

St Petersburg's two long-distance bus stations are Avtovokzal 1, at naberezhnaya Obvodnogo Kanala 118 (Map 6, near Baltiyskaya metro), which serves northern destinations such as Vyborg, Karelia etc; and Avtovokzal 2, at naberezhnaya Obvodnogo Kanala 36 (Map 7, approximately 250m from Ligovsky Prospekt metro), which serves Baltic countries and destinations to the south and east such as Novgorod, Pskov, Vologda, Moscow and beyond.

Finland

There are three bus companies offering shuttle services between Helsinki's bus station and St Petersburg (a seven-hour journey). St Petersburg Express is the cheapest of the bus services; at the time of writing it charged US$43.50 for the St Petersburg-Helsinki trip. Buses leave from the Hotel Astoria at 12.30 pm and arrive in Helsinki at 7.35 pm.

Finnord (☎ 314 89 51) runs buses to Helsinki via Vyborg and Lahti from its office at ulitsa Italyanskaya 37 (Map 8), and from the Hotel Astoria. At the time of writing the cost of a one-way ticket to Helsinki was US$46. Buses leave the Astoria at 3.10 pm and arrive in Helsinki at 10.15 pm.

Sovtransavto Express Bus (☎ 264 51 25) has daily coaches to Helsinki and Lappeenranta, as well as a Vyborg-Lappeenranta service. As a way of saving money (but not time), take the electric train from St Petersburg to Vyborg (see information under Train) and then the bus to Lappeenranta. In St Petersburg, buses leave from the Hotel Pulkovskaya, Hotel Astoria, Grand Hotel Europe and St Petersburg Hotel. The bus for Helsinki costs US$46 and leaves from the Grand Hotel Europe at 8.45 am, arriving at 3.45 pm. See the service desk or concierge at these hotels for more information, or call Sovtransavto.

From Helsinki, buses leave the bus station for St Petersburg at 7.15 am, 9 am, noon and 11 pm – the companies that run buses at these times change daily, but the times are always valid.

TRAIN

The main international rail gateways to St Petersburg are Helsinki, Tallinn, Warsaw and Berlin. Trains leave daily from St Petersburg to these and, by connections, to many European capitals. You can also use Moscow as a gateway, opening up the possibility of more connections. Rail passes are not valid in Russia.

Moscow

Most of the 12 or more daily trains to Moscow take seven to 8½ hours to complete the journey. Several are overnight sleepers, which save time and a night's accommodation costs. To Moscow, the best overnight trains are Nos 1 (11.55 pm), 3 (11.59 pm) and 5 (11.33 pm). From Moscow, Nos 2 (11.55 pm), 4 (11.59 pm) and 6 (11.10 pm) are the best. All of these trains cost approximately US$50/77 each way for 2nd/1st class.

There's also the once-weekly, high-speed ER200, which covers the 650km between the two cities in less than five hours – it leaves from St Petersburg on Thursday at 12.15 pm, and from Moscow on Friday at 12.22 pm. Second/1st class tickets cost US$56/74, or US$54/71 for students.

In St Petersburg, tickets to Moscow can be purchased at the Central Train Ticket Office, the Intourist counter inside Moscow Station, Sindbad Travel and, at a huge mark-up, from any luxury hotel. Foreigners are required to pay the foreigner rate for tickets between Moscow and St Petersburg; many (non-Russian speaking) foreigners trying to use the cheaper tickets are told they must pay the conductor the difference between the Russian and foreigner tickets or they cannot board the train. If your Russian is good, give it a shot, but if you're caught, the fine can be higher than the face-value of the foreigner tickets.

Security Reports of robberies on the overnight trains between St Petersburg and Moscow have decreased substantially.

Nevertheless, try to get a bottom bunk and place your belongings in the bin beneath your bed when you go to sleep. Make sure that the lock on your door is operational, and flip up the steel latch – about two-thirds of the way up on the left hand side of the door – to prevent entry by thieves who may have a skeleton key to carriages. Jam a piece of paper or cork underneath the latch to prevent it being flipped down again by the keener thieves who use bent coat-hangers for that purpose. To go slightly over the top (but not much), I always carry a couple of metres of climbing rope and a couple of karabiners (metal clips available at any good sporting goods store for under US$6) in case the lock or latch doesn't work. Slip the karabiners over the lock switch (thus placing steel, as opposed to rope, in any opening of the door if it's forced) and tie them off to one of the steel handles secured to the wall.

Finland

On the heavily travelled Helsinki-Vyborg-St Petersburg corridor the rail crossing is at Vainikkala (Luzhayka on the Russian side). There are two daily trains between St Petersburg and Helsinki. The *Repin*, a Russian-run train that's cleaner than most, departs from St Petersburg's Finland Station (Finlyandsky vokzal) at the mellow hour of 7.14 am and arrives in Helsinki at 12.30 pm. The return train leaves Helsinki at 3.34 pm and arrives in St Petersburg at 10.45 pm. The *Repin* costs US$53 each way in 2nd class, US$94.25 for 1st class.

The *Sibelius*, a quite civilised Finnish Railways-run train that's more convenient, more pleasant, faster and, if you're travelling in 1st class, cheaper, leaves St Petersburg at 4.35 pm, arriving in Helsinki at 9.34 pm. It leaves Helsinki at 6.30 am and arrives in St Petersburg at 1.15 pm. At the time of writing, 2nd-class tickets are the same price as for the *Repin*, while 1st-class tickets are US$84 each way.

On the way back you can save yourself about US$15 by spending a lot of time: from St Pete's Finland Station, take any *elektrichka* (suburban train) to Vyborg Station, where you can meet the Helsinki-bound *Repin* at 10.16 am, and the *Sibelius* at 6.15 pm. The trip to Vyborg takes approximately 2½ hours and costs about US$2.

In St Petersburg's Finland Station, buy tickets in the Foreign Ticket Office, separate from the main hall, alongside platform 1 (from where the Helsinki trains arrive and depart); the ticket booth is open Monday to Saturday from 6.30 am to 7 pm, and on Sunday from 8 am to 1 pm and from 2 to 4 pm. In Helsinki's main station, tickets are sold in the long-distance ticket room at the international counter; take a number from the middle number generator near the door and walk straight to the back of the hall – get there early: midday waits of up to two hours are common. You can buy tickets on board the *Sibelius* but it's problematic (read: dicey) on the *Repin*, where you may be charged a special penalty by greedy conductors.

For stays in Finland of up to three months, no visa is required for US, Canadian, UK, Australian or NZ passport holders.

Czech Republic

Prague to St Petersburg trains (US$119/116 for adults/students) connect through Warsaw's Central Station (Warszawa Centralna); the night train from Prague arrives in Warsaw at 6.50 am and connects with the 9 am Warsaw-Moscow train (24 hours). Alternatively, you can stick around for the day (check out Warsaw's Old Town) and catch the night train at 12.44 am from Warsaw's Gdansk station to St Petersburg (29 to 39 hours).

UK, US and Western European passport holders need no visa to enter the Czech Republic; those with Canadian, Australian and NZ passports do need one.

Poland

There's a service from St Petersburg to Warsaw (US$65/100 for adults in 2nd/1st class, or US$62/98.50 for students) leaving Warsaw Station at 2.19 pm on Tuesday, Thursday, Friday and Sunday, and a daily service from Warsaw to St Petersburg (29 to 39 hours). These trains cross at Kuznica which is near Hrodna (Grodno) in Belarus. You'll change wheels (this takes about three hours) just east of Bialystok station.

No visa is needed for entry for citizens of the USA, Germany or the Netherlands, but UK, Canadian, Australian, French and New Zealand citizens need a visa. If you are just passing through Belarus from Europe your Russian visa will serve as a transit visa as long as you don't leave the train. On the return trip, you should be issued a transit visa at the Russia-Belarus border at no cost, but many travellers report having been charged around US$20. All I can say is that they've tried it with me and I found that telling them in hostile Russian that I'm just passing through has worked every time – I've never paid.

Estonia

From St Petersburg the Tallinn sleeper (US$36.50/57 adult 2nd/1st class, US$34/55 student) leaves at 11.10 pm. There's a daily sleeper to St Petersburg that leaves Tallinn at 8.10 pm and arrives in St Petersburg at around 7 am.

Arriving in St Petersburg by Train

St Petersburg has four chief main-line stations. Finland Station (Finlyandsky vokzal, Map 5) at ploshchad Lenina, Vyborg Side, serves trains on the Helsinki line. South of the river, Moscow Station (Moskovsky vokzal, Map 8), at ploshchad Vosstania on Nevsky prospekt, handles trains to/from Moscow, the far north, Crimea, the Caucasus, Georgia and Central Asia; Vitebsk Station (Vitebsky vokzal, Map 7), at Zagorodny prospekt 52, deals with Smolensk, Belarus, Kiev, Odessa and Moldova; and Warsaw Station (Varshavsky vokzal, Map 6), at naberezhnaya Obvodnogo Kanala 118, covers the Baltic republics, Pskov, Lvir (Lvov) and Eastern Europe.

Baltic Station (Baltiysky vokzal, Map 6), just along the road from Warsaw Station, is mainly for suburban trains. Obukhovo

Station, at the extreme south-east of the city, has short-hop regional services to tiny villages and most travellers (including me) have never seen its interior.

Leaving St Petersburg by Train

Domestic and international train information is available from the Intourist counter (No 13) at the Central Train Ticket Office (Map 8), naberezhnaya Kanala Griboedova 24, between the Kazan Cathedral and the Bankovsky Most. It's open Monday to Saturday from 8 am to 4 pm; Sunday from 9 am to 4 pm. It always has the most up-to-date information on prices but sometimes charges you a small fee for the information. You can also get information about domestic trains from the Intourist counter at Moscow Station, which is inside the main hall – the first small door on the right after you pass the schedules if you enter from ploshchad Vosstania.

Sindbad Travel at the HI St Petersburg Hostel issues Moscow tickets and discounted Helsinki tickets on the spot. It also has a ticket-buying service for those who just can't cope with the folk at the station (it tacks a straight US$5 charge on to the ticket price).

CAR & MOTORCYCLE

See the Getting Around chapter for specific driving tips for St Petersburg.

Foreigners can legally drive on almost all of Russia's highways and can even ride motorcycles. On the down side, driving in Russia is *truly* an unfiltered Russian experience. Poor roads, maddeningly inadequate signposting (except in St Petersburg's centre), low-quality petrol (in town and along the highway from Vyborg to St Petersburg 95 octane is readily available, but outside town 76 octane is the norm) and keen highway patrollers (see the boxed text in the Getting Around chapter) can lead to frustration and dismay.

Motorbikes will undergo vigorous scrutiny by border officials and highway police, especially if you're riding anything vaguely Ninja-ish. But one traveller said that while riding his hand-built motorcycle across the entire former Soviet Union, the only attention he attracted from the police consisted of admiring questions and comments.

It's definitely not wise to ride a motorcycle in St Petersburg, where crime is high and traffic police are widespread. Finally, while foreign automobile companies now have an established presence in Moscow, St Petersburg and other cities, motorcycles in the former Soviet Union are almost exclusively Russian or East German-made – it is to be doubted that a Ural-brand carb will fit your Hog.

Departure Tax

A departure road tax of about US$10 is collected at the border.

The Basics

To be allowed to drive your own or a rented car/motorcycle in Russia you'll need to be 18 years old and have a full driving licence. In addition, you'll need an International Driving Permit with a Russian translation of your licence, or a certified Russian translation of your full licence (you can certify translations at a Russian embassy or consulate).

You will also need your vehicle's registration papers and proof of insurance. Be sure your insurance covers you in Russia. Your insurance agent at home or one in Finland may also be able to get you a policy covering driving in Russia. In the UK, Black Sea and Baltic Insurance (☎ 0171-709 9202) can provide you with all you need.

Finally, a customs declaration promising that you will take your vehicle with you when you leave is also required.

Speed limits are generally 60km/h in cities and between 80 and 100km/h on highways. Russians drive on the right and traffic coming from the right has the right of way. Children under 12 may not travel in the front seat, and safety belt use is mandatory. Motorcyclists (and passengers) must wear a crash helmet.

Technically, it is legal to have a blood-alcohol level of up to 0.04%, but in practice

Not So Fast, Bud

Almost every rental company on earth precludes you from taking your rented car into Russia. If you do drive a car in and it's not permitted under your rental agreement, you immediately void your agreement, along with your insurance policy. And if the company finds out it may even report the car as stolen.

The only car rental outfit I could find in Helsinki that rents cars that can be taken into Russia is Transvell (☎ 09-351 33 00, or toll free in Finland ☎ 0800-8000 7000). It ain't cheap though; see the Getting Around chapter for more information.

it's illegal to drive after you have consumed *any* alcohol at all. This is a rule that is strictly enforced.

Filling stations are located throughout the city.

Border Crossings

You'll first pass the neighbouring country's border point where you'll need to show your vehicle registration and insurance papers (including Finnish proof of coverage if you're coming from Finland), your driving licence, passport and visa. These formalities are usually minimal for Western citizens.

On the Russian side, chances are your vehicle will be subjected to a cursory inspection by border guards (your life will be made much easier if you open all doors and the boot yourself, and shine a torch for the guards at night). You pass through customs separately from your car, walking through a metal detector and possibly having hand luggage X-rayed.

Finland Highways cross at the Finnish border posts of Nuijamaa and Vaalimaa (Brusnichnoe and Torfyanovka respectively on the Russian side). From these towns to St Petersburg the road is said to be infested with modern-day highwaymen (though we've driven it literally dozens of times and never had any difficulties). Don't stop for anybody, fill up with petrol on the Finnish side (preferably before you get to the border filling station, which is more expensive than others and closes early). There's a radar speed-trap just outside the St Petersburg city line where the limit is 60km/h (hint: radar detectors are legal in Russia). Be sure and watch for all road signs; a few involve tricky curves and signposting is not all it should be. It's best to make this drive for the first time during daylight hours.

Estonia The nearest border crossing from Tallinn is at Narva and the road from there is uneventful, if not particularly fast.

Ukraine & Belarus The border crossings into Russia are open to foreign drivers.

BOAT

If you thought the break-up of Aeroflot was something, wait till you see what's happened to Russian shipping services. The state services are being pared down further and further, and boats are being handed over to private enterprises. Shipping services to St Petersburg have been seriously curtailed over the past couple of years. This information can change drastically, so do check ahead.

Passenger ships dock at the Sea Terminal (Morskoy vokzal, Map 6) at the west end of Bolshoy prospekt on Vasilevsky Island (take bus No 128 from Vasileostrovskaya metro or trolleybus No 10 from Nevsky Prospekt or Primorskaya metro stations).

Baltic Lines' (☎ 355 16 16 or 355 61 40) *Inzhenir* is a cargo ship that sails on Thursday and Sunday from St Petersburg to Stockholm, returning on Friday and Monday. There are 12 spartan passenger berths aboard and the fare for the 30 hour trip is US$153 per person. For complete scheduling information, contact Baltic Lines at their office at the Sea Terminal. Baltic Line's US agent (EuroCruises) can

be contacted on ☎ 212-366-4747 or (toll-free) ☎ 800-688-3876.

River Cruises to/from Moscow

In summer, passenger boats ply the rivers and canals between Moscow and St Petersburg. The route follows the Neva River to Lake Ladoga, to the Svir River and Lake Onega, the Volga-Baltic canal to the Rybinskoe Reservoir and through some of the Golden Ring along the Volga to Moscow.

These cruises take 11 days to Moscow, and 12 days back. You usually will have had to book outside Russia, as getting tickets once inside the country is extremely difficult. In a pinch, Sindbad Travel (☎ 327 8384) may be able to get tickets (if there are any left over) for cruises aboard the *Kirov*, *Pakhomov*, *Surkov*, and *Lomonosov*.

Generally, tickets cost US$110 per person per day. In the US, agents for cruises are Berrier Enterprises (☎ 415-398-7947), 1 Sutter St, Suite 910, San Francisco, CA 94104, and in Switzerland, contact Reiseburo Mittelthurgau (☎ 41-71-626-8585) CH 8570, Weinfelden.

The St Petersburg Travel Company (☎ 315 51 29), naberezhnaya reki Moyki 60B, can also arrange cruises and tours.

River cruises to Moscow leave from the St Petersburg River Station at prospekt Obukhovskoy oborony 195 near metro Proletarskaya (turn right upon exiting and take any tram one stop), and sometimes from the Sea Terminal on Vasilevsky Island (see earlier in this section).

The Moscow terminus for these sailings is the Northern River Station (Severny Rechnoy vokzal) at Leningradskoe shosse 51 (metro Rechnoy Vokzal).

Cruises to Valaam and Kizhi are available; see the Excursions chapter for more information.

TRAVEL AGENTS

This is a fledgling field and dozens of agencies are popping out of the woodwork (check the *St Petersburg Times* for adverts). Be careful, and check with the airlines to see if the agent is actually getting you a better deal before you commit to one. Concierges at the better hotels can perform some standard booking services, though these come at a price.

Sindbad Travel, owned by the HI St Petersburg Hostel, has two offices in town. The first is on the ground floor of the hostel itself (Map 8, ☎ 327 83 84, fax 329 80 19, sindbad@sindbad.ru, www.sindbad.ru), at 3-ya Sovetskaya ulitsa 28; the second (☎ 324 08 80) is inside the green St Petersburg Philological Faculty building on Vasilevsky Island, Universitetskaya naberezhnaya 11 (Map 6). Both are genuine Western-style student (and adult) discount air ticket offices, specialising in one-way and short or no advance-purchase tickets. Sindbad operates as a full-service ticketing centre for STA and Kilroy Travel, sells and issues train tickets, can service any student-issued tickets regardless of source and can book youth hostel accommodation through the IBN system. Basically it offers all the same services as the big guys it represents, and it has friendly service from people who understand what they're booking. It also sells ISIC cards.

American Express at the Grand Hotel Europe (Map 8) sells discounted return tickets to European and American destinations. Check their specials, sometimes advertised in the *St Petersburg Times*.

ORGANISED TOURS
The UK
Travel For The Arts (☎ 0171-483 4466, fax 0171-586 0639; www.travelforthearts.co.uk) 117 Regent's Park Rd, London NW1 8UR, organises luxury 'culture'-based tours to St Petersburg and other European cities for people with a specific interest in opera and ballet. It runs themed tours, like the five-day Tchaikovsky trip which includes sightseeing, city tours, museums, Tchaikovsky lore and performances at the Mariinsky and the Maly theatres for £1295, including airfare, transfers, half-board and accommodation at the Astoria hotel.

Exodus Adventure (☎ 0181-675 5550; fax 0181-673 0779; www.exodustravel.co.uk),

9 Weir Rd, London SW12 0LT, organises heaps of fantastic adventure stuff in the former Soviet Union; walking trips around Lake Baikal, trips to the Caucasus, Samarkand, Kamchatka – pretty much everywhere. They use Moscow and St Petersburg as their hubs – a few days in each – and offer city tours and excursions.

North America
REI Adventures, PO Box 1938, Sumner, Washington 98389-0880 (☎ 253-395-8111, toll-free in the US and Canada ☎ 800-622-2236, fax 253-395-4744, www.rei.com), offers a huge array of adventure tourism packages for Russia and the former Soviet Union.

General Tours (☎ 603-357-5033, toll-free ☎ 800-221-2216), 53 Summer St, Keene, NH 03431, is a well established company offering 'to your right is the Kremlin'-style packages to Moscow, St Petersburg and the Golden Ring for a wide range of prices. My dad used them and says they were tops. Their eight-day Price Buster Russia tours – including flights, transfers, stays at the Sofitel in Moscow and the Pribaltiyskaya in St Pete, with breakfast, two dinners, city, palace and Hermitage tours – start at US$1400/2200 in winter/summer.

Pioneer East-West Tours (☎ 617-547-1127), 203 Allston St, Cambridge, MA 02142, specialises in independent travel packages which can consist of airfares and á la carte hotel bookings or homestays.

EuroCruises (☎ 212-366-4747 or toll-free in the US 800-688-3876), 303 W 13th St, New York, NY 10032, is the US agent for Baltic Lines, the Russian company that runs a cargo ship between St Petersburg and Stockholm – see the Boat section in this chapter.

Australia
Eastern Europe Travel Bureau (☎ 02-9262 1144, fax 02-9262 4479), 75 King St, Sydney 2000, does budget tours (airfares not included): Moscow, four days from A$250 (twin share); Moscow and St Petersburg, eight days from A$845; Moscow

to St Petersburg cruise by river and canal, 15 days from A$2040. They also offer visa assistance, and homestays in Moscow or St Petersburg can be arranged.

Passport Travel, the representative of Red Bear Tours (☎ 03-9867 3888, fax 03-9867 1055, passport@werple.net.au, www.travel centre.com.au), is at 11a, 410 St Kilda Rd, Melbourne 3004. They can arrange visa invitations, independent travel, language courses, trans-Siberian railway tours and much more.

Russian Gateway Tours (☎ 02-9745 3333, fax 02-9745 3237, gatrav@magna.com.au), 48 The Boulevarde, Strathfield, NSW 2135, arranges homestays, B&Bs, youth hostels, apartments and hotels from A$40 to A$215, and can also arrange tours, cruises and railway journeys.

Finland

The very helpful and friendly Eurohostel (☎ 09-66 44 52, fax 09-65 50 44) works closely with the Russian Youth Hostel Association and can help with paperwork and visa support. It can provide bus and train schedules and assist with car rental. It's also on the IBN HI reservations system. It's located just off the Silja Lines port in Helsinki at Linnankatu 9 and is a key source in Helsinki for Russia-related travel information.

RTT Matkapalvelut Travel Agency (☎ 09-65 90 52), Laivasillankatu 14, Helsinki (near the Russian embassy), has a very handy deal on its visa invitations (see Visas in the Facts for the Visitor chapter) and can also book discounted hotel rooms in St Petersburg.

Finnsov Tours (☎ 09-694 20 11), Eeri-kinkatu 3, Helsinki, offers short package tours from Helsinki to St Petersburg and other Russian cities by train, bus and ship. It has a three-day and two-night train tour to

St Petersburg for US$410 to US$670, all inclusive of tours, hotel, meals and transport. It also runs a four-day, three-night bus tour for US$425 inclusive.

Estonia

Karol (☎ 2-454 900 or 446 240, fax 6-313 918) was a major player in the establishment of a St Petersburg-Helsinki-Tallinn youth hostel network. It specialises in cheap independent travel to Russia, including full visa support, and it's located at Lembitu 4, Tallinn EE0001.

WARNING

The information in this chapter is particularly vulnerable to change: prices for international travel are volatile, routes are introduced and cancelled, schedules change, special deals come and go, and rules and visa requirements are amended. Airlines and governments seem to take a perverse pleasure in making price structures and regulations as complicated as possible. You should check directly with the airline or a travel agent to make sure you understand how a fare (and ticket you may buy) works. In addition, the travel industry is highly competitive and there are many lurks and perks.

The upshot of this is that you should get opinions, quotes and advice from as many airlines and travel agents as possible before you part with your hard-earned cash. The details given in this chapter should be regarded as pointers and are not a substitute for your own careful, up-to-date research.

Getting Around

St Petersburg's excellent public transport system makes getting around the centre very simple and inexpensive. Outlying areas are served, albeit less efficiently, and if you're staying at the end of any metro line in a 'microregion' your journey to the centre will probably be a combination of bus and metro. The centre, especially Nevsky prospekt, is best seen on foot.

TO/FROM THE AIRPORT

St Petersburg's airport is at Pulkovo, about 17km south of the centre (see Map 3). The cheapest do-it-yourself transport is metro plus bus. From Moskovskaya metro (not Moskovskie Vorota), bus No 39 runs to Pulkovo-1, the domestic terminal, and bus No 13 runs to Pulkovo-2, the international terminal, stopping at the Hotel Pulkovskaya en route. They go whenever they feel like it, take 15 minutes and cost less than US$0.50. From the airport, take bus No 13 to Moskovskaya metro and the metro from there into the city.

Shuttle buses run between the domestic and international terminals, but you'll probably have to pay about US$2 to US$5.

It's cheaper to get a taxi to the airport (about US$10) than from it (at least US$25 unless your Russian's great, then at least US$15). One good way to reduce the bill is metro-plus-taxi; from Moskovskaya metro to the centre a taxi will cost about US$5.

The drivers that hang out at the airport are your introduction to what everyone calls the 'Mafia' – actually just a bunch of thugs who control who can park and wait for fares there.

When friends can't meet me I arrange to be picked up at the airport by faxing one of the more reliable (read expensive) taxi services in advance – I prefer Hertz (US$35) but there are several options. When you arrive, they are waiting with your name on a sign. Expect to pay US$30 to US$40 for a ride to the centre using these services (see the Taxi section later in this chapter for contact numbers), but for this price you won't have to hassle and haggle after your arrival and possible customs ordeal.

If you're staying at any of the luxury hotels in town, or if your hotel package includes transfers, you'll be met by bus or minivan.

TO/FROM THE SEAPORT

The Vasilevsky Island seaport (Map 6) is on the bus No 7 and trolleybus No 10 routes which leave from near the Hermitage. The St Petersburg Travel Company, as well as the more expensive taxi services, offers transfers to/from train stations, hotels and the seaport for about US$35 per car load. Every train terminus has a metro station next door, and taxis are easy to get if you walk a block or two away from the station.

BUS, TROLLEYBUS & TRAM

A US$0.25 ticket (*talony*) is used on all buses, trolleybuses (electric buses) and trams. They're sold in kiosks at major interchanges, by hawkers at the train stations, and often in strips of 10 by drivers. Punch the ticket in the ticket-punch boxes; failure to do so results in on-the-spot fines should you be so unlucky as to run into one of the plain-clothes ticket inspectors.

Bus stops are marked by '**A**' signs (for avtobus), trolleybus stops by '**П**' (representing a handwritten Russian 'T') or signs by the roadside, tram stops by a '**T**' sign over the roadway, all usually indicating the line numbers too. Stops may also have roadside signs with little pictures of a bus, trolleybus or tram. Most transport runs from 6 am to 1 am.

The following are some important long routes across the city:

Along Nevsky prospekt between the Admiralty and Moscow Station: bus Nos 7, 44; trolleybus Nos 1, 7, 10, 22. Trolleybus Nos 1 and 22 continue out to Hotel Moskva and Alexandr Nevsky Monastery.

To The Hostels!

Lots of people have written to Lonely Planet saying that they found it difficult to get from the airport to the hostels; many more wrote to say that I made it sound far more complex than it actually was. And still more wrote or emailed me – or harangued me in the hostels during my visit – about how they got ripped off coming from a station.

In my defence, I will say that the information you need *was* in the first edition, as was the advice to bring only pristine, new US dollar notes – so lay off, OK?

Let's review:

You're standing at the airport and a bunch of thugs is trying to charge you scads of cash for a lift to town. Wait in front of the terminal for bus No 13, which will be along shortly, and take that to Moskovskaya (Московская) metro.

From Moskovskaya metro, head to Tekhnologichesky Institut (Технологический Институт) station and then change for a Line 1 metro to Ploshchad Vosstania (Площадь Восстания) station. This is right in the heart of the centre and it's a five-minute walk to the HI St Petersburg Hostel – see Map 8. For the Holiday Hostel, stay on Line 1 for two more stops, to Ploshchad Lenina (Площадь Ленина) station – see Map 5.

If you arrive by train, Moscow Station is on ploshchad Vosstania, so you're close to the HI St Petersburg Hostel and two metro stops from the Holiday Hostel. From Warsaw or Baltic Stations, take a Line 1 metro directly to Ploshchad Vosstania or Ploshchad Lenina metro stations, or take a taxi – and don't pay more than US$5 to the former and US$7 to the latter. From Finland Station you're within walking distance of the Holiday Hostel, or take a Line 1 metro two stops south to Ploshchad Vosstania (or a taxi for no more than US$5).

And if for some reason you find yourself stuck at Obukhovo Station, take a Line 3 train to Ploshchad Vosstania (or a taxi for no more than US$8).

Any questions?

Around the Sadovaya ulitsa ring road south of Nevsky prospekt: tram Nos 3, 13, 14. Tram No 3 continues north of Nevsky prospekt and crosses the Kirovsky Bridge into Petrograd Side.

From the Hermitage to the Pribaltiyskaya Hotel on Vasilevsky Island: bus Nos 7, 30, 44; trolleybus No 12.

From the Hermitage to Krestovsky Island (Petrograd Side): bus No 45 terminates at the bridge to Yelagin Island. From metro Gostiny Dvor via Liteyny Bridge to the same terminus: tram No 12.

From the Hermitage via prospekt Kronverksky to Kamennoostrovsky prospekt (Petrograd Side): tram No 63.

Along Kamennoostrovsky prospekt (Petrograd Side): bus Nos 46, 65. These cross the Neva on the Troitsky Bridge.

Along Lesnoy prospekt (Vyborg Side): trolleybus No 23; tram Nos 20, 32. These all cross the Neva on the Liteyny Bridge.

Bridges

Most transport shuts down between 1 and 6 am and, when the river isn't frozen, the following Neva bridges *(mosty)* are raised at night to let seagoing ships through. All St Petersburgers (and many visitors) have stories of being marooned, and the fun of paying triple price to have a taxi race at break-neck speed to try to beat a bridge opening wears thin quickly – don't get caught on the wrong side! Below are times when the bridges are up:

- Alexandra Nevskogo (Map 7), 2.35 to 4.50 am
- Bolshoy Okhtinsky (Map 7), 2.45 to 4.45 am
- Liteyny (Map 5), 2.10 to 4.35 am
- Troitsky (Map 5), 2 to 4.40 am
- Dvortsovy (Map 6), 1.55 to 3.05 and 3.15 to 4.45 am
- Leytenanta Shmidta (Map 6), 1.55 to 4.50 am

- Birzhevoy (Map 4), 2.25 to 3.20 and 3.40 to 4.40 am
- Tuchkov (Map 4), 2.20 to 3.10 and 3.40 to 4.40 am

Exceptions to the schedule are only made during all-night festivals such as White Nights.

METRO

Though less majestic than Moscow's, the St Petersburg metro leaves most of the world's other 'undergrounds' for dead. You'll rarely wait more than three minutes for a train (even at 6 am on a Sunday), and the clock at the end of the platform shows time elapsed since the last train departed.

Taking the metro is the quickest way around the wider city and, in 1998, tokens *(zhetony)* cost US$0.25! Buy your tokens from the booths in the stations, place them in the entry gates, wait for the coins to drop, and walk through. Multi-ride pass-cards are sold at all metro stations in multiples of 10, 15 and 20 rides. The cards are encoded with a magnetic strip and are good for a specified period, usually 15 days. All metro stations have card-reading turnstiles – place your card in the slot and when it comes back out you'll have a green light to proceed if there's sufficient credit left on the card.

Metro lines are numbered; colours given to them vary, depending on the map you're looking at, but at the southern (bottom) half of the map, Line 1 is always at the left; Line 4 at the right (refer to Map 1 at the beginning of this book). The grandest stations are on Line 1. Stations open at 5.30 am and close at 1 am, and the metro begins closing down at about 12.30 am.

Despite the two new metro stations opened on Line 3 (Sportivnaya/Спортивная and Chkalovskaya/Чкаловская, both on Petrograd Side), St Petersburg's metro is not as extensive as Moscow's, nor as user-friendly. In addition, a section of the metro in the north-east of the city is closed due to a tunnel collapse (see the boxed text).

Many station platforms (eg on Line 3 to Vasilevsky Island, and many stations on

Line 2 north of Nevsky prospekt) have outer safety doors, so you can't see the station from an arriving train; also, you can't rely on spotting the signs on the platforms as you pull in. Furthermore, the announcements in the carriages are confusing: just before a departing train's doors close, a recorded voice announces '*Ostorozhno! Dveri zakryvayutsya. Sleduyushchaya stantsia* (name of next station)'. This means 'Caution! The doors are closing. Next station (name of next station).' Just before the train stops at the next station, its name is announced. In case you don't catch these, or they come confusingly close together (as they often do in St Petersburg), the surest way of getting off at the right station is to count the stops. Another small annoyance (actually it's quite funny) is when the tape-playback units wow and flutter, making the voice sound like either Mickey Mouse or Louis Armstrong.

You're expected to give your seat to the elderly – stand up, point to your seat and say '*pazhalsta*'. On crowded (this means all) public transport, people also usually give up seats to women with children or a lot of baggage. People manoeuvre their way out by confronting anyone in the way with '*Vy vykhodite seychas?*' (*'vih vih-KHO-deetyeh sih-SHASS?*'), meaning 'Are you getting off now?'), or just '*Vykhodite?*' ('Getting off?'). If you're asked this and you're not getting off, step aside – quickly.

Metro stations are mostly identified from outside by big 'M' signs. To exit to the street, follow signs saying 'Выход в город'

Metro Closures

Due to a cave-in of a section of tunnel, there is an interruption in Line 1 service north of the city centre. Lesnaya (Лесная) and Politekhnicheskaya (Политехническая) metro stations are connected by a free shuttle-bus service. Allow extra time when travelling on this route. The situation is expected to remain like this till well past the turn of the century.

'*Vykhod v gorod*', meaning 'Exit to the city'. If there's more than one exit, each sign names the street you will come out on. If you need to change to another line, the process is much the same – whether the line passes through the same station or through a nearby one linked by underground walkways. The word to look for is 'Переход' '*perekhod*', meaning 'change', often with a blue-background man-on-stairs sign, followed by 'на станцию ...' '*na stantsiyu ...*' (to ... station) or 'на линию ...' '*na ... liniyu*' (to ... line), then usually 'к поездам до станций ...' '*ke poezdam do stantsiy ...*' (to trains to ... stations).

CAR & MOTORCYCLE

It's true: the best way of getting around the city by road is on a bus. St Petersburg's roads are gnarled, its laws are strange, and the *semper vigilans* eyes of the GAI guys (traffic cops; see the boxed aside), who are empowered to stop you and fine you on the spot, are always on you. Oh, yeah, they can also *shoot* at your vehicle if you don't heed their command to pull over, which is a wave of their striped (sometimes lighted) stick towards your car. While shooting is not common, neither is it unheard of: one trouble-making American expatriate resident had 18 bullet holes put in his car after he refused to stop! OK, maybe they're lousy shots (he lived, only to be incarcerated later in the US, but that's another story), but it's pr obably best to pull over. The GAI claim to shoot at about 15 cars a month(!).

GAI officers are stationed all over the city, and during major events they can literally be on every street corner in the centre.

Driving Tips

See the Getting There & Away chapter for information on national driving regulations and border crossings with your car. Left turns are illegal except where posted; you'll have to make three rights or a short U-turn (this is safer?). Street signs, except in the centre (where they have been sponsored by advertisers), are woefully inadequate, street lights are almost nonexistent, and Russian drivers make Italian drivers seem downright courteous! Watch out for drivers overtaking on the inside, which would appear to be the national sport. There are potholes everywhere – straddle them.

Traffic Jams

These days, St Petersburg's streets are heavily congested during rush hours, from 8 to 9.30 am and 4 to 6.30 pm; major arteries can be jammed throughout the day.

Rental

Renting a car here is now a pretty simple thing, though as with most simple things in Russia, it's inordinately expensive; below are some agencies offering self-drive and chauffeured vehicles:

Astoria-Service
 (☎ 112 15 83), Hotel Astoria.
 Rents cars with or without drivers for about US$100 per day.
Hertz
 (☎ 272 50 45), Nekrasova ulitsa 40.
 Has chauffer-driven cars for US$155 for 10 hours, and US$17 per hour after. They're looking to begin self-drive and possibly Zil limo services as well.
Svit
 (☎ 356 93 29), Pribaltiyskaya Hotel.
 Rents Fords with drivers; they cost US$25 per hour.
Transvell
 (☎ 09-351 33 00, or toll-free in Finland ☎ 0800-8000 7000), Helsinki.
 Rents cars that you can take in to St Petersburg. Rates are outrageous: about US$90 a day for the car and another US$90 a day for insurance.

Fuel

At the time of writing, petrol prices here are wonderfully low: about US$0.40 a litre for 95 octane fuel, which is now readily available. In addition to state-run filling stations, Neste, a Finnish firm, currently operates over 15 full-service filling stations in and around St Petersburg that charge more for petrol but offer faster service and accept major credit cards. You can get leaded and unleaded fuel at the following places in St Petersburg:

- Teatralnaya ploshchad
- Aleksandrovsky park
- naberezhnaya reki Fontanki 156
- Maly prospekt (Vasilevsky Island) 68 (Neste)
- Pulkovskoe shosse 44 (Neste)
- Moskovsky prospekt 100 (Neste)
- Avangardnaya ulitsa 36 (Neste)
- Savushkina ulitsa 87 (Neste)

Parking

In the town's centre uniformed parking attendants charge about US$1 to watch your car for you. There are guarded parking lots

outside many hotels now – use them when you can. Never leave anything of value, including sunglasses, cassette tapes and cigarettes, in a car. Street parking is pretty much legal wherever it seems to be; it's illegal anywhere on Nevsky prospekt. Use common sense – avoid parking in dark side streets and isolated areas.

Emergencies

The law says that when you have an accident you're supposed to remain at the scene until the GAI arrive; in practice, if the damage

A Day with One of Russia's Most Hated Public Servants

NICK SELBY

'But officer, I can explain ...'

In the United States, it's the IRS. In the Soviet Union, it was the KGB. In England it's Manchester United fans, but in the new Russia, it's the ubiquitous members of the Gosavtoinspektsia – GAI – whom motorists and passengers alike loathe, fear and despise.

GAI ('gah-yee') are traffic officers who stand at intersections throughout the country looking for signs of vehicular misbehaviour. Actually, they can pull you over for anything they want. And they do. But what makes them really annoying is that they're entitled to impose on-the-spot fines. Oh, yeah, one more thing: if you don't stop when they wave you over, they can shoot at your vehicle.

While researching the last edition of this book I got pulled over twice in one day while riding in two separate vehicles. I thought, 'What makes these guys tick? How do they decide who to pull over? And is it exciting to be an armed traffic cop?' I mean, their New York City counterparts would give a limb for the opportunity. In the interests of fair play, I spent a rainy Monday morning with some of the guys at St Petersburg GAI Central.

7 am. Roll Call No big surprise, kinda like *Hill Street Blues* with shabbier uniforms. Hotsheet covered, accidents discussed, criminal element lamented. I learn that GAI guys work two days on, two days off, and they have regular beats.

9 am. Upstairs Office Meeting with Sergey (not his real name), a captain. Yes, we can shoot at your car. No, I can't tell you how many officers we have, but there are enough to keep control of the situation. I asked him what a foreigner can do if he should disagree with an officer's charges against him. 'Well, his documents will be confiscated and then he can go to the address on the ticket the officer gives him and get them back ...' Oh.

10 am. Parking Lot Sergey leads the way to his spanking new Ford Escort GAImobile. We're off to check out the boys on patrol. Obeying the seat-belt law, I fasten mine. Sergey ignores isn't major, most people would rather leave than add insult (a fine) to injury. Spas 001 (☎ 001) is a towing company that will come and get you 24 hours a day. They may speak German better than English, but Russian's your best bet.

There are a number of foreign car service centres in town (check *Luchshee V Sankt Peterburge*); they include Chrysler (☎ 591 07 50), Swed-Mobil (Volvo) (☎ 225 40 51) and Pats (GM and Opel) (☎ 260 20 57).

TAXI

There are two main types: official ones (four-door Volga sedans with a chequerboard strip down the side and a green light in the front window) and 'private' taxis (any other vehicle you may see).

Official taxis have a meter that they use more often than not, though you can almost always negotiate a meter-off price.

If currency devaluation has reintroduced a 'multiplier', it will probably be the same as it was prior to the rouble revamp: a printed

---

his, peels out of the parking space, turns on the revolving blue light and, in blatant violation of every St Petersburg traffic law, does 120km/h (80mph) through narrow city streets; he runs all red traffic lights, honks and shoots truly terrifying looks at motorists he passes – which is all of them.

10.30 am. Checkpoint on the St Petersburg-Murmansk Highway There are GAI checkpoints at all major roads leading out of the city. We arrive in time to see one incoming and one outgoing car being tossed by Kalashnikov-wielding officers. They salute Sergey, who leads me into the checkpoint station house where he proudly shows off the station sauna (it's a four-seater). He has another officer demonstrate the state-of-the-art computer system (it's a 386 running MTEZ). They dial in to the GAI server and the officer stumbles through the log-in – after five minutes he gives up and instead proffers the handwritten hotsheet.

11.15 am. Through the City Screeching through residential neighbourhoods, Sergey is explaining how the officers we're whizzing by are trained professionals – they spend six months in the GAI academy after their army service. We pass about half a dozen stopped cars and Sergey is saying, 'He's checking documents ... this one's checking insurance ... that one's investigating a stolen car ...' He can tell all that by passing them at speed. Amazing. Sergey says he's been in 'many' high-speed car chases and I believe him. Not out of idle curiosity, I ask him how long it takes to fill in an accident report. He says a minimum of one hour.

11.40 am. Checkpoint on the St Petersburg-Vyborg Highway This is exactly the same as the first checkpoint, except this one is on the road leading to Finland and there's no sauna. There's an enormous pile of cash on the desk. The checkpoint officer tells me that their radar gun is 'out for repair', but helpfully points out one of the other pieces of crime-fighting equipment present: the telephone. Sergey says that radar detectors are 'unfortunately not prohibited here'. That's Russian cop lingo for: 'They're legal'.

12.10 pm. Petrograd Side As we careen home, Sergey spots a stalled pick-up truck at an intersection. His face a mask of pure anger, he screeches to a halt, tickets the hapless driver, radios his number plates (to ensure follow-up action) and we drive away. As we tear back to the station house, Sergey suddenly stops to let a dump truck, for whom the signal is green, pass through an intersection, and (I swear) says solemnly, 'You know, even though I have this siren on, I still have a responsibility to maintain safety on the roads.' ·

And people say these guys aren't dedicated public servants.

NICK SELBY

No, it's not an imported German car, it's the brand new 1998 Volga!

notice on the glove box showing a number. Multiply the amount shown on the meter by the multiplier to calculate the fare (so if the metered fare is R6.50 and the multiplier is 10, the total fare will be R65).

Extra charges are incurred for radio calls and some night calls.

Unofficial taxis are anything you can stop. They're used more often than official taxis and are a legitimate form of transport in Russia (though St Petersburg traffic police have been cracking down on cars that stop along major thoroughfares to pick up passengers). Stand at the side of the road, extend your arm and wait until something stops – it could be an ambulance, off-duty city or tour bus, army Jeep or passenger car (I once stopped an off-duty *tram*).

When something stops for you, it's common to negotiate destination by speaking to the driver through either the passenger-side window or a partially open door. State your destination and, if the driver's game, one of a couple of things will

happen. If the driver asks you to *sadites* (sit down), just get in, and when you reach the destination you pay what you feel the ride was worth. If the driver states a price, you can negotiate – your offer has been rejected if the driver drives off in a huff.

Another possibility is that the driver may just ask you how much it's worth to you. For this you'll need to speak with locals to determine the average taxi fare at the time of your visit. Practise saying your destination and the amount you want to pay so it comes out properly; the smoother you speak, the lower the fare.

Telephone booking a taxi is usually a reliable way to get one. If you're a Russian speaker or you know one, the city-run taxis are the easiest. Call only when you need the taxi, as calling far in advance just makes the dispatcher cranky.

City Taxi Service
 (☎ 265 13 33)
Hertz
 (☎ 272 50 45), Nekrasova ulitsa 40

Has dependable chauffer-driven Volgas that will pick you up from the airport for US$35 (they'll take you to the airport from anywhere in town for US$25) if you reserve a couple of hours in advance.

SVIT
(☎ 356 93 29, fax 356 00 94 or 356 38 45) Will arrange to meet you at the airport if you fax them a day in advance.

Prices

In 1998 official taxi rates were US$0.35 flagfall, US$0.35 per kilometre; US$0.75 fee for reservation and US$2 an hour waiting time.

A short trip through the centre of St Petersburg was about US$2; from Pulkovo-2 (the airport) to the HI St Petersburg Hostel it was US$25 to US$35; from metro Petrogradskaya to Pulkovo-2 it was US$15, from Finland Station to the HI St Petersburg Hostel it cost US$2. If you can, have a Russian friend negotiate for you: they'll do better than you will.

Risks & Precautions

Generally speaking both standard and private taxis are safe. Now and then tales crop up of rip-offs or robberies in taxis. Russian citizens rather than foreigners seem to be the chief victims, but you are advised to take sensible precautions.

The following tips refer to both official and unofficial taxis, though the former are generally safer than the latter.

- Avoid taxis lurking outside foreign-run establishments, luxury hotels etc – they charge far too much and get uppity when you try to talk them down.
- Know your route – be familiar with how to get there and how long it should take.
- Never get into a taxi with more than one person in it, especially after dark.
- Keep your fare money in a separate pocket to avoid flashing large wads of cash.
- Have the taxi stop at the corner nearest your destination, not the specific address, if you're staying at a private residence.
- Check the back seat of the car for hidden friends before you get in.
- Finally, trust your instincts: if a driver looks creepy, take the next car.

BOAT

In this 'Venice of the North' there is surprisingly no water-based public transport other than river tour boats (see Organised Tours) and hydrofoil and ferry services to Petrodvorets, Kronstadt and Lomonosov.

BICYCLE

St Petersburg's not really a good place to ride a bike – bumpy, pothole-filled roads and lunatic drivers not accustomed to seeing cyclists make it a dangerous proposition. It's a very nice pastime outside the centre or through the parks, but as a method of transport it's not recommended. That said, the number of bicycles on St Petersburg's streets has been increasing of late.

One wonderful bicycle ride – wonderful, that is, once you are south of the airport – is to head due south on Moskovsky prospekt. Once you pass the airport, you're suddenly in lovely countryside. At the turnoff (there's a statue of Pushkin and the sign points south to Kiev and east to the town of Pushkin) turn left and you'll soon be at Pushkin Palace. It's a long (about 25km) ride, but you can take the elektrichka train back to St Petersburg.

Lock your bike before you leave it, preferably with a Kryptonite or other 'U'-type lock and not just a chain and padlock.

WALKING

The best way to get around St Petersburg is to combine walking with public transport. Distances are not too taxing but the roads and footpaths are not in the best condition. Bring good, comfortable walking shoes, and watch out for open manholes and potholes (see the Dangers & Annoyances section in the Facts for the Visitor chapter).

ORGANISED TOURS
City Tours

See the Tourist Offices & Information section of the Facts for the Visitor chapter for addresses of tour companies. Peter Kosyrev runs the excellent Peter's Tours (☎ 329 80 18, pkozyrev@hotmail.com), which leave daily from the HI St Petersburg Hostel. His walking tours last four hours and cost about US$8.50 per person. He also offers several cool variations, including a rooftops tour which gives you a great view from a number of interesting vantage points, a Dostoevsky walking tour and, during White Nights, midnight tours through the city.

The St Petersburg Travel Company has the most reliable tour schedule – tours leave its offices at Nevsky prospekt 16 daily and include city orientation tours by coach; the Peter & Paul Fortress and St Isaac's Cathedral; the Hermitage; and jaunts by bus to Pushkin, Pavlovsk, Petrodvorets and Gatchina. Tours start at about US$10 but average US$18.

There are so many other agencies offering tours of the city that there's no point in trying to list them all; check the *St Petersburg Times* or *Pulse* for tour agencies and special offers.

River & Canal Tours

In summer – roughly from May to September – excursion boats leave the Anichkov Bridge landing on the Fontanka River, just off Nevsky prospekt, every 15 minutes from 10.45 am to 8 pm. They offer a 75-minute, US$8 tootle round the canals and smaller rivers, sometimes with commentary in Russian.

There are also 80-minute City on the Neva cruises, up the river and back from Hermitage No 2 landing, every 40 minutes or so for US$5. There are also 40-minute trips from Letny sad (Summer Garden), though these aren't as reliably scheduled. You'll generally putter into the Neva,

heading east, go around the horn and south to Smolny, where you turn back and head for home. The boats' cafés sell snacks, beer and champagne – bring an ice bucket *and* ice.

Queues for these public boats can be long but, should you be feeling wealthy or are in a group of four, you can hire a water taxi (motorboat) at various landings throughout the city, particularly just north of Nevsky prospekt at the Griboedova Canal, and further south, at the landing just north of the Bankovsky Most. You can also catch water taxis on the Moyka at Nevsky prospekt and, one landing south of there, near ulitsa Gorokhavaya. The benefit of this (other than the obvious lack of screaming children and sometimes belligerent and/or vomiting co-passengers) is that you can choose the canals you want to see and take them at a pace you set yourself.

The price for trips on a water taxi is as much as you're willing to pay, with a rock-bottom starting price of about US$30; expect to pay at least US$35 unless you're a good negotiator.

Helicopter Tours

Now that aviation restrictions have been loosened, helicopter tours are much more common. You still can't fly directly over the city centre, but you can fly over the Neva, between the Admiralty and the Peter & Paul Fortress and over to Smolny. Baltic Airlines (☎ 311 00 84) flights leave from the beach in front of the Peter & Paul Fortress on weekends; just show up and wait to join a tour (about US$30 for 10 to 15 minutes).

Things to See & Do

Highlights

The Top Ten
Things you'll kick yourself for missing are:

1. The Hermitage and Dvortsovaya Ploshchad
2. St Isaac's Cathedral
3. The Peter & Paul Fortress
4. The Smolny Cathedral
5. The Admiralty
6. The Alexandr Nevsky Monastery
7. The Summer Garden and Palace
8. The Church of the Resurrection of Christ
9. The Kazan Cathedral
10. Gostiny Dvor and Passazh department stores

THE HISTORIC HEART

For two centuries the Russian government was centred in the half-kilometre strip of territory that stretches from the Winter Palace to ploshchad Dekabristov. Today its great buildings are devoid of political muscle but stand as monuments to the extravagant splendours of tsardom.

Dvortsovaya Ploshchad (Map 8)

From Nevsky Prospekt or Gostiny Dvor metro, a 15 minute walk along Nevsky prospekt (or a quick bus or trolleybus ride) brings you to Dvortsovaya ploshchad (Palace Square) where the stunning green, white and gold **Winter Palace** (Zimny dvorets) appears like a mirage, its rococo profusion of columns, windows and recesses topped by rows of larger-than-life statues. A residence of tsars from 1762 to 1917, it's now the biggest part of the Hermitage art museum.

On Bloody Sunday (9 January 1905), tsarist troops fired on workers who had peaceably gathered in the square, thus spark-

ing the 1905 revolution. And it was across Dvortsovaya ploshchad that the much-exaggerated storming of the Winter Palace took place during the 1917 October Revolution. Indeed there *was* gunfire before the Provisional Government surrendered to the revolutionaries, but the famous charge across the square was largely invented by film maker Sergey Eisenstein.

The 47.5m **Alexander Column** in the square commemorates the 1812 victory over Napoleon and is named after Alexander I. On windy days, contemplate that the pillar is said to be held on its pedestal by gravity alone!

The former **General Staff building** of the Russian army (1819-29) curves around the south of the square in two great blocks joined by arches over ulitsa Bolshaya Morskaya. The arches are topped by a chariot of victory, another monument to the Napoleonic wars.

Admiralty (Map 6)

The gilded spire of the old Admiralty across the road from Dvortsovaya ploshchad is an unmistakeable St Petersburg landmark, currently under renovation. It's visible along most of Gorokhovaya ulitsa, Voznesensky prospekt and Nevsky prospekt, the three streets that originate practically at the Admiralty's front door. This spot was the headquarters of the Russian navy from 1711 to 1917. Despite the spire's solid gold appearance, it's actually made from wood, and was almost rotted through before restoration efforts began in 1996.

The present building houses a naval college. It was constructed in 1806-23 to the designs of Andreyan Zakharov, and with its rows of white columns and plentiful reliefs and statuary it is a foremost example of the Russian Empire style of classical architecture. One feature you can get a close look at is the nymphs holding giant globes flanking the main gate. Its gardens and fountains are particularly lovely in summer – it's worth walking three or four blocks out of your way to or from the Hermitage to see these.

Ploshchad Dekabristov (Map 6)

West of the Admiralty, ploshchad Dekabristov (Decembrists' Square) is named after the first feeble attempt at a Russian revolution – the Decembrists' Uprising of 14 December 1825. Inspired by radical ideas from France during the Napoleonic campaigns, young officers tried to depose the new tsar, Nicholas I, by drawing up troops in the square. But they were ineptly led, and after repeated attempts by Nicholas to reason with the rebels, they were finally dispersed with grapeshot. Most of the leaders ended up on the gallows or in Siberia.

The most famous statue of Peter the Great, the **Bronze Horseman**, with his mount rearing above the snake of treason, stands at the river end of the square. This statue was cast for Catherine the Great by Frenchman Etienne Falconet. Its inscription reads 'To Peter I from Catherine II – 1782'. The statue, along with the view of the Peter & Paul Fortress against raised drawbridges during summer white nights, has become the trademark image of the new spirit of St Petersburg.

Most of the west side of the square is occupied by the Central State Historical Archives in the former Senate and Synod buildings, built in 1829-34. These institutions were set up by Peter the Great to run the civil administration and the Orthodox Church.

The **Manege Central Exhibition Hall** (☎ 314 82 53) across the street used to be the Horse Guards' Riding School (constructed in 1804-07 from a design by Quarenghi). It now has rotating exhibitions and is open daily from 11 am to 7 pm (closed Thursday). Admission for foreigners is US$1.

St Isaac's Cathedral (Map 6)

The golden dome of bulky St Isaac's Cathedral (Isaakievsky sobor), looming just south of ploshchad Dekabristov, dominates the St Petersburg skyline. French designer Ricard de Montferrand won a competition organised by Alexander I to design the cathedral in 1818. It took so long to build (until 1858) that Nicholas I (Alexander's successor) was able to insist on a more grandiose structure than Montferrand had planned. Special ships and a railway had to be built to carry the granite from Finland for the huge pillars. There's a statue of Montferrand holding a model of the cathedral on the west façade.

Since 1990, after a 62-year gap, services have been held here on major religious holidays and St Isaac's may return to full Church control before long.

St Isaac's obscenely lavish interior is open as a museum on Thursday to Monday from 11 am to 6 pm, Tuesday from 11 am to 5 pm (closed Wednesday and the last Monday of the month). Admission is about US$8.50 (US$4.25 for ISIC holders); photos (no tripods or flashes) cost another US$8.50 and video camera usage commands a whopping US$21.

Don't miss the sublime city views from the colonnade (kolonnada) around the drum of the dome, which is open Thursday to Monday from 11 am to 5 pm, Tuesday from 11 am to 4 pm (closed Wednesday). You need to purchase separate tickets for the colonnade, and there are often long queues to pay the US$2.80 (US$1 for ISIC holders), another US$3.10 for photos and US$10.50 for video. You could avoid the crowds by joining any tour from the usual suspects – try St Petersburg Travel Company across the street (St Isaac's is often combined with the Peter & Paul Fortress). Note that it's several hundred steps up the spiral staircase to the colonnade. Every printed resource on this matter seems to come up with a different number of steps; I got bored after counting 180, though 262 seems reasonable (and Søren Bjelke from Copenhagen backs me up on that), but a couple of guides put the number at 562; send your totals to Lonely Planet Steps Contest, c/o the Federal Counter-Intelligence Service, Lubyanka ulitsa 1/3, Moscow.

Palace of Matrimony (Map 6)

At Angliyskaya naberezhnaya 28, just east of the Leytenanta Schmidta bridge, is the Palace of Matrimony (☎ 314 98 48). It's a fascinating place to visit, especially on Friday, the most popular day for marriages (to allow the happy couple an entire weekend of partying). The couples and their entourages emerge from the palace and head round the city to pose for photos at ploshchad Mira, by the Cruiser *Aurora* and other significant and/or photogenic spots.

St Petersburg History Museum (Map 6)

About 600m west of ploshchad Dekabristov, at Angliyskaya naberezhnaya 44, this museum focuses on St Petersburg since the 1917 revolution. Though there's no material in English, it has good coverage of the 1941-44 siege; it's open daily from 11 am to 5 or 6 pm (closed Wednesday).

New Holland (Map 6)

About a five minute walk west alongside the Moyka River, where it meets the Kryukov and Admiralteysky canals, is the island of **Novaya Gollandiya**, or New Holland. The buildings on this sweet and serene (but closed) little island were used to store wood.

THE HERMITAGE

Set in a magnificent palace from which tsars ruled Russia for one-and-a-half centuries, the State Hermitage (Gosudarstvenny ermitazh) fully lives up to its reputation as one of the world's great art museums. You can be absorbed for days by its treasures and still come out wishing for more time.

The enormous collection almost amounts to a history of Western European art, displaying the full range of artists such as Rembrandt, Rubens, Picasso and Matisse, and schools including the Florentine and Venetian Renaissance, impressionism and post-impressionism. There are also Prehistoric, Ancient Classical, Egyptian, Russian and Oriental sections, plus excellent temporary exhibitions.

The vastness of the place – five main buildings, of which the Winter Palace alone has 1057 rooms and 117 staircases – and its huge number of visitors (more than three million annually) demand a little planning. It may be useful to make a reconnaissance tour first, then return another day to enjoy your favourite parts.

The State Hermitage consists of five linked buildings along riverside Dvortsovaya naberezhnaya – from west to east they are the **Winter Palace**, the **Little Hermitage**, the **Old** and **New Hermitages** (sometimes grouped together and called the Large Hermitage) and the **Hermitage Theatre**. The art collection is on all three floors of the Winter Palace and the main two floors of the Little and Large Hermitages. The Hermitage Theatre isn't generally open.

History

The present baroque/rococo Winter Palace was commissioned from Rastrelli in 1754 by Empress Elizabeth. Catherine the Great and her successors had most of the interior remodelled in classical style by 1837. That year a fire destroyed most of the interior, but it was restored virtually identically. It remained an imperial home until 1917, though the last two tsars spent more time in other St Petersburg palaces.

The classical Little Hermitage was built for Catherine the Great as a retreat that would also house the art collection started by Peter the Great, which she expanded through her purchase of over 4000 Old Master paintings, tens of thousands of engraved gems, drawings, sketches and engravings, a large sculpture collection and the commission of imperial decorative arts. At the river end of the Large Hermitage is the Old Hermitage, which also dates from her time. At its south end, facing ulitsa Millionnaya, is the New Hermitage, which was built for Nicholas I to hold the still-growing art collection and was opened to the public for the first time in 1852. The Hermitage Theatre was built in the 1780s by the classicist Quarenghi, who thought it one of his finest works.

The art collection benefited when the State took over aristocrats' collections after the revolution, but Stalin sold some treasures, including about 15 Rembrandts, for foreign currency. The famous impressionist and post-impressionist collections of the pre-revolutionary Moscow industrialists Sergey Shchukin and Ivan Morozov were moved to the Hermitage in 1948.

In 1995 the Hermitage began displaying a highly controversial temporary display called 'Hidden Treasures Revealed'. The exhibition is composed entirely of art captured from private collections by the Red Army in 1945. Originally slated to run until October 1995, the exhibition has been somewhat reduced and extended to run at least through to the end of 1998, and probably longer. The exhibition includes works by Monet, Degas, Renoir, Cézanne, Picasso and Matisse – almost all of which have never been publicly displayed. The political debate as to whether the paintings belong back in Germany has only heated up in the past few years.

Admission

The Hermitage (☎ 311 34 65) is open Tuesday to Saturday from 10.30 am to 5.30 or 6 pm, and Sunday from 10.30 am to 5.00 pm (closed Monday). The main ticket hall is inside the main entrance on the river side of the Winter Palace. In summer there are also ticket kiosks outside a second entrance at the west end of the Winter Palace, but neither the kiosks nor the second entrance are always open.

The dual pricing system (whereby Westerners pay the rouble equivalent of about US$10 while Russians pay about US$2.25 – though note that students with any valid student identification including ISIC are admitted, for the time being, free of charge) infuriates many visitors, but it is not about to change. Unless your Russian's good, forget about getting in for the Russian price – these babushkas have an eagle eye for Western running shoes, bum bags, University of Whatever sweatshirts etc. Still photographs, but not tripods or flashes, are permitted, though you'll have to pay a US$1.25 charge; if you wish to bring in a video camera you will need to pay an additional US$5.

Admission tickets entitle you to wander freely through the museum (crowds permitting), and the last tickets are sold an hour before closing time. At busy times the queues can be horrendous and you might wait well over an hour to get in. On a wet November Tuesday, there'll hardly be a queue at all.

To avoid queues altogether, you can join a tour, which whizzes round the main parts in about 1½ hours but at least provides an introduction to the place in English. It's easy enough to 'lose' the group and stay on till closing time. The tours take place most afternoons and can be arranged at hotels, the St Petersburg Travel Company, other travel agents, or with the Hermitage itself; the museum's rude tours office is down the corridor to the right as you enter, up the stairs and through the last door on the left.

At the top of the Jordan Staircase you can rent a Walkman with recorded tours in English or German, including a general orientation (US$5), and tours of the Flemish and Dutch collections, Impressionism to Picasso, and Unknown Masterpieces Revealed, each US$3.50. The same tours in Russian are US$1.50/0.75.

There's an exchange office inside the museum; as you enter go up the stairs to the right, walk back and through the archway to the right, and it's on the right. Toilets are near the coat check (ie before ticket control), so once you're inside, hold it in.

Much of the Hermitage is now wheelchair accessible, though that may entail having you and your wheelchair carried upstairs by museum staff.

The café, just off the Jordan Staircase, is hardly worth queuing for. The hot dogs and hamburgers are highly overpriced at US$1.25; if you plan a long visit, take your own snacks and buy a Coke (US$0.50) or a beer (US$2.25) and sit at the café's pleasant tables.

continued on page 99

GUIDE
TO THE
HERMITAGE

INSIDE THE HERMITAGE

The Hermitage exhibits listed within this section were verified in June 1998. While changes do occur, Dr Vladimir Yurievich Matveev, Deputy Director for Exhibitions, says things should remain static for the next few years. That said, consider his parting words of wisdom: 'Everything will remain exactly where it is, except for those things which do not.'

Winter Palace, First Floor

1-33 Russian prehistoric artefacts 11: Paleolithic (from three million years ago to the the 12th millennium BC) and Mesolithic (from the 12th to the 3rd millennium BC); **12:** Neolithic (from the 4th millennium BC to 2400 BC) and Bronge Age (from 2000 to 500 BC), including petroglyphs from 2500 to 2000 BC taken from the north-eastern shores of Lake Ozero; **13:** Bronze Age, western steppes, 4th to 2nd millennium BC; **14:** Bronze Age, southern Siberia and Kazakhstan, 2nd millennium to 9th century BC, fine bronze animals; **15-18:** Scythian culture, 7th to 3rd century BC – but the best Scythian material is in the Golden Rooms Special Collection; **19 & 20:** Forest steppes, 7th to 4th century BC; **21-23 & 26:** Material from Altai Mountains burial mounds, including **26:** Human and horse corpses preserved for over 2000 years complete with hair and teeth; **24:** Iron Age, Eastern Europe, including Finno-Ugrians and Balts, 8th century BC to 12th century AD; **33:** Southern steppes tribes 3rd century BC to 10th century AD – some fine Sarmatian gold.

34-40 & 46-69 The Russian East 34-39: Central Asia, 4th century BC to 13th century AD; **55-66:** Caucasus and Transcaucasia, 10th century BC to 16th century AD, including **56:** Urartu, 9th to 7th century BC, **59:** Dagestan, 6th to 11th century AD, **66:** 14th century Italian colonies in Crimea, **67-69:** Golden Horde, 13th to 14th century.

100 Ancient Egypt A fine collection, much of it uncovered by Russian archaeologists; sadly there is no labelling in English except the signs saying 'Please Do Not Touch'.

Little Hermitage, First Floor

101 & 102 Roman marble.
105 Closed at the time of researching.

Large Hermitage, First Floor

105-131 Ancient Classical culture 106-109 & 127: Roman sculpture, 1st century BC to 4th century AD; **111-114:** Ancient Greece, 8th to 2nd century BC, mostly ceramics and sculpture; **115-117 & 121:** Greek colonies around northern Black Sea, 7th century BC to 3rd century AD; **128:** The huge 19th century jasper Kolyvanskaya Vase from Siberia; **130 & 131:** Ancient Italy, 7th to 2nd century BC, including Etruscan vases and bronze mirrors.

HERMITAGE - FIRST FLOOR ЭРМИТАЖ - ПЕРВЫЙ ЭТАЖ

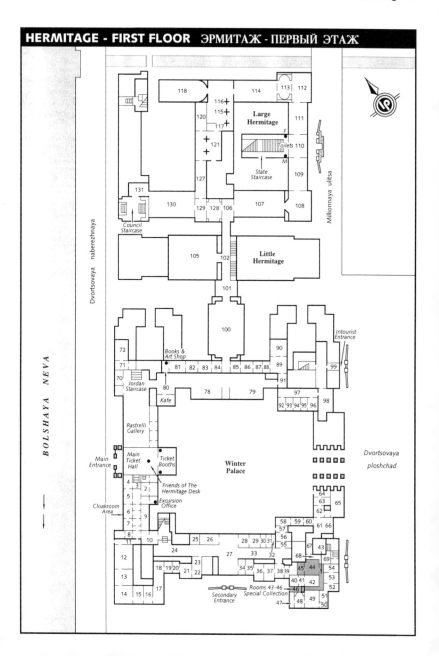

Winter Palace, Second Floor

143-146 Hidden Treasures Revealed An exhibit of paintings captured by the Red Army from private collections in Germany, including works by Monet, Degas, Renoir, Cézanne, Picasso and Matisse, almost all never before publicly displayed.

147-189 Russian culture and art 147-150: 10th to 15th century; **151:** 15th to 17th century; **152:** Icons, ceramics, jewellery etc from 'Moscow Baroque' period, first half of the 17th century; **153:** Items relating to Peter the Great; **155-166:** Late 17th and early 18th century, including **155:** Moorish Dining Room and **156:** Rotunda, with a bust of Peter the Great and a brass Triumphal Pillar, topped by a Rastrelli-created statue of Peter; **157-first half of 161:** Petrovskaya Gallereya, including lathing machinery used by Peter; **161:** A chandelier partly built by the Great Guy and **162:** Mosaic of Peter by Lomonosov; **167-73:** Mid to end 18th century – spot the bizarre 1772 tapestry image of Australia (**167**); **175-187:** (Start at 187 and work your way back.) Rooms occupied by the last imperial family, now displaying 19th century interior design, including **178:** Nicholas II's Gothic library; **188:** Small Dining Room (Malaya stolovaya), where the Provisional Government was arrested by the Bolsheviks on 26 October 1917; **189:** Malachite Hall (Malakhitovy zal) with two tonnes of gorgeous green malachite columns, boxes, bowls and urns.

190-192 Neva Enfilade One of two sets of state rooms for ceremonies and balls: **190:** Concert Hall (Kontsertny zal) for small balls, with an 18th century silver coffin for the remains of Alexandr Nevsky; **191:** Great or Nicholas Hall (Bolshoy zal), scene of great winter balls, and **192:** The Fore Hall; all are now used for temporary exhibitions.

193-198 Great Enfilade The second series of state rooms: **193:** Field Marshals' Hall; **194:** Peter the Great's Hall (Petrovsky zal), with his throne; **195:** Armorial Hall, bright and gilt encrusted, displaying 16th to 19th century Western European silver; **197:** The 1812 Gallery, hung with portraits of Russian and allied Napoleonic war leaders; **198:** Hall of St George or Great Throne Room – once a state room, now used for temporary exhibitions.

200-202 Western European tapestry, 16th to 19th century.

263-268 German art, 15th to 18th century, including Dürer and Lucas Cranach the Elder. **269-271: Western European porcelain,** 18th century (**271** was the tsars' cathedral).

272-289 French art, 15th to 18th century, including **272-273:** Tapestries, ceramics, metalwork; **279:** Paintings by Poussin; **280:** Lorrain; **284:** Watteau.

298-302 British art, 16th to 19th century, including **299:** Reynolds; **300:** Gainsborough's *Lady in Blue.*

303 'Dark Corridor' containing Western European tapestry, 16th to 18th century, mainly from Flanders. Follow the confusing trail through 167 and 308 to get to **304:** A wonderful collection of **Western European stone engravings** from the 13th to the 19th century; **305:** The Burgundy Hall, containing English and French Porcelain; **306:** Maria Alexandrovna's bedroom; **307:** the Blue Bedroom, containing French, Austrian and German porcelain, with a temporary exhibition of Grand Fabergé (no eggs) accessories, cigarette holders, etc which continues until 1999, possibly longer.

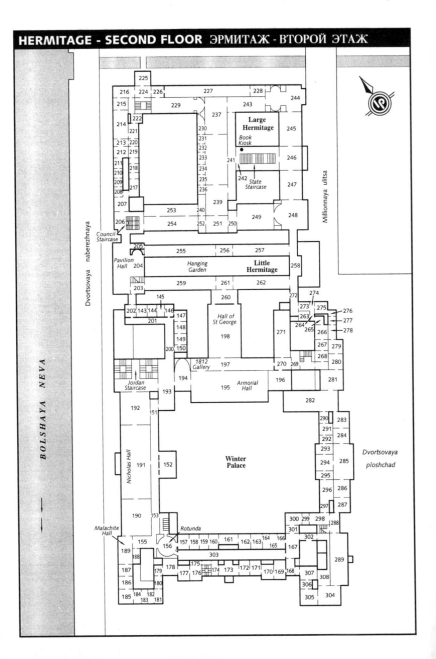

Little Hermitage, Second Floor

204 Pavilion Hall (Pavilonny zal) A sparkling white-and-gold room with lovely chandeliers, tables, galleries, and columns. The south windows look on to Catherine the Great's hanging garden; the floor mosaic in front of them is copied from a Roman bath. Roman and Florentine mosaics from the 18th and 19th centuries, and the amazing Peacock Clock – a revolving dial in one of the toadstools tells the time, and on the hour (when it's working) the peacock, toadstools, owl and cock come to life.

258 Flemish art, 17th century.

259 Western European applied art, 11th to 15th centuries.

261-262 Dutch art, 15th and 16th centuries.

Large Hermitage, Second Floor

206 Next to the Council (Soviet) Staircase with a marble, Malachite and glass triumphal arch; **207-215: Florentine art,** 13th to 16th centuries, including: **209:** 15th century paintings, including Fra Angelico; **213:** 15th and early 16th centuries, including two small Botticellis, Filippino Lippi, Perugino; **214:** Russia's only two paintings by Leonardo da Vinci – the *Benois Madonna* and the strikingly different *Madonna Litta*, both named after their last owners; **215:** Art by Leonardo's pupils, including Correggio and Andrea del Sarto.

216 Italian Mannerist art, 16th century, and a view over the little Winter Canal to the Hermitage Theatre.

217-222 Venetian art, mainly 16th century: **217:** Giorgione's *Judith* (*Yudif*); **219:** Titian's *Portrait of a Young Woman* (*Portret molodoy zhenshchinu*) and *Flight into Egypt* (*Begstvo v Egipet*), and more by Giorgione; **221:** More Titian, including *Dana* and *St Sebastian*; **222:** Paolo Veronese's *Mourning of Christ* (*Oplakivanie Khrista*).

Mounted horseman from Kul Oba, 4th century BC.

226-227 Loggia of Raphael Quarenghi's 1780s copy of a gallery in the Vatican with murals by Raphael.

228-238 Italian art, 16th to 18th centuries: **228:** 16th century ceramics; **229:** Raphael and disciples, including his *Madonna Conestabile* and *Holy Family* (*Svyatoe Semeystvo*), plus wonderful ceramics and decorations, as well as Russia's only Michelangelo, a marble statue of a crouching boy; **230-236:** These rooms always seem to be closed, but they should contain Caravaggio and Bernini (**232**). **237:** 16th century paintings, including Paolo Veronese and Tintoretto; **238:** 17th and 18th century painters including Canaletto and Tiepolo; also two huge 19th century Russian malachite vases. **237 & 238:** have lovely ceilings.

239-240 (temporarily in **143-146**) **Spanish art,** 16th to 18th centuries: **239:** Goya's *Portrait of the Actress Antonia Zaŕate* (*Antonii Sarate*), Murillo's *Boy with a Dog*, Diego Velazquez' *Breakfast*; **240:** El Greco's marvellous *St Peter and St Paul.*

241 Marble sculptures, Antonio Canova and Albert Thorwaldsen; **243:** The Giddyap Room; Western European armour and weaponry from the 15th to 17th centuries, featuring four 16th century German suits of armour atop armoured (and, thankfully, stuffed) horses.

244-247 Flemish art, 17th century: **245:** Savage hunting and market scenes by Snyders; **246:** Van Dyck portraits; **247:** A large room displaying the amazing range of Rubens. It includes *Descent from the Cross* (*Snyatie c kresta*), *Bacchus* (*Bakkh*), *The Union of Earth and Water* (*Soyuz zemli i vody*), *Portrait of a Curly-Haired Old Man* (*Golova starika*), and *Roman Charity* (*Ottselyubie rimlyanki*).

248-252 & 254 Dutch art, 17th century: **249:** Landscapes and portraits by Ruisdael, Hals, Bol and others; **250:** 18th century Delft ceramics; **254:** More than 20 Rembrandts ranging from lighter, more detailed early canvases like *Abraham's Sacrifice of Isaac* (*Zhertvoprinoshenie Avraama*) and *Dana* to *The Holy Family* (*Svyatoe semeystvo*) of 1645, and darker, penetrating late works like *The Return of the Prodigal Son* and two canvases entitled *Portrait of an Old Man* (*Portret starika*). There's also work by Rembrandt's pupils, including Bol.

The giant foot of Atlas, outside the New Hermitage building (adjacent to the Winter Palace)

ROGER HAYNE

Winter Palace, Third Floor

An approximate chronological order in which to view the French art collection is 314, 332-328, 325-315 and 343-350. The staircase beside room 269 on Floor 2 brings you out by room 314.

314-320, 330-332 French art, 19th century: **321-325, 328, 329:** mostly Barbizon School, including Corot, Courbet, Millet, though closed when we visited in 1998; **331:** Delacroix and Vernet.

315 Impressionists and post-impressionists: 315: Rodin sculptures; **316:** Gauguin's Tahitian works; **317:** Van Gogh, Rousseau, Forain, Latour; **318:** Cézanne, Pissarro; **319:** Pissarro, Monet, Sisley; **320:** Renoir, Degas.

334 Works by Vincent van Gogh

334-342 European art, 19th century, including landscapes by Caspar David Friedrich.

343, 349-350 French art, 19th to 20th centuries: Bonnard, Vlaminck, Marquet, Leger and others.

344 & 345 Picasso: 344: Mainly his blue and Cubist periods; **345:** Cubist and later periods.

346-348 Matisse.

351-371, 381-396 Oriental culture and art: 351-357, 359-364: Art of China and Tibet, an excellent collection; **358:** Indonesia; **365-367:** Mongolia; **368-371:** India; **381-387:** Byzantium, Near and Middle East.

398 & 400 Coins.

The two-tonne Cauldron of Tamerlane, cast in bronze in 1399 by mastersmith Abdal-Aziz for a mosque in present-day Kazakhstan, and now part of the Hermitage's Central Asian Collection.

For information on current exhibitions and other events at the Hermitage, visit the museum's website at www.hermitage-museum.com

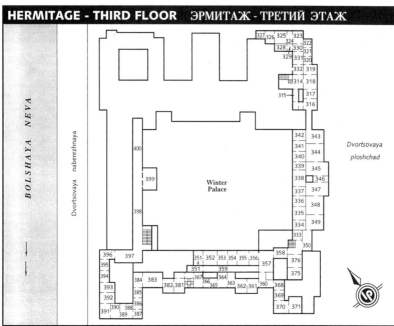

HERMITAGE - THIRD FLOOR   ЭРМИТАЖ - ТРЕТИЙ ЭТАЖ

BOLSHAYA NEVA

Dvortsovaya naberezhnaya

Winter
Palace

Dvortsovaya
ploshchad

Hermitage Pavilion Hall

ROGER HAYNE

ROGER HAYNE

Hermitage (Winter
Palace) from the
Neva River.

Protecting the Hermitage

Complain though we will about the high price of Hermitage
tickets for foreigners, the museum is under extreme financial
pressure and many cost-cutting measures are in effect. The
museum's budget has been slashed in recent years, a victim of
federal and regional austerity measures. Unfortunately, many
visitors are now complaining about the conditions – for the
patrons as well as the artworks – within the Hermitage.

Some visitors were appalled to note that many paintings
were hanging in direct sunlight and not behind glass. Still, far
more complain that glass blocks the view of the paintings,
forcing rooms of people to walk round bobbing like chickens,
their heads curiously cocked to one side as they try to see
through the glare.

But the cost cutting, says the Hermitage, in no way jeopar-
dises the safety of the paintings. It just irritates people: I was
more than put out to enter the 1812 room and find it in almost
pitch blackness because all the lights had been turned out.

Guests, including me, also complain of draughts in winter,
excessive heat in summer and a generally dilapidated appearance within the museum and even outside.

Well, instead of complaining, how about doing something
about it: join Friends of the Hermitage, the museum's last-ditch
attempt to secure funding from the public. A US$100 gift gets
you unlimited entry for a year. For US$200 you can take a
friend. Of course, you can give as much as you'd like.

Unless you're living here you probably won't get your
money's worth as far as admission is concerned, but you'll have
the satisfaction of knowing that your money (the museum
says) is going directly to support the museum – and you can
eartag gifts to go towards reconstruction of the museum, renovation of the artworks, education programs or improvement of
visitors' facilities. To join, see the volunteers in the main entry
hall near the cash desks.

continued from page 88

Orientation

The river is on the north side and Dvortso-vaya ploshchad is south. Rooms inside are numbered. There's only space to show up to 10% of the collection at any given time, so the works on view are changed from time to time and sometimes rooms are closed. Relatively few sections have English labelling.

From the main ticket hall, the Rastrelli Gallery (which has a few book and card stalls usually selling small Hermitage plans in Russian) leads to the white marble Jordan Staircase, with windows and mirrors on all sides, which takes you up to the 2nd floor of the Winter Palace. The staircase is one of the few parts of the interior to maintain its original Rastrelli appearance.

Note that Russians number their levels in the same way as in the US. There is no 'ground floor' as such – the ground level is known as the first floor. We have followed the Russian/US system in this book.

See the special guide to the Hermitage for a more thorough run-down on what's in all the rooms at the time of writing. If your time is limited, the following route takes in the major highlights (room numbers are in bold type):

Winter Palace, 2nd floor
189: Malachite Hall; **190-198:** Great state rooms.

Little Hermitage, 2nd floor
204: Pavilion Hall, with its view onto the 'Hanging Garden'.

Large Hermitage, 2nd floor
207-215: Florentine art, 13th to 16th centuries; **217-222 & 237:** Venetian art, 16th century; **229-236:** More Italian art, 16th century; **238:** Italian art of the 17th and 18th centuries; **239-240:** (temporarily located in **143-146**) Spanish art, 16th to 18th centuries; **245-247:** Flemish art, 17th century; **249-252 & 254:** Dutch art, 17th century.

Winter Palace, 3rd floor
315-320: Impressionists and post-impressionists; **344-348:** Picasso and Matisse.

Golden Rooms Special Collection

To get into this mind-bending display of crafted gold, silver and jewels in rooms **41-45** you must either book with a group at hotel concierge desks or at the St Petersburg Travel Company, or hire a guide from the hostile bureaucrats in the Hermitage's excursion office (see Admission, earlier). Prices vary depending on who you book your tour through, but an average would be US$10 to US$20, and even at these prices places are scarce (and days on which you can enter are limited), so book as soon as you reach St Petersburg.

You'll also need to pass through a special security checkpoint within the museum, and cameras and video cameras are not permitted inside.

The focus is a hoard of fabulously worked Scythian and Greek gold and silver from the Caucasus, Crimea and Ukraine, dating from the 7th to 2nd centuries BC when the Scythians, who dominated the region, and the Greeks, in colonies around the northern Black Sea, crafted the pieces to accompany the dead into the afterlife.

The treasure was unearthed from graves in the late 19th century. The rest of the collection is European jewellery, precious metals and stones of the 16th to 19th centuries, amassed by tsars from Peter the Great onwards.

The exhibit is planned to expand in the coming years. Currently there are labels in English.

NEVSKY PROSPEKT (MAP 8)

Russia's most famous street runs 4km from the Admiralty to the Alexandr Nevsky Lavra (monastery), from which it takes its name. The inner 2.5km to Moscow Station is St Petersburg's seething main avenue, the city's shopping centre and the focus of its entertainment and street life. Pushing through its crowds is an essential St Petersburg experience.

A walk down Nevsky is a walk into the heart of the new Russia: a buzzing, swirling mishmash of new and colourful shop fronts, restaurants, bars, toy shops, art galleries, banks and perfumeries that's packed to overflowing with tourists and natives, workers and beggars, scamrunners, pickpockets, purse snatchers, yahoos and religious fanatics – and all of them are shoving past on their way to the action.

Nevsky prospekt was laid out in the early years of St Petersburg as the start of the main road to Novgorod, and it soon became dotted with fine buildings, squares and bridges. Today five metro stations – Nevsky Prospekt, Gostiny Dvor, Mayakovskaya, Ploshchad Vosstania and Ploshchad Alexandra Nevskogo – are scattered along its length, and buses and trolleybuses hunt in packs (see the Getting Around chapter for useful public transport routes).

Nevsky's brightly coloured buildings – including the Sheraton Nevskij Palace Hotel, the House of Journalists, Yeliseevsky Food Shop (back in private hands), the Grand Hotel Europe, Dom Knigi and the Kazan Cathedral – have not looked this good since St Petersburg's heyday at the turn of the 20th century. Too bad the 1995 painting of the Beloselsky-Belozersky Palace used such low quality red paint: it's completely faded again and sorely needs redoing. Fellas, two coats next time, okay?

Admiralty End

Inner Nevsky, ulitsa Malaya Morskaya and ulitsa Bolshaya Morskaya were the heart of the pre-revolutionary financial district, and if Credit Lyonnais Russie (back in Russia after the 'late unpleasantness'), The Russian Bank of Trade and Industry, and Baltiysky Bank get their way, it will be again; all of these institutions have headquarters or offices in this area.

Points of interest include ulitsa Malaya Morskaya 13, where Tchaikovsky died in 1893. The wall of the school at **Nevsky prospekt 14** (1939) bears a blue-and-white stencilled sign maintained since WWII. Beginning Граждане! *(`Grazhdane!')*, it translates: 'Citizens! At times of artillery bombardment this side of the street is most dangerous!'

Close to the Moyka River, the **Kafe Literaturnoe** is, despite its repugnant food, worth peeping into for its Pushkin associations and ambience. Across the Moyka, Rastrelli's green **Stroganov Palace** (1752-54), Nevsky prospekt 17, has kept most of its original baroque appearance. The Stroganovs were a prominent family in pre-revolutionary Russia and were noted art collectors (and yes, if you absolutely must know, their chef *did* create a certain beef dish). Inside the palace is a small museum of the family's paintings and icons, open daily from 10 am to 6 pm (closed Tuesday).

Kazan Cathedral Area

A block east of the Moyka, the great colonnaded arms of the neo-classical Kazan Cathedral (Kazansky sobor, 1801-11) reach out towards the avenue. Its design, by Andrey Voronikhin, a former serf, was influenced by St Peter's in Rome. It's named after the supposedly miraculous Kazan icon which it once housed. The square in front of it has been a site for political demonstrations since before the revolution.

The cathedral houses the **Museum of the History of Religion** (☎ 311 04 95); it genuinely covers the history and infamies of many religions. There's no explanatory material in English, so if you're particularly interested, go with a group. The museum is open weekdays (except Wednesday) from 11 am to 6 pm, Saturday from noon to 6 pm, Sunday from 12.30 to 6 pm. Entrance fees for foreigners are US$3 (US$1.50 for ISIC holders, children and pensioners), and the Russian rate is US$0.75/0.40 (it's easy to get this). Pikers can enter the cathedral from the front (free of charge) which enables you to see the interior, if not the exhibits up close.

Opposite, St Petersburg's biggest bookshop, **Dom Knigi**, is topped by the globe emblem of the Singer sewing machine company, which constructed the building in 1902-04.

Just behind the Kazan Cathedral, a bit south of the central train ticket office, sits the **Bankovsky Most**, one of St Petersburg's loveliest bridges. Suspended by cables emerging from the mouths of golden-winged griffins, the wooden bridge affords a splendid view north up the Griboedova Canal past Nevsky prospekt to the Church of the Resurrection of Christ.

In the next block of Nevsky prospekt, pavement artists cluster in front of the **Central Art Salon** (Tsentralny khudozhestvenny salon).

Griboedova Canal to the Fontanka River

The area around this section of Nevsky is perhaps the busiest; a whirlwind of activity and colour of which the **Grand Hotel Europe** (the Yevropeyska under the Soviets) is the epicentre. The lavish hotel was completely renovated from 1989-91 and is again one of the city's architectural gems, boasting serious splendour: marble and gilt, sweeping staircases, four restaurants, a caviar bar, a shopping arcade and a pool and health club. You can lounge in the mezzanine listening to the harpist – coffee is $4,

but staff are so inattentive you probably won't have the chance to order.

Diagonally across Nevsky, the arcades of the **Gostiny Dvor** department store stand across ulitsa Dumskaya from the clock tower of the former **Town Duma**, seat of the pre-revolutionary city government. One of the world's first indoor shopping malls, Gostiny Dvor (literally 'merchant yard') dates from 1757-85, and is another Rastrelli creation. The St Petersburg equivalent of Moscow's GUM, it housed hundreds of small shops, counters and stalls. Under the Sovs, of course, it became one giant place in which to find the same nothing stretched out over a large area that was freezing in winter, broiling in summer and inconvenient all year round. In recent years, though, it's been progressively improving, and the façade has been completely restored.

On the other side of Nevsky, in the arcade at No 48, the **Passazh** department store was the first St Petersburg shop to move to self-financing, independent of the state supply network. Today, Passazh is everything that Gostiny Dvor wants to be: stylish, packed

Lunatic Central

The area in front of Gostiny Dvor along Nevsky prospekt has become a kind of Hyde Park Speaker's Corner, attracting representatives of the most reprehensible lunatic-fringe political groups, religious proselytisers, and purveyors of posters featuring a range of subjects from smut to 1970s vintage Fonzy.

In other words, it's fabulous entertainment. On any given day, young flag-waving communists sell newspapers and denounce capitalism, older flag-waving communists mouth off about how much better things were under Stalin or how much bread was in the shops under Brezhnev, and anarchists of all ages stand spookily under their own (black) flags, talking to anyone who'll listen. It's great fun, free, and there are kiosks selling snacks and drinks – make an afternoon of it!

NICK SELBY

Young communists in action again.

with desirable goods and, more important, shoppers with cash to spend. There's a well-stocked supermarket in the basement (see Self-Catering in the Places to Eat chapter).

Tucked in a recess between the banks and the café near ulitsa Mikhailovskaya, the **Armenian Church** (1771-80), one of two in St Petersburg, is open though under extensive renovation. The Soviets deemed it reasonable to bash the place to bits and install a 2nd floor, which blocked the view of the cupola. The renovation, performed by members of the congregation, has included removal of the 2nd floor and restoration of the cupola and several icons, but there is still a long way to go. They're in the process of creating a new iconostasis as well.

The **Vorontsov Palace** on Sadovaya ulitsa, opposite the south-east side of Gostiny Dvor, is another noble town house designed by Rastrelli. It's now a military school.

Ploshchad Ostrovskogo

An enormous statue of **Catherine the Great** stands amid the chess, backgammon and sometimes even mahjong players that crowd the benches here. The statue depicts, according to the *Blue Guide*, 'The towering figure of the Empress [standing] above her close associates ...' Well, among those 'close associates' are at least three known lovers of Catherine's – Orlov, Potyomkin and Suvorov – and it would probably be safe to assume that the rest were, too.

Formerly the home of a 'tourist art market', this airy square was created by Carlo Rossi in the 1820s and 30s and its west side is taken up by the **Saltykov-Shchedrin Public Library**, St Petersburg's biggest – it's even got an English-language section. Rossi's **Pushkin Theatre** (formerly the Alexandrinsky) at the south end is one of Russia's most important. In 1896 the opening night of Chekhov's *The Seagull* was so badly received here that the playwright fled to wander anonymously among the crowds on Nevsky prospekt.

Behind the theatre, on ulitsa Zodchego Rossi, is a continuation of Rossi's ensemble. It is proportion deified: 22m wide and high and 220m long. The **Vaganova School of Choreography** situated here is the Kirov Ballet's training school, where Anna Pavlova, Vaslaw Nijinsky, Rudolf Nureyev, Mikhail Baryshnikov and others learned their art.

The cream-coloured **Anichkov Palace**, between ploshchad Ostrovskogo and the Fontanka River (its main façade faces the river), was the home of several imperial favourites, including Catherine the Great's lover Grigory Potyomkin.

Anichkov Bridge & Beyond

Nevsky prospekt crosses the Fontanka on the **Anichkovsky Most**, with famous 1840s statues of rearing horses at its four corners. Note the genitals of the horse at the south-western corner bear the profile of Napoleon (and you said this wasn't a classy book ... What do you mean how did I notice that? I'm a trained professional).

A photogenic baroque backdrop is provided by the (currently rather faded) red 1840s **Beloselsky-Belozersky Palace**, Nevsky prospekt 41. The palace was formerly a home of Communist Party officials and now to the St Petersburg Historic Museum (☎ 315 56 36), where a political **Wax Museum** is a hoot; if you ever questioned the legitimacy of the 'body' in Lenin's tomb in Moscow, you'll know for sure after you see this. There are two displays: Russia from the 7th to 18th Centuries and From Alexander to Boris Yeltsin, each US$5/2.50 for foreigners/students, US$2.50/1.25 for Russians. Both are open daily from 11 am to 7 pm.

Between the Fontanka and Moscow Station, Nevsky prospekt has fewer historic buildings but heaps more shops and cinemas. This is one of the most concentrated areas of chi-chi shops and restaurants, and in the centre of the strip is the **Sheraton Nevskij Palace Hotel**, with fine restaurants, bars and nightclubs, and a very flash atrium lobby.

Marking the division of Nevsky prospekt and Stary (old) Nevsky prospekt is ploshchad **Vosstania** (Uprising Square), whose landmarks are the giant granite pillar with the Commie star, Moscow Station and the huge colour animation screen atop the building next to the station.

Stary Nevsky juts off the square at a 45° angle and heads south-east to the Alexandra Nevskogo bridge (Map 7). Its charm lies in its relative desolation; despite the appearance of some tourist-oriented art galleries and the California Grill (see the Places to Eat chapter), the mood on Stary Nevsky is far more laid back.

Alexandr Nevsky Monastery (Map 7)

The working Alexandr Nevsky Lavra (☎ 274 36 05), with the graves of some of Russia's most famous artistic figures, is entered from ploshchad Alexandra Nevskogo opposite the Hotel Moskva. It was founded in 1713 by Peter the Great, who wrongly thought this was where Alexandr of Novgorod had beaten the Swedes in 1240. In 1797 it became a lavra (superior monastery). Today it is open to the public and, sadly, the courtyard is filled with homeless beggars.

You can wander freely around most of the grounds, but there's a fee to enter the two most important graveyards. Tickets for foreigners cost US$2 or US$1 for ISIC holders, and US$1/0.50 for Russians; taking photographs costs an additional US$2 (though I didn't pay and took pictures anyway). Tickets are sold outside the main gate (to your right as you enter) and in summer you may have to book an hour or two ahead. Opening hours are from 11 am to 6 pm daily (closed Monday).

The **Tikhvin Cemetery** (Tikhvinskoe kladbishche), on the right as you enter, contains the most famous graves. In the far right-hand corner from its gate, a bust of Tchaikovsky marks his grave. Nearby are Rubinshteyn, Borodin, Mussorgsky, Rimsky-Korsakov and Glinka. Following the wall back towards the gate you reach the tomb of Dostoevsky.

The **Lazarus Cemetery** (Lazarevskoe kladbishche), facing the Tikhvin across the entrance path, contains several late great St Petersburg architects – among them Starov, Voronikhin, Quarenghi, Zakharov and Rossi.

Across the canal in the main lavra complex, the first main building on the left is the 1717-22 baroque **Annunciation Church** (Blagoveshchenskaya tserkov), now the City Sculpture Museum (Muzey gorodskoy skulptury) and (still) closed for renovation.

About 100m further on is the monastery's 1776-90 classical **Trinity Cathedral** (Troitsky sobor). It is open for worship on Saturday, Sunday and holidays from 6 am to the end of evening services (closed for cleaning between 2 and 5 pm); early liturgy is from 7 am, late liturgy from 10 am and all-night vigils begin at 6 pm. Hundreds crowd in on 12 September to celebrate the feast of Saint Alexandr Nevsky.

Opposite the cathedral is the St Petersburg **Metropolitan's House**, residence of Metropolitan Vladimir, the spiritual leader of St Petersburg's Russian Orthodox community. On the far right of the grounds facing the canal is St Petersburg's **Orthodox Academy**, one of only a handful in Russia (the main one is at Zagorsk, near Moscow).

BETWEEN NEVSKY & THE NEVA

It's a pleasure to stroll in the gardens, waterways and squares of the old area north of Nevsky prospekt and west of the Fontanka River. Some of St Petersburg's best museums are located here.

Ploshchad Iskusstv (Map 8)

Just a block north of Nevsky Prospekt metro station, quiet ploshchad Iskusstv (Arts Square) is named after its cluster of museums and concert halls: the **Russian Museum**, one of St Petersburg's best; the **Museum of Ethnography**; the **Large Hall** (Bolshoy zal) of the St Petersburg Philharmonic, venue for top classical concerts; and the **Maly Theatre**, the city's second fiddle to the Mariinsky for opera and ballet. Two of our walks pass through here (see St Petersburg Walks later in this chapter).

The **Brodsky House-Museum** at No 3 is a former home of Isaak Brodsky, one of the favoured artists of the revolution. It has works by top 19th century painters like Repin, Levitan and Kramskoy, but the Russian Museum has better collections by the same artists.

A statue of Pushkin stands in the middle of ploshchad Iskusstv. The square, and ulitsa Mikhailovskaya which joins it to Nevsky prospekt, were designed as a unit by Rossi in the 1820s and 1830s.

Russian Museum The former Mikhail Palace, now the Russian Museum (Gosudarstvenny Russky muzey), houses one of the country's two finest collections of Russian art (the other is in Moscow's Tretyakov Gallery). It's open daily from 10 am to 6 pm; to 5 pm Monday (closed Tuesday). Staff are absolutely adorable, going out of their way to be understood even though many don't speak English (many do). There's a little café outside in summer. Admission is US$8/4 for foreigners/foreign students, US$1.20/0.40 for Russians. Photography permission costs US$4.20. An audio tour (a Walkman with a cassette) in English is US$2.50, in Russian US$1.80.

Note that the façade of the palace is illuminated at night, making that the best time to photograph it. It was designed by Carlo Rossi and built in 1819-29 for Grand Duke Mikhail, brother of Tsars Alexander I and Nicholas I. The museum was founded in 1898, under Alexander II. The Benois Building, now connected to the original palace and accessible through an entrance on naberezhnaya Kanala Griboedova, was constructed in 1916.

The museum has finally emerged from a long renovation and looks wonderful; that said, lighting and climate control are awful and someone should be criminally prosecuted for the placement of my favourite painting, *Barge Haulers on the Volga* by Ilya Repin, in a manner that makes you strut back and forth like a big pigeon trying to see the details obscured by the reflected sunlight.

The boxed text shows highlights of the rooms as they were laid out when I visited in summer 1998; things change slightly from time to time, and after the return of a small portion of the museum's collection (albeit an important one, including the museum's entire Chagall collection, currently on world tour) they will change again from the current configuration.

Room numbering in the museum is not always chronological. The boxed text is a straightforward walk through the rooms open to the public at the time of writing. Rooms 1-15 are on the 2nd floor (upstairs from the State Vestibule, originally the main entrance), and rooms 18-38 are on the 1st floor of the Mikhail Palace. Rooms 39-54 are on the 1st floor and rooms 66-113 are on the 2nd floor of the Benois Building. Note that we use the Russian/US system of floor numbering (there is no 'ground floor' as such).

Ethnography Museum The State Museum of Ethnography (☎ 219 11 74) displays the traditional crafts, customs and beliefs of many of the peoples who make up Russia's impossibly fragile ethnic mosaic. There's a good deal of blatant propaganda going on here, but there are some notable exceptions: the sections on Transcaucasia and Central Asia, upstairs, are fascinating, with wonderful rugs and two full-size *yurts* (nomad's portable tent-house). A guide makes a lot of difference to how much you understand on your visit.

It's open daily from 10 am to 6 pm (closed Monday and the last Friday of the month). Admission for foreigners is US$3.50 (US$1 for Russians). The special exhibition of gold and jewellery rates a separate admission charge of US$3.25 for foreigners, US$1.60 for Russians.

Winter Stadium (Map 8)

East of the Ethnography Museum, the **Winter Stadium** (Zimny stadion) is an Olympic-class arena, with an indoor track and a terrific scoreboard in both Cyrillic and English courtesy of the 1994 Goodwill

Games. Events such as karate, wrestling, races etc are held regularly. The hall is also used for various exhibitions. Admission for events that charge it (many don't) is about US$1 per person at the door. There's a video arcade in the front.

Resurrection Church (Map 7)

The multi-domed **Church of the Resurrection of Christ** (Khram Voskresenia Khristova), on the Griboedova Canal just off ploshchad Iskusstv, was built in 1883-1907 on the spot where Alexander II, despite his reforms, was blown up by the People's Will terrorist group in 1881. Because of its site it's also known as the Church of the Saviour of the Spilled Blood (Khram Spasa na Krovi), and because various translations of *that* term float around you may hear it called several other names by tour guides and hotel concierges, such as 'Church of the Spilled Blood', 'Church of the Bleeding Saviour' etc. It can get confusing.

The church was partly modelled on St Basil's in Moscow in an effort to revive earlier Russian architecture, and it was seriously damaged during the 1940s Siege of Leningrad. Artisans began work in the 1970s to restore the church's spectacular onion domes and its rich treasure of mosaics; the exterior was uncovered (it had been entombed in scaffolding for decades) in 1995, and the inside opened in 1996. Outside you can see one of its etched tablets that has been left unrestored to remind visitors of the devastation.

Inside, the 7000 sq metres of mosaics are the work of over 30 artists working between 1895-1907. And, on the very spot of the assassination is a marble *Shatrovy Cen*, a monument to Alexander.

The museum is open daily from 11 am to 7 pm. Admission for all nationalities is US$2.50, US$1.20 for students. Photographs are not permitted inside.

Pushkin Flat-Museum (Map 7)

Pushkin's last home (he only lived here for a year), at naberezhnaya reki Moyki 12, is beside one of the prettiest curves of the Moyka River – between two small bridges and almost opposite the little Winter Canal, which branches off to join the Neva beneath the Hermitage arches. This is where the poet died after his duel in 1837.

His killer was a French soldier of fortune, D'Anthés, who had been publicly courting Pushkin's beautiful wife, Natalya. The affair was widely seen as a put-up job on behalf of the tsar, who found the famed poet's radical politics inconvenient and who, gossip said, may have been the one actually stalking Natalya.

The little house is now the Pushkin Flat-Museum (☎ 314 00 06), open daily from 11 am to 6 pm (closed Tuesday and the last Friday of the month). Admission for foreigners is about US$3 (US$1 for ISIC holders, children and pensioners) including a Russian-language tour (English tours can be arranged on advance notice).

Mars Field (Map 5)

The Mars Field (Marsovo pole) is the open space south of the Troitsky bridge. Don't take a short cut across the grass – you may be walking on graves from the 1917 revolution, the civil war, or later communist luminaries also buried here. There's a monument to the luminaries in the middle. The field is so named (after Mars, the Roman god of war) because it was the scene of 19th century military parades.

Across ulitsa Millionnaya, in the courtyard of the Marble Palace, there's a pedestal which once displayed the armoured car from which Vlad Lenin uttered his rallying call '*Da zdrastvuet sotsialisticheskaya revolyutsia*' ('Long live socialist revolution') at the Finland Station on 3 April 1917.

The **Marble Palace**, built for Catherine the Great's lover Grigory Orlov in 1768-85, formerly housed a Lenin Museum; currently it is a branch of the Russian Museum (☎ 312 91 96) featuring rotating exhibitions. It's open daily from 10 am to 6 pm (closed Tuesday); admission for foreigners is US$8 (US$2.25 for ISIC holders, children and pensioners), use of photo and video cameras costs US$2.25.

The Russian Museum (A Room-by-Room Tour)

Highlights and personal favourites in the Russian museum include (room numbers in **bold** – note that rooms 1 to 17 and 66 to 99 are on the second floor):

Rooms 1-4: 12th to 15th century icons. I liked *Apostle Peter* and *Apostle Paul* by Andrey Rublyov and others; **5-9:** 17th to 18th century sculpture, portraits and tapestries, and Rastrelli's enormous *Anna Joannovna and an Arab boy* (**7**). **10, 12, 14:** Late 18th century, early 19th century paintings and sculpture. **11:** The White Hall, the finest in the palace, with period furniture by Rossi. **15:** Big 19th century canvases mainly by graduates of the official Academy – Aivazovsky's Crimea seascapes stand out.

18-22: 19th century works focusing (**19**) on the beginnings of the socially aware 'Critical Realist' tradition. **23-38:** Peredvizhniki and associated artists including **24, 27, 28:** Landscapes; **25:** Kramskoy; **26:** Nikolai Ge, including his fearsome *Peter I interrogating Tsarevich Alexey at Peterhof*, **27:** Shishkin and **31:** KA Savitsky's *To The War*.

32: Poleneov, including his *Christ and the Sinner*; Antakolsky sculptures.

33-35, 54: A permanent exhibition of the work of Repin, probably Russia's best-loved artist; **33** has portraits and the incomparable *Barge Haulers on the Volga* (when it's not out on loan or at the Tretyakov in Moscow), an indictment of Russian 'social justice'; **34** has *Zaporozhie Cossacks Writing a Letter to the Turkish Sultan* (officially entitled *Zaprozhtse*); **35** has Mikhail Mikeshin's model of the *Millennium of Russia*; and **54** contains the massive *Meeting of the State Council*, Repin's rendering of the meeting at the Mariinsky Palace on 7 May 1901 (it's full of tsarist hot shots; there's a scheme in the room to help you tell who's who).

36: Russian history, portraits by Surikov, a national revivalist. **37, 38:** Landscapes by Kuinzhi.

39: Popular 19th century painter Malyavin's depictions of Russian mothers and maidens.

41: Vasnetsov, including *Russian Knight at the Crossroads* and other 'sketches' for his mosaics. **42-47:** Currently under renovation and will be used to permanently exhibit works by Levitan and other late 19th century painters, and **45:** Ryabushkin on pre-Peter the Great 17th century Russian history, includes the very telling and humorous *Yedut*, or *They Are Coming*, depicting the perturbed-looking reception committee for the first foreigners allowed in Russia

48: Antakolski sculptures. (Exits straight ahead lead to the 10 halls of Russian folk art exhibition, including handicrafts, wood work, carvings, pottery, toys etc; exits to the right lead to the Benois building.) **49:** Actually a long corridor that houses temporary exhibitions.

50-65: Closed at the time of researching.

66-79: 20th century art, including **66:** Vrubel, with his epic *Russian Hero*, and *Venice* and Artemiy Ober's terrifying bronze *Calamity*; **67:** Nesterov's religious paintings of the history of the Orthodox Church; Konenkov sculptures and Vasnetsov's *The Entombing*; **70, 71:** Serov, portraits of Russian aristocracy (like one of *SM Botkina*) and other high-rollers; Trubitskoy sculptures of same including *Isaak Levitan and Children*; **72:** Impressionists Korovin, Grabar and Serebryakova; Trubitskoy's *Moscow Carriage Driver* and Boris Kustodiev's *Holiday on the Volga*; **73:** Kustodiev's paintings of stereotypical Russians; **74:** The Rerikh Room.

75-79: Russian avant-garde, symbolism, neoclassical works of artists, including Saryan Kuznetsov, Petrov-Vodkin, Grigoriev, Shukhaev, Altman, Lenturov etc; **78** features Natalia Goncharova's series of four panels, *Evangelist* and **79** has Kazimir Malevich's *Aviator*. Note that **79** will be home to the museum's Chagall and Malevich collection as soon as the works return from revenue-producing exhibitions abroad (don't hold your breath).

83-113: Halls for rotating exhibitions.

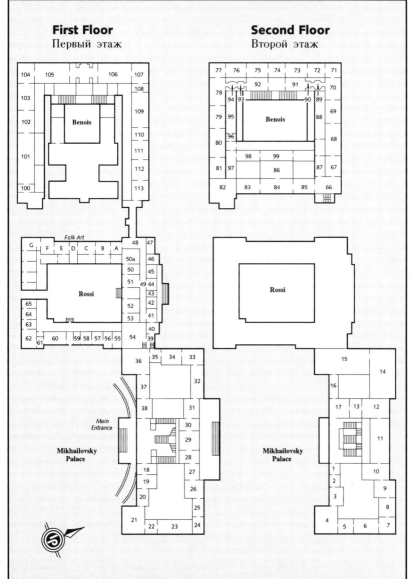

Summer Garden (Map 5)

Perhaps St Petersburg's loveliest park, the Summer Garden (Letny sad) is located between the Mars Field and the Fontanka River. You can enter at the north or south ends. It opens at 8 am daily and closes at 10 pm from May to August, 8 pm in September and 7 pm from October to March. It's closed during the month of April.

Laid out for Peter the Great with fountains, pavilions and a geometrical plan to resemble the park at Versailles, the garden became a strolling place for St Petersburg's 19th-century leisured classes. Though changed since that era, it maintains a formal elegance, with thousands of lime trees shading its straight paths and lines of statues. In winter individual wooden huts are placed over the statues to protect them from the cold.

The modest, two-storey **Summer Palace** in the north-eastern corner was St Petersburg's first palace, built for Peter in 1704-14, and is pretty well intact. Little reliefs around the walls depict Russian naval victories. Today it's open as a museum (Muzey Letny Dvorets Petra I; ☎ 314 04 56) from early May to early November daily from 11 am to 6 pm (closed Tuesday and the last Monday of the month). Many rooms are stocked with early 18th century furnishings. Tickets are sold in the nearby **Tea House** (Chayny domik) for Russian-language group tours, usually from 11 am to late afternoon. Admission for foreigners is US$4, US$1 for children and students.

Neither the Tea House nor the Coffee House (Kofeyny domik) behind it offers tea, coffee or anything else to eat or drink (nor does anywhere else in the garden). But they do hold various small exhibitions – art openings and the like. Buy tickets from the Tea House, or the little kiosk near the palace.

South of the Summer Garden (Map 7)

A much greater Summer Palace used to stand across the canal from the south end of the Summer Garden. But Rastrelli's almost fairy-tale, wooden creation for Empress Elizabeth was knocked down in the 1790s to make way for the bulky, brick **Engineers' Castle** of Paul I, an insanely cruel tsar who lived in fear of assassination and was indeed suffocated in his bed a month after moving in. Later it became a military engineering school (hence the name). The pleasant **Mikhail Gardens** are over the road.

Chyzhik (Map 7)

'*Chyzhik, Chyzhik, gde tyi byl*?' begins a famous Russian folk song, 'Little bird, little bird, where have you been? Down at the Fontanka, sipping water' (well, hell; it rhymes in Russian). Anyway, the charming song inspired a wonderfully charming little monument by Mikhail Shemyakin (the same sculptor who created the controversially proportioned statue of Peter the Great at the Peter & Paul Fortress) that's exceptionally easy to miss: a little bird perched just above the river. You can see it best if you stand on the south-west side of the Inzhenerny most (bridge) and look to the south (towards Nevsky prospekt). People believe it's good luck to throw coins: if it lands on the bird's perch you get a wish fulfilled (and it's appreciated by the kids who hang round with magnets and gum at the end of string fishing for coins all day!).

Akhmatova Museum (Map 8)

Across the Fontanka, the yellow **Sheremetev Palace** (1750-55) houses a lovely little museum to the great, long-persecuted poet Anna Akhmatova (see Literature in the Facts about St Petersburg chapter). The flat, on the 2nd floor, is filled with mementos of the poet, including her bedroom and her study, and correspondence with Pasternak. Downstairs is an excellent little bookshop and a small video room where you can watch Russian-language documentaries on her life while drinking tea or coffee (US$0.25). They also sell audiotapes of Akhmatova's works read by famous Russian actors (US$3). A memorial to Akhmatova is being discussed, and contoversy surrounds the site: it will probably be near Kresty Prison (see Vyborg Side, later in this chapter), where her son was imprisoned, as she requested in her own *Requiem* when speaking of the possibility of a memorial to her:

... there, where I queued for three hundred hours ...
And where the door was never unlocked

Admission to the museum is US$2 for foreigners, US$1/0.40 for Russians/Russian students. The museum is open Tuesday to Sunday from 10.30 am to 5.30 pm (closed Monday). From the Fontanka, enter the Sheremetev Palace, walk through the lobby and into the courtyard, to the right along the path and follow the signs. Two more Akhmatova museums are in the town of Pushkin; see the Excursions chapter for more information.

SMOLNY REGION (MAP 5)
Tauride Gardens

The Tauride Gardens (Tavrichesky sad), encompassing the **City Children's Park** (Gorodskoy detsky park), are worth a stop on the way to Smolny. It's a great place for children under 10; the kiddie rides are among the best in Russia. Even though the beauty of this lovely park's canals and little bridges has been somewhat marred, you can watch Russians enjoying themselves and have a look across the lake at the fine **Tauride Palace** (Tavrichesky dvorets), built in 1783-89 for Catherine the Great's lover Potyomkin.

The palace takes its name from the region of Crimea (once called Tavria), which Potyomkin was responsible for conquering. Between 1905 and 1917 the State Duma, the Provisional Government and the Petrograd Soviet all met here. Today it's home to the Parliamentary Assembly of the Member States of the CIS and the St Petersburg Economic Forum, an international group of chin-waggers. The gardens are a block and a half east of Chernyshevskaya metro. Bus Nos 5, 46, 58 and 134 to Smolny pass alongside here.

Anna Akhmatova began writing verse at the age of 11 and went on to become the greatest female poet in Russian literature.

Flowers Exhibition Hall

One of the finest ways to escape momentarily from a St Petersburg winter is to head for the Flowers Exhibition Hall, an indoor tropical paradise just north-west of the City Children's Park at the corner of Potyomkinskaya ulitsa and Shpalernaya ulitsa. It has a wishing well, and there's a flower-selling stall at the front of the building. It's open year-round, daily from 11 am to 7 pm (closed Monday and Thursday). There's a florist next door, and one diagonally across the street as well.

Smolny

The **cathedral** at Smolny, 3km east of the Summer Garden, is one of the most fabulous of all Rastrelli's buildings, and the Smolny Institute next door was the hub of the October Revolution. Buses here include No 6 from the Admiralty via much of Nevsky prospekt, and trolleybus No 5 or 7 from ploshchad Vosstania.

The cathedral is the centrepiece of a convent mostly built, to Rastrelli's designs, in 1748-57. His inspiration was to combine baroque details with the forests of towers and onion domes typical of an old Russian monastery. There's special genius in the proportions of the cathedral, to which the convent buildings are a perfect foil. Rastrelli also planned a gigantic bell tower needling up at the west end of the convent, facing down Shpalernaya ulitsa, but funds ran out. Today the convent houses the city administration's offices while the cathedral is a concert hall, usually open only for performances.

The **Smolny Institute**, built by Quarenghi in 1806-08 as a school for aristocratic girls, had fame thrust upon it in 1917 when Trotsky and Lenin directed the October Revolution from the headquarters of the Bolshevik Central Committee and the Petrograd Soviet, both of which had been set up here. In its Hall of Acts (Aktovy zal) on 25 October, the All-Russian Congress of Soviets conferred power on a Bolshevik government led by Lenin, which ran the country from here until March 1918.

About 100m west of the Smolny Cathedral, on Shpalernaya ulitsa, is the former home of General Kikhin (one-time naval advisor to Peter the Great), today known as **Music School No 2**. Kikhin, who built this house about the same time as the Menshikov Palace was being constructed across town, fell from Peter's graces and was dropped from the pages of St Petersburg history. The house was formerly a branch of the Kunstkammer (see Museum of Anthropology & Ethnography, later), as well as a Soviet sports school.

Further west, near the corner of Tavricheskaya ulitsa, stands one of the last remaining statues of **Felix Dzerzhinsky**, founder of the infamous Cheka, predecessor to the KGB (it was a statue of Dzerzhinsky in front of Moscow KGB headquarters that was so famously ripped down by crowds in the 1991 coup). You can, by the way, buy eggs just one block away at the little shop on the corner of ulitsas Tavricheskaya and Tverskaya.

The Big House

Speaking of the KGB, their headquarters were a bit west of here in the enormous **Bolshoy dom** (Liteyny prospekt 4, the vicious-looking granite cube festooned with radio antennae), now home to the St Petersburg GUVD (Glavnoe Upravlenie Vnutrennikh Del; ☎ 311 18 51). These days it's still packed with spooks, though now they prefer to be referred to as 'Interior Ministry' and 'Counter Espionage' personnel.

SOUTH & WEST OF NEVSKY PROSPEKT
Sennaya Ploshchad Area (Map 6)

This teeming market square, dominated by what seems to be a permanent exhibition of construction equipment, is the gateway to Dostoevskyville – despite the McDonald's and the kiosk city that sells everything from bootlegged software to vodka to flowers. The peripatetic Dostoevsky, who occupied around 20 residences in his 28-year stay in the city, once spent a couple of days in debtors' prison in what is now called the **Senior Officers' Barracks**, just across the square from the Sennaya Ploshchad metro station. Dostoevsky had been thrown in there by his publisher, for missing a deadline ('Had we but thought of it ...' – Tony Wheeler). At the site of the metro station there was once a large cathedral that dominated the square.

Just west of the square and across the river at ulitsa Kaznacheyskaya 7 is the flat where Dostoevsky wrote *Crime and Punishment*; Raskolnikov's route to the murder passed directly under the author's window (see St Petersburg Walks later in this chapter).

And due west of the square along Sadovaya ulitsa is the charming **Yusupovsky Sad**, a hugely pleasant park.

Vladimirskaya Ploshchad Area (Map 7)

Around Vladimirskaya ploshchad are the indoor **Kuznechny market**, St Petersburg's biggest and best stocked (open daily), plus a clutch of entertainment venues, a bitchin' Irish pub, small museums and a smattering of eateries and shops. The onion-domed working **Vladimir Church** (1761-83) dominates the square.

Dostoevsky wrote most of *The Brothers Karamazov* in a flat at Kuznechny pereulok 5, just past the market, and he died there in 1881. It's now a small **Dostoevsky Museum** (☎ 164 69 50), open daily from 11 am to 5 pm (closed Monday and the last Wednesday of the month). Admission for foreigners is US$2.80, US$1.20 for students. Nearby, outside the Dostoevskaya/Vladimirskaya metro station is a **monument** to the writer.

The **Arctic & Antarctic Museum** (☎ 311 25 49) on ulitsa Marata focuses on Soviet polar exploration, with taxidermy exhibitions – great fun for the kids. Admission is US$1.60/0.30 for foreigners/students, US$0.90/0.30 for Russians. It's open Wednesday to Sunday from 10 am to 5 pm.

There's a small **Rimsky-Korsakov Flat-Museum** (☎ 113 32 08), Zagorodny prospekt 28, open from 9 am to 8 pm Wednesday to Saturday, 11 am to 6 pm Sunday. There are also chamber music and other concerts here each Wednesday evening and on weekends; check the *St Petersburg Times* for more information.

Zagorodny prospekt continues past Pionerskaya ploshchad, where in 1849 Fyodor Dostoevsky and 20 others, sentenced to death for socialist leanings, were lined up to be shot – only to be told at the last moment that their sentences had been commuted. Most of them were transported to Siberia.

Teatralnaya Ploshchad Area (Map 6)

Known throughout the world during the Soviet reign as the Kirov, the **Mariinsky Theatre** resumed its original name in 1992, though the ballet company still uses the name Kirov. Its home, at Teatralnaya ploshchad, is an area of quiet, old canal-side streets (and a nice Irish pub). Teatralnaya ploshchad has been a St Petersburg entertainment centre since fairs were held here in the mid-18th century.

North-east of Teatralnaya ploshchad, before it twists south-west, the canal runs under yet another beautiful beast-supported suspension bridge, the **Lviny Most**, with chains emerging from the mouths of lions.

Bus Nos 3, 22 and 27 from Nevsky prospekt, Nos 2 and 100 from Ploshchad Lenina via the Mars Field and Nevsky prospekt, and tram No 31 from Kronverksky prospekt on the Petrograd side via the Admiralty, all serve Teatralnaya ploshchad.

Built in 1860, the Mariinsky has played a pivotal role in Russian ballet and opera ever since. The St Petersburg Conservatory faces it, and a monument to Rimsky-Korsakov is diagonally opposite it in the small park.

Outside performance times you can usually wander into the Mariinsky Theatre's (☎ 114 12 11 or 314 90 83) foyer, and maybe peep into its lovely auditorium. Tickets to performances can be a problem, as Westerners are charged as much as they possibly can be, and official tickets are rationed out to the larger hotels and tour companies well

Rimsky-Korsakov had a fascination with the sea, and oceanic scenes feature heavily in his operas and symphonies.

The Life and Death of Rasputin

A good way to get to Teatralnaya ploshchad is to walk along the Moyka River from Isaakievskaya ploshchad. On the way, you'll pass the old **Yusupov Palace** (Map 6, ☎ 314 98 83) at naberezhnaya reki Moyki 94. (Note that there are two Yusupov Palaces in the city; the other is in the Yusupovsky Gardens by the Fontanka River.) Grigory Rasputin was invited to dinner here on the night of 16 December 1916 by Prince Felix Yusupov and friends.

Rasputin, born Grigory Yefimovich Novykh, was a failed monk (he was never actually ordained), charlatan and party-animal whose spooky hold over the Imperial family of Nicholas and Alexandra granted him the effective run of Russia for over a decade. Rasputin came to believe, as did the contemporary Khylst (whip) sect, that sinning (especially through sex) and then repenting could bring people close to God. Early in the 20th century, Rasputin reached St Petersburg, where some sectors of high society, with little better to do, took a big interest in holy peasants. Rasputin's soothing talk, compassion and generosity, and his teaching that promiscuity could bring redemption, made him very popular with some aristocratic women. His magnetic personality was apparently heightened by what the French ambassador called a 'strong animal smell, like that of a goat'.

Tsarina Alexandra was most fond of Rasputin, though it's unclear whether there was any sexual relationship (though Rasputin and Alexandra were alone quite often when Nicholas was off botching up WWI). Rasputin endeared himself to the court by somehow treating Alexandra and Nicholas' son, Alexey, for haemophilia. As he continued his drunken, lecherous life, replete with famous orgies, Rasputin's influence on the royal family grew to the point that he could make or break the careers of ministers and generals. Very soon, the upper echelons of St Petersburg society began to feel their territory quite invaded and finally got together to do something about it.

The 1916 dinner at the Prince's place was ostensibly to introduce Rasputin to Yusupov's wife (to whom the priest was allegedly attracted). During the meal, Rasputin was fed poisoned food, cakes, cookies and drink. After he ate and drank all this and was happily (and healthily) licking his fingers, the Yusupov gang did what they probably should have done in the first place: shot ol' Raspy repeatedly.

But like a tsarist-era Terminator, the mystic refused to die and when Yusupov knelt over him, Rasputin grabbed him by the throat. At that point, Yusupov did what any sane man would do: he ran away. When he returned with reinforcements, they found the mystic had dragged himself outside. They shot him a few more times, beat him with sticks for good measure, and finally stuffed him through the ice of the frozen river. Legend has it that the Rasputin did not die until he was submerged – water was found in his lungs.

Yusupov Palace's 1st and 2nd floors are open to visitors, but to see the basement chamber in which Rasputin ate the poisoned food, you'll need to arrange a 'Rasputin Tour' with the museum administrator, who generally wants about US$10 per person in a group of at least three. Consolation: you'll see wax figures of the priest and Prince Felix.

Monument to Pushkin

NICK SELBY

GEORGI SHABLOVSKY

ROGER HAYNE

Streetlamp near Winter Palace

Museum of Anthropology & Ethnography

GEORGI SHABLOVSKY

Engineers' Castle, built in the 1790s for Tsar Paul I

NICK SELBY

View from Millionnaya ulitsa

Clothing stall at one of St Petersburg's many markets

Decisions, decisions ...   'Wanna buy a goat?'   Michael Jordan and friends

Prunes and ... brooms?

Magazine seller, Nevsky prospekt

in advance. You can try at the box office, where the face price of tickets is about US$4. Go as early as you can (the booking office is open from 11 am to 7 pm; performances start at 7 pm). Should you get turned away from there you have several choices, including the *teatralnaya kassi* (theatre ticket booths) around town, tourist agencies like the St Petersburg Travel Company and concierge desks at the larger hotels (see Tickets in the Entertainment chapter for more information).

The baroque spires and domes of **St Nicholas' Cathedral** (1753-62), rising among the trees at the bottom of ulitsa Glinki, shelter many 18th century icons and a fine carved wooden iconostasis. A graceful bell tower overlooks the Kryukov Canal, crossed by the Staro-Nikolsky bridge. South along this canal and across a footbridge over the Fontanka is blue-domed **Trinity Cathedral** on Izmaylovsky prospekt, an impressive 1828-35 classical edifice; sadly, it was boarded up at the time of writing.

The flat where Alexandr Blok spent the last eight years of his life, at Dekabristov ulitsa 57, is now a museum (☎ 113 86 16) open Thursday to Tuesday from 11 am to 5 pm (closed Wednesday and the last Tuesday of the month).

Moskovsky Prospekt (Map 3)

This long avenue south from Sennaya ploshchad is the start of the main road to Moscow. The iron **Moscow Triumphal Arch**, 3.5km out, looking very like Berlin's Brandenburg Gate, was built in 1838 to mark victories over Turks, Persians and Poles. It was demolished in 1936 then rebuilt in 1959-60. Local legend has it that the gate is built on the spot where travellers entering the city in the early days had to show that they had brought with them bricks or stones to be used in the construction of buildings.

A couple of kilometres further south, east off Moskovsky prospekt on ulitsa Gastello, is the **Chesma Palace**. Built for Catherine the Great to rest en route to the city of Tsarskoe Selo (now Pushkin) it has a

ground plan like a radiation warning sign. More interesting is the red-and-white 18th-century Gothic **Chesma Church**, behind the Hotel Mir at ulitsa Gastello 17. The church, built in honour of the Battle of Çesme (1770), when the Russian fleet sailed from the Baltic to the Aegean to beat the Turks, has just emerged from a lengthy renovation (and the roof *still* leaks!). Its museum of the battle has been moved to Yekaterinsky Park in the city of Pushkin.

Wide Moskovskaya ploshchad, a little way south of ulitsa Gastello, was intended under a 1930s plan to become the centre of St Petersburg, replacing the old tsarist centre. It is a testament to the stubbornness of St Petersburgers that during the time of Stalin's terror, this plan was universally ignored. Moskovsky prospekt ends a few hundred metres further on at ploshchad Pobedy, where the **Monument to the Heroic Defenders of Leningrad**, commemorating the siege of WWII, makes a striking first impression on entering St Petersburg.

VASILEVSKY ISLAND

The interesting parts of Vasilevsky Island are its eastern 'nose', the Strelka (Tongue of Land), where Peter the Great first wanted his new city's administrative and intellectual centre, and the embankment facing the Admiralty.

In fact, the Strelka became the focus of St Petersburg's maritime trade, symbolised by the white colonnaded Stock Exchange. The two Rostral Columns on the point, studded with ships' prows, were oil-fired navigation beacons in the 1800s (on some holidays gas torches are still lit on them). The area remains an intellectual centre, with the St Petersburg State University, the Academy of Arts and a veritable 'museum ghetto'.

The Strelka also has one of the best views in the city: you look left to the Peter & Paul Fortress and right to the Hermitage, the Admiralty and St Isaac's Cathedral.

At the inner end of the island many north-south streets have separate names and independent numbering for each side or 'line' (linia). Thus the street beside Menshikov Palace is Sezdovskaya linia on the east side and 1-ya (*pervaya*, first) linia on the west, the next street is 2-ya linia on the east and 3-ya on the west, and so on.

Museums near the Strelka (Maps 4 & 6)

The Stock Exchange is now the **Central Naval Museum** (Tsentralny Voenno-Morskoy muzey; Map 4, ☎ 218 25 02), full of maps, excellent model-ships, flags and photos of and about the Russian navy right up to the present. Also on display is the *Botik*, Peter's first boat (the granddaddy of them all), a pre-turn-of-the-century submarine (it's a two-seater) and some big oars. It's open from 10.30 am to 5.30 pm; last entry is at 4.45 pm (closed Monday, Tuesday and the last Thursday of the month). Admission is US$3.20/1.60 for foreigners/students, Russians pay US$1.30/0.65.

To the right (north) of the old Exchange is a former maritime warehouse and former Museum of Agriculture (Map 4). Beyond this the old Customs House, topped with statues and a dome, is now called Pushkin House (Pushkinsky dom), and is home to the **Institute of Russian Literature** and a Literary Museum with exhibits on Tolstoy, Gogol, Lermontov, Turgenev, Gorky and others (Map 4). It's open on weekdays from 11 am to 5 pm (closed Saturday and Sunday).

To the left (south) of the Exchange, in another former warehouse, is the **Museum of Zoology** (Zoologichesky muzey; Map 6, ☎ 218 01 12), said to be one of the biggest and best in the world, with more stuffed animals than you can shake a stick at, plus insects and fish from all over the world. Among the dioramas and the tens of thousands of mounted beasties is a complete woolly mammoth(!) thawed out of the Siberian ice in 1902.

The museum is open from 11 am to 6 pm; last entry is at 5 pm (closed Friday). And it's a bargain – admission for foreigners is US$1.60 (US$0.80 for ISIC holders, children and pensioners). The administrator told me that admission is free on Thursday

(except for tours). Pay at the microscopic cash window just west of the main entrance.

Museum of Anthropology & Ethnography (Map 6)

The blue-and-white building with the steeple was the city's first museum, founded in 1714 by Peter himself. In contrast to the State Museum of Ethnography, this museum (Muzey Antropologii i Etnografii; ☎ 218 14 12) is about peoples outside the former USSR, with wonderfully kitsch dioramas and displays on the cultures of Asia, Oceania, Africa and the Americas. The old anatomy theatre is the big draw, with selections from Peter's original *Kunstkammer*. While this translates from German to 'art chamber', the bloodthirsty crowds are really here to see Peter's collection of 'curiosities': bugs and snakes, gold ornaments from Siberian tombs and a truly ghoulish collection of preserved freaks, foetuses and body parts. The displays are fun for the whole family.

The museum is open from 11 am to 5 pm; last entry is at 4.45 pm (closed Thursday). Admission for everyone is US$2.40/1.80. The entrance is around the corner on Tamozhyonny pereulok.

Menshikov Palace (Map 6)

Alexandr Menshikov was a close friend (many now say lover) of Peter the Great. For helping the tsar defeat the Swedes he was made Governor General of St Petersburg and given Vasilevsky Island. Peter later took the island back, but in 1707 Menshikov put up one of the city's first buildings, a riverside palace (Dvorets Menshikova) just west of the Twelve Colleges. He effectively ran Russia from here for three years between Peter's death and his own exile.

Later the palace was a military academy and then it went to seed until Lenin suggested it be saved. Now its lavish interiors are again filled with period art and furniture as a museum of 'Russian Culture of the First Third of the 18th century' (☎ 213 11 12). It's open daily from 10.30 am to 4.30 pm (closed Monday). Admission for foreigners is US$5 (US$3 for ISIC holders and children) with extra charges for photography. Russian-language tours, which start every 10 minutes, are included in the price.

Academy of Arts Museum (Map 6)

Two blocks west of the Menshikov Palace, at Universitetskaya naberezhnaya 17, is the Russian Academy of Arts' Research Museum (Muzey Akademii Khudozhestv; ☎ 213 64 96, tour desk ☎ 213 35 78), guarded by two imported Egyptian sphinxes said to be about 3500 years old. Inside are works by Academy students and faculty since its founding, plus changing exhibitions, sometimes by foreign artists. The classical entrance hall with its dusty statues is a sight in itself. It's open from 11 am to 6 pm; last entry is at 5 pm (closed Monday and Tuesday). Admission for foreigners is US$4.85 (US$2.50 for ISIC holders, children and pensioners), or US$0.80/0.40 for Russians.

Churches (Map 6)

Four untended, mostly unused classical churches are located in the blocks just west of the university. The handsomest is the former Lutheran **Church of St Catherine** (Tserkov Yekateriny, 1771, Map 6) at Bolshoy prospekt 1, now a sound studio owned by record company Melodia.

More intriguing is what looks like a homage to Istanbul's Sancta Sofia, behind high walls at the west end of Bolshoy prospekt. This Byzantine mystery is now a naval training school so there's no way in. Take bus No 7 or trolleybus No 10 from the Hermitage if you wish to take a look.

Twelve Colleges (Map 6)

West of the Anthropology Museum and marked by a statue of scientist-poet Mikhail Lomonosov (1711-65) is Mendeleevskaya linia and the skinny, 400m-long Twelve Colleges building. One of St Petersburg's oldest buildings, it was meant originally for Peter's government ministries, and is now part of the university, which stretches out behind it.

Monuments (Map 6)

Outside the main Vasilevsky Island fire station, at Bolshoy prospekt 73 just east of 22-23-ya linii, is a **monument** commemorating the firemen who died fighting the 1991 blaze in the Hotel Leningrad (now Hotel St Petersburg). And there's a pretty good statue of **Lenin** just east of 16-17-ya linii on the north side of Bolshoy prospekt.

PETROGRAD SIDE

Petrograd Side (Petrogradskaya storona) is a cluster of delta islands between the Malaya Neva and Bolshaya Nevka channels. On little Zayachy Island, Peter the Great first broke ground for St Petersburg and built the Peter & Paul Fortress. Most of Petrograd Side's other sights are near the fortress, though the Kirovsky Islands feature some vast parklands and old dacha-palaces which are currently the stomping ground of government big-wigs, large gentlemen of indeterminate occupation who drive Mercedes Benzes, rich foreign businessmen, and a presidential dacha.

Peter & Paul Fortress

Founded in 1703, the Peter & Paul Fortress (Petropavlovskaya krepost, see the Peter & Paul Fortress map on the following page) is the oldest building in St Petersburg. Peter planned it as a defence against the Swedes but defeated them before it was finished. Its main use up to 1917 was as a political prison; one of its first inmates was Peter's own son Alexey, whose torture Peter is said to have personally overseen. Other famous residents were Dostoevsky, Gorky, Trotsky and Lenin's older brother, Alexandr. The entrance to the fortress is on the eastern side of the island, and most worth seeing are the **SS Peter & Paul Cathedral**, with its landmark needle-thin spire, and the **Trubetskoy Bastion**.

The cathedral, though plain on the outside, was radically different from traditional Orthodox churches. If you haven't overdosed on churches, don't miss its magnificent baroque interior. All of Russia's pre-revolutionary rulers from Peter the

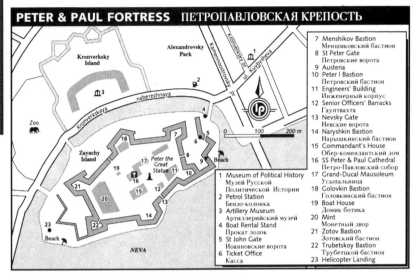

PETER & PAUL FORTRESS ПЕТРОПАВЛОВСКАЯ КРЕПОСТЬ

7   Menshikov Bastion
    Меншиковский бастион
8   St Peter Gate
    Петровские ворота
9   Austeria
10 Peter I Bastion
    Петровский бастион
11 Engineers' Building
    Инженерный корпус
12 Senior Officers' Barracks
    Гауптвахта
13 Nevsky Gate
    Невские ворота
14 Naryshkin Bastion
    Нарышкинский бастион
15 Commandant's House
    Обер-комендантский дом
16 SS Peter & Paul Cathedral
    Петро-Павловский собор
17 Grand-Ducal Mausoleum
    Усыпальница
18 Golovkin Bastion
    Головкинский бастион
19 Boat House
    Домик ботика
20 Mint
    Монетный двор
21 Zotov Bastion
    Зотовский бастион
22 Trubetskoy Bastion
    Трубецкой бастион
23 Helicopter Landing

1   Museum of Political History
    Музей Русской
    Политической Истории
2   Petrol Station
    Бензо-колонка
3   Artillery Museum
    Артиллерийский музей
4   Boat Rental Stand
    Прокат лодок
5   St John Gate
    Иоанновские ворота
6   Ticket Office
    Касса

Great onwards (except Peter II and Ivan VI) are buried here – a controversial ceremony held in 1998 re-buried Nicholas II, his wife Alexandra and three of their five children here (Alexey and either Maria or Tatyana are missing), having been exhumed from their mass grave near the Ural Mountains (for the full story see the boxed aside entitled 'Reburying the Past' in the Facts about St Petersburg chapter). Peter I's grave is at the front on the right, and people still pay their respects by leaving fresh flowers on it. Individuals might avoid queues by discreetly moving upstream through the crowds exiting, into the adjoining **Grand-Ducal Mausoleum**. The mausoleum, built at the turn of this century, has a free exhibit on the reconstruction of the fortress. Between the cathedral and the **Senior Officers' Barracks** is a statue of a seated Peter the Great, with somewhat interestingly proportioned head and hands.

In the fort's south-west corner are reconstructions of the grim cells of the **Trubetskoy Bastion**, where Peter supervised the torture to death of his son. The cells were used by later tsars to keep a lid on original thinking in the empire.

In the south wall is **Nevsky Gate**, a later addition, where prisoners were loaded on boats for execution elsewhere. Notice the plaques showing water levels of famous floods. Outside are fine views of the whole central waterfront. Around to the left in summer is a fascinating collection of anglers, joggers and standing sunbathers (standing's said to give you a *proper* tan), and in winter you might see people swimming in holes cut through the ice (an activity that's said to be 'good for the health'). Above this, on the artillery platform, is a summer café serving chicken, sandwiches, beer and soft drinks. At noon every day a cannon is fired from **Naryshkin Bastion**, scaring the daylights out of tourists.

The **Commandant's House** is a Museum of the History of St Petersburg up to the 1917 revolution and includes a room restored to its 1820s appearance. It's been under renovation for quite some time. The **Engineers' Building** has a museum on the city's architecture.

Entry to the fort is free but for most buildings inside you'll need to either obtain a ticket from the kiosk at the east end, or make a payment at the door.

The fort is open daily from 11 am to 6 pm (to 4 pm Tuesday), and is closed Wednesday and the last Tuesday of the month. The closest you can get by bus from near the Hermitage is on a No 10 or 45 to the zoo, but it's a very pleasant walk along Dvortsovaya naberezhnaya, and across the Troitsky bridge to Kamennoostrovsky prospekt and the entrance. Gorkóvskaya metro is in Alexandrovsky Park.

Behind the Fortress

Across the moat, in the fort's original arsenal, is the **Artillery Museum** (Artilleriysky muzey; ☎ 232 02 96), open daily from 11 am to 6 pm (closed Monday and Tuesday). It's a great place if you like weapons: it seems to have one of everything right back to the Stone Age. It also has Lenin's armoured car parked in the driveway. Admission for foreigners is US$4.

West of that is the **St Petersburg Zoo** (☎ 232 28 39), which, while full of miserable animals and happy kids, has improved the conditions of its exhibits now that money's coming in again (but the zoo still suffers from a lack of funds). It's open daily from 10 am to 5 pm; admission is about US$1 for adults and US$0.35 for children.

Just north of the zoo is a new permanent **amusement park**, complete with bumper cars, petrol-powered go-carts, small roller coasters and the like; rides cost about US$0.50, the go-carts US$1.30 for 10 minutes.

East and behind the museum is thriving **Alexandrovsky Park**, cool in summer but too close to traffic and thronged with people to be peaceful.

The **Planetarium** (Map 4) has reopened as just that (it was a disco for a while) and offers 50-minute star shows for US$1.50. Nearby is a **wax museum** (US$2.50/1.60 for adults/students) that's good for kids: Greek

mythological heroes, Yeti – a monster who roams the Kola Peninsula – etc, etc.

Mosque (Map 5)

East of the park across Kamennoostrovsky prospekt is a working mosque, built in 1912 and modelled on Samarkand's Gur Emir Mausoleum where Timur (Tamerlaine) is buried. Its fluted azure dome and minarets have emerged from a painstaking renovation and are stunning. Entering is difficult: jamat (congregation) members are highly protective of their mosque, which is a serious place of worship and decidedly not a tourist attraction. Women without a keemar (head covering) may not be admitted at all; men need to look neat, dress in long pants and preferably a collared shirt and politely ask the guard for entry: saying you're a student of religion or architecture is best. If you are asked in, remove your shoes at the stairs (and hope your socks are clean – dirty socks, like dirty feet, may be an insult to the mosque) and do not talk inside. Forget photography. To enter, walk through the gate at the north-east side.

Museum of Political History (Map 5)

East of Kamennoostrovsky prospekt at ulitsa Kuybysheva 4 is the Kshesinskaya Palace containing the Museum of Political History in Russia (Muzey Politicheskoy Istorii Rossii; ☎ 233 70 48), which is more interesting than it sounds. The Bolsheviks made their headquarters – Lenin often gave speeches from the balcony – in this elegant Art-Nouveau palace that once belonged to Matilda Kshesinskaya, famous ballet dancer and one-time lover of Tsar Nicholas II. Even if you can't read Russian go in to see the house itself, the paintings and photos from the lead up to the revolution, and the glossy dioramas and mini-films. It has good information on Lenin and Brezhnev and probably the best collection of Soviet kitsch in town. It's open daily from 10 am to 6 pm (closed Thursday). Admission is US$2.50/1.30 for foreign adults/students, US$0.80/0.30 for Russians.

Peter's Cabin (Map 5)

In a patch of trees east of the fortress at Petrovskaya naberezhnaya 6 is a little stone building. In here is preserved St Petersburg's first residence, a log cabin where Peter lived in 1703 while supervising the construction of the fortress and city. It feels more like a shrine than a museum. Peter's Cabin (Domik Petra; ☎ 232 45 76) is open daily from 10 am to 5 pm (closed Tuesday and the last Monday of the month). Admission is about US$2.50/1.20 for foreigners/students, US$0.65/0.20 for Russians.

Cruiser *Aurora* (Map 5)

In the Nevka opposite the Hotel St Petersburg is the *Aurora* (or *Avrora*), a mothballed cruiser from the Russo-Japanese War. From a downstream mooring on the night of 25 October 1917, its crew fired a blank round from the forward gun, demoralising the Winter Palace's defenders and marking the start of the October Revolution. During WWII, the Russians sank it to protect it from German bombs. Now refloated, restored and painted in awfully pretty colours, it's a museum, free of charge and open from 10.30 am to 4 pm (closed Monday, Tuesday and the last Wednesday of the month). It's swarming with kids on weekends.

Kirov Museum (Map 4)

Sergei Mironovich Kirov, one of Stalin's leading henchmen after whom countless parks, plazas, squares and a town are named, spent the last days of his life at his decidedly unproletarian apartment at Kamennoostrovsky prospekt 26-28. Now open as a museum (☎ 346 14 81), the apartment is a quick journey back to the days of Soviet glory, right down to the sombre and reverential babushkas who lead you through each room, describing in detail all the great guy's artefacts.

It's worth stopping in to his lovely study (with its enormous polar and brown bear rugs) if only to see the choice examples of late 1920s Soviet technology, a lot of books (120,000 of them) and medals, all on display here. It's open daily from 11 am to

6 pm; to 5 pm Thursday and Friday (closed Wednesday). Admission is about US$1 for foreigners. The museum is on the 4th floor. Be polite to the babushka-guards – they're some of the last defenders of the former Soviet Union.

Botanical Gardens (Map 5)

This quiet jungle in eastern Aptekarsky (Apothecary) Island, just north-east of the Petrogradskaya metro station and across the Karpovka River, was once a garden of medicinal plants which gave the island its name. The Botanichesky sad (botanical gardens) on the site today offer one of St Petersburg's most peaceful strolling grounds. The Dutch-built greenhouse is difficult to get into but the lovely gardens are, for now, free. The entrance is at ulitsa Professora Popova 2, but if they decide to start charging, there are holes in the fence near the intersection of the Karpovka River and Aptekarskaya naberezhnaya, on the river side.

Television Antenna (Map 5)

Here's a weird one – the Leningrad Radio-Tele Broadcasting Centre's antenna (☎ 234 78 87), at the northern end of Petrograd Side, is open for tours by appointment. The 50,000-watt transmitter tower stands 310m over the city. It's a great place to bring kids (hang on tight); it offers excellent views of the entire city and environs, and you can take photos.

The tower was originally 316m (taller than the Eiffel Tower), but they had to lop off the top six due to stress from high winds.It was the first of its kind in the Soviet Union when constructed in 1963, so they weren't thinking about revolving restaurants or other amenities yet (the Ostankino tower in Moscow is modelled on this one), but these days there's a bar/café on the 2nd observation level (200m).

The itty-bitty lift (once the fastest in the country) makes the trip from ground level to the first viewing platform (197m) in 1¾ minutes; from there you can walk up to the café level, where you can access the outside catwalk. The tower sways up to 50cm on windy days, and you can feel it! A fun fact: the tower's construction was supervised by an all-female crew; the forewoman still lives in St Petersburg.

All the city's TV and radio signals originate here, but residents within a kilometre of the antenna still get bad reception, as the signal goes right over their heads.

To enter, call (in Russian) Tuesday to Saturday from 10 am to 5 pm for an appointment. It's US$50 for up to 10 people – get a group together at the hostels if necessary. Or you can book a tour through city travel agents, including Sindbad Travel at the HI St Petersburg Hostel.

To reach the television antenna start at Petrogradskaya metro, take trolleybus No 31 two stops north up Bolshoy prospekt from the stop in front of Teatr Mironova; get off when you see the tower (if you cross the big bridge you've missed it). Walk down to naberezhnaya Kantemirovsky, turn right and walk to the city centre gates facing the river.

KIROVSKY ISLANDS (MAP 4)

This is the collective name for the outer delta islands of Petrograd Side – Kamenny, Yelagin and Krestovsky. Once marshy jungles, the islands were granted to 18th and 19th century court favourites and developed into elegant playgrounds. But they're still mostly parkland – huge leafy venues for picnics, river sports and white nights cavorting.

Kamenny Island

Kamenny (Stone) Island's charm, seclusion and turn-of-the-century dachas, combined with winding lanes and a series of canals, lakes and ponds, make a stroll here pleasant at any time of year (though the walk across the bridge from the Aptekarsky side gets a mite chilly in winter). At the east end of the island the **Church of St John the Baptist** (Tserkov Ioanna Predtechi, 1778) seems to have found better use as a basketball court. Behind it the big, classical **Kamennoostrovsky Palace**, built by Catherine the Great for her son, is now a weedy military sanatorium.

Extending west across the island from the roundabout off Kamennoostrovsky prospekt, 2-ya Beryozovaya alleya sports some lovely dachas, including former party and KGB retreats, which now rent out space to wealthy Russians and foreigners, as well as some of the upper strata of the St Petersburg mafiagentsia.

The island also boasts a **government retreat**, used by the president when he's in town, and by other big wigs when he's not. Look for the **tree**, said to have been planted by Peter the Great, almost blocking naberezhnaya reki Krestovki just west of its intersection with 2-ya Beryozovaya alleya.

The centre of the island has lots of turn-of-the-century summer houses. A pretty example is the **Yeltsin cottage** – a wooden gingerbread mansion with high gables like hats. It's at the end of Polevaya alleya, next to the kindergarten. A grander example on the north-west shore is the lavish **mansion** of one Senator Polovtsev, who had barely moved in when the Bolsheviks took it away. Nearby is the ungainly, though sweet, wooden **Kamenny Island Theatre** first put up in the 1820s, and a footbridge to Yelagin Island. The **Danish Consulate-General** has, hands-down, the coolest diplomat property in town: a massive dacha on Bolshaya alleya, towards the centre of the island.

Kamenny Island is a short walk from Yelagin Island, 15 minutes walk north of metro Petrogradskaya and 10 minutes south of metro Chyornaya Rechka.

Yelagin Island

This island's centrepiece is the **Yelagin Palace** (Yelaginsky dvorets), built for his mother by Tsar Alexander I, who had architect Carlo Rossi landscape the entire island while he was at it. The palace is to your right as you cross the footbridge from Kamenny Island.

The very beautiful restored interiors of the main house include old furnishings on loan from the Europe and Astoria hotels; don't miss the stupendous 1890s carved-walnut study ensemble from Europe and the incredible inlaid-wood floors. The house is open from 10 am to 6 pm (closed Monday and Tuesday). Admission is US$3.60/1.80 for foreigners/students, US$1/0.20 for Russians. Other nearby estate buildings sometimes have exhibitions, too.

The rest of the island is a lovely network of paths, greenery, lakes and channels – you can rent rowing boats – and a plaza at the west end looking out to the Gulf of Finland. It's all now the **Central Park of Culture & Rest** (still named after Kirov), 2km long and pedestrian only. Several small cafés are open in summer.

The rowing boat rental stand is in the north of the island, at the 3-ya Yelagin bridge, which runs between the island and Primorsky prospekt to the north. The water bicycle rental stand is almost due south of the Yelagin Palace. Rates are about US$5 per hour, and you can explore the network of canals and lakes on the island. If you stop for a picnic, keep the boat in sight!

Krestovsky Island

Krestovsky Island, the biggest of the three Kirovsky islands, consists mostly of the vast **Seaside Park of Victory** (Primorsky Park Pobedy), dotted with sports fields and the 100,000-seat **Kirov Stadium**, where you can see St Petersburg's reprehensible football team, Zenit (see the Entertainment chapter).

Bus No 71a from metro Petrogradskaya goes the length of Krestovsky Island to Kirov Stadium. Bus No 71 from near metro Petrogradskaya, No 45 from inner Nevsky prospekt and the Hermitage, and tram No 12 from metro Gostiny Dvor or metro Gorkovskaya all terminate on Krestovsky near the footbridge to Yelagin.

Buddhist Temple

From Yelagin Island a footbridge crosses north to the mainland. There, at Primorsky prospekt 91 by Lipovaya alleya, is a Buddhist *datsan* (temple), of all things. (Russia's Buddhist community is centred in the Buryatia Republic in Siberia.) A neglected but handsome and richly coloured three-storey building with walls sloping in

Tibetan style, it was built from 1900-15 at the instigation of Pyotr Badmaev, a Buddhist physician to Tsar Nicholas II.

Enter the datsan from the door on the west side of the building; walk up the stone staircase to the right, avoiding the unbelievably smelly toilet under the staircase. There's an exhibition in Russian on Buddhism and the Dalai Lama. A small kiosk sells incense and pamphlets.

To reach the datsan, take any tram or trolleybus west from metro Chyornaya Rechka to the Lipovaya alleya stop.

CHYORNAYA RECHKA (MAP 4)

There's nothing really to draw you up here unless you've been in the city for a while or are visiting friends, but if you get up to Svetlonovskaya ploshchad, at the intersection of prospekt Engelsa and Murinsky prospekt, there's something worth looking at. Stand with your back to the grassy area and look east. On your left, the sign on top of the building says 'Glory to the Soviet People'. On your right, the sign on top of the building says 'If you smell gas, dial 09'.

VYBORG SIDE (MAP 5)

Peter the Great had no apparent interest in the far side of the Neva, and today, beyond the embankment and Finland Station, among the factories and railway lines, there are few attractions, though if you're looking for a fur hat, the **Kondratevsky Market** (Map 5) at Polyustrovsky prospekt is just the ticket.

Finland Station

Finland Station (Finlyandsky vokzal) is where, in 1917, Lenin arrived from exile in Switzerland (having ridden in a sealed railway carriage through Germany, Sweden and Finland) and gave his legendary speech from the top of an armoured car, in the square where his statue now stands. After fleeing a second time he again arrived here from Finland, this time disguised as a rail fireman, and the locomotive he rode in is displayed on the platform. It's not really the same station, having been rebuilt following

WWII. There's a statue outside: Vlad's pointing across the Neva to the Big House (former KGB headquarters)! The Ploshchad Lenina metro station is next door.

Kresty Prison

Kresty is St Petersburg's main holding prison; if you're busted while in the city, Kresty is where they take you to await whatever it is that awaits you (it's conveniently located just next door to the Holiday Hostel). But what distinguishes Kresty from, say, New York's Riker's Island, is that Kresty is located on a main boulevard, and prisoners can get to the windows. Russian families are quite close, and with true Russian exuberance, the families of the accused line the street outside, bonding with their inmates.

On any given day you can see dozens of these well-wishers lining Arsenalnaya naberezhnaya. Mothers, fathers and drunken friends stand crying. Wives and girlfriends stand close to the concrete fence, moving their arms in what may look like complicated dance moves, but what is in fact a crude code, known to inmates and prison guards alike.

The prisoner makes himself known by holding an article of clothing out the window (they stick their arms through the bars or through holes in the steel mesh). When the visitor, down on the street, identifies their man, they start waving their arms about, tracing Cyrillic characters in the air.

The prisoner waves up and down to signal 'I understand', and side to side to signal 'repeat'. Under this method, after three or four minutes of waving, one can clearly discern the message, 'I c-a-l-l-e-d y-o-u-r f-r-i-e-n-d M-i-s-h-a'!

The process, understandably, is time consuming (a message like 'I called your lawyer but he was out to lunch' could take a good while), but the family and friends on the street below (again in true Russian style) bring along sausage, bread, cheese and thermoses filled with hot tea. Of course, some bring along a bottle of vodka just to pass the time. The best time to observe this activity is in the early evening – try not to be obtrusive or rude.

Inside the prison itself, there's said to be a **Police and Crime Museum** containing gruesome exhibitions like embalmed severed limbs and the usual murder weapons. It's only open to cops and their ilk (forget about it).

St Sampson's Cathedral

Peter the Great defeated the Swedes at Poltava in 1709, on the feast day of St Sampson. In commemoration a wooden church (Sampsonevsky sobor) was built at what is now prospekt Sampsonevsky 41, and the five-domed stone church that replaced it in the 1730s is now among the city's oldest buildings. The comely church, with galleries on either side and a kerb-side bell tower, is closed and in the hands of a team of Polish restorers.

Piskaryovka Cemetery

The Germans besieged Leningrad for two and a half years during WWII, and between 500,000 and one million people died, mostly of cold and starvation. Almost half a million were buried in mass graves in this cemetery (Piskaryovskoe memorialnoe kladbishche, arrowed off Map 5). With acres of slightly raised mounds marked by year, it's a sobering place. Here you'll understand the Russian obsession with that war. At the back, against the backdrop of a granite wall inscribed with a promise that Russians will never forget the sacrifice of the *blokadeniks*, is a **statue** of the Mother Russian, holding a wreath.

The cemetery is a fair way out of town (see Map 3); about a 40-minute trip from the city centre on public transport. From Ploshchad Muzhestva metro station turn left, cross prospekt Nepokoryonnykh and take bus No 123 about seven minutes east to the square granite pavilion.

ST PETERSBURG WALKS

These are some basic orientation walks through the centre and a bit south. They're not meant to take you through everything, but they do pass by much of St Petersburg's most stunning or at least landmark architecture, sights and points of interest. They also afford some great photo opportunities.

Walk 1: Dvortsovaya Ploshchad to Ploshchad Iskusstv

To start this walk, refer to Map 6. Time: about an hour, more if you stop for a snack or a drink.

After standing around and cursing the difficulty of photographing the Hermitage, which refuses to fit into frame until you're far enough away to make the rooftop statues look like gold smears, start this walk with Photo Opportunity No 1. Walk north-east to the start of Millionnaya ulitsa, and from there into the porch covering the south entrance of the **New Hermitage**. This is one of several buildings in the city that has a façade supported by musclemen: if you play this right you can get a shot from the north-east corner of the porch that includes a healthy slice of St Isaac's Cathedral past the Winter Palace and some of its statuary, including the three musclemen.

Tip: a good way to get a photo of the Hermitage is from the river; the exterior is fitted with floodlights – catch a late-evening river cruise or water taxi.

Walking north-east again, make the first right turn and walk along the **Zimny Canal** the short block to the **Moyka River**. This is one of its loveliest stretches: to your right, Nevsky prospekt is crossed by the **Norodny bridge**, and across Nevsky, catch a glimpse of the **Stroganov Palace**.

Along the Moyka Hope you enjoyed the glimpse, because that's not where you're going to turn left. On the left side of the Moyka embankment is the **Japanese Embassy**, and directly opposite that is one of the St Petersburg Philharmonic's two concert

---

Moscow versus St Petersburg

The friendly competition between residents of Moscow and St Petersburg can get quite heated. Muscovites will claim that St Petersburgers are a bunch of foppish bumpkins who sit in the provinces drinking tea, looking at portraits and discussing the state of the world crisis. Similarly, St Petersburgers paint an image of Muscovites as opportunistic greedheads who would sell their own mothers in order to raise enough cash to import cigarettes that they'd then sell to school children.

But most visitors who come to St Petersburg from Moscow agree that life in the former capital is certainly more laid back than in the present one, and that St Petersburg residents carry themselves with a brand of dignity not seen elsewhere in the country. A popular joke offers a unique insight into the differences between residents of the two big cities.

A young man from St Petersburg was lucky enough to have found a seat on the Moscow metro during rush hour. After he had gone a stop or two, an elderly woman carrying shopping bags got on the train and stood in front of him. The young man immediately got up and offered his seat to the old woman, who sat down contentedly.

'You must be from St Petersburg,' the old woman said.

'Yes, I am,' said the young man, 'but how did you know?'

'No Muscovite would ever be so polite as to give an old woman his seat,' the woman said. The young man considered this for a moment and then said, 'And you are from Moscow.'

'Yes, I am,' replied the woman, 'but how did you know?'

'Well,' replied the young man, 'in St Petersburg, when someone gives us a seat on the metro, we always say thank you.'

halls – the **Glinka Capella** (Akademich-eskaya khorovaya kapela imeni MI Glinki). Cross the little footbridge to the west side of the river, turn left and walk past **Pushkin's last home**, diagonally opposite the French Consulate at naberezhnaya reki Moyki 12, to the little Konyushennaya pereulok, which brings you to one of Imperial St Petersburg's flashiest streets, Bolshaya Konyushennaya ulitsa. This street has been, at various times, home to Turgenev, Rimsky-Korsakov and Chernyshevsky, and the former location of the court stables (from which the street's name is taken). On the west side of the street is **DLT**, one of St Petersburg's best depart-ment stores, and opposite it, the little **Finnish Church** (1803-05).

The Konyushennayas There are two op-tions as to the next leg of the walk: do a little browsing at DLT and maybe grab a snack in the upstairs café or at the excellent dough-nut shop next door; or walk around to Nevsky prospekt and have a beer at the outdoor beer garden in front of the **Luther-an Church**.

Whatever you choose, in either case (by walking down Shvedsky pereulok or down to Nevsky and making two lefts) walk to the northern end of **ulitsa Malaya Konyushen-naya** one block east – taking note of the bizarre **statue** of a well-endowed Imperial police officer by Albert Charkin – and turn into the tiny alley that runs between it and naberezhnaya Kanala Griboedova.

The Griboedova As you emerge onto the embankment, to your right will be Nevsky prospekt and the golden colonnades of the **Kazan Cathedral**, past which you can just make out the **Bankovsky Most** with its golden-winged griffins, before the canal twists south-west. To your left is the spec-tacular **Church of the Resurrection of Christ** (1887-1907), built on the spot where Alexander II, despite his actually caving in and doing exactly what they wanted (the establishment of an elective assembly), was blown up by the People's Will terrorist group in 1881.

If you didn't stop for a bit of something back near DLT, walking north on the west side of the canal, you'll pass the little café adjacent to the Restaurant St Petersburg, famous for its inexpensive and wonderful mushrooms in cream sauce. Otherwise turn south towards Nevsky prospekt, and cross the canal on the lovely little 22m **Italyansky Mostik**. From the middle of this bridge is 'Perfect Photo Opportunity No 2', of the cathedral and the canal (a better shot, though, is in Walk 3).

Walk towards the cathedral on the east side of the canal (being sure to turn before you reach the fur hat and military watch purveyors at the souvenir market) and turn right onto Inzhenernaya ulitsa. This short block opens into **ploshchad Iskusstv** (Arts Square), where the walk concludes. If you haven't been into the **Russian Museum**, now's the perfect time to do so.

Walk 2: Crime & Punishment

To start this walk, refer to Map 6. Time: about an hour.

Looking at **Sennaya ploshchad** today, it's not hard to imagine that in Dostoevsky's time it was a teeming madhouse, filled with drunks, layabouts and guttersnipes. Though the present-day metro station is built on the site of the former Church of the Assump-tion, the major landmarks of the day were seedy pubs and inns.

The border between reality and fantasy has been smudged irrevocably here: Peters-burgers will point out where Dostoevsky lived as quickly as they will the home of his protagonist Raskolnikov and the old pawn broker. And snatches of the grim reality of slum life in the mid-19th century can still be had during an hour's walk. The omnipresent stray cats, as permanent a fixture in St Pe-tersburg courtyards as dim light, foul odours and pockmarked cement, are the gatekeep-ers to a neighbourhood whose gloominess and squalor has been preserved well enough to make it instantly recognisable, even to Fyodor himself.

For *Crime and Punishment* fans, even those with limited time on their hands, the area is a wonderful opportunity to get a better feel for the neighbourhood in which it was set. Die-hard fans argue to this day about where the '730 steps' would place Raskolnikov's attic, and it's come down to a choice between two possible addresses.

Raskolnikov's Flat(s) From Sennaya ploshchad, walk north on Grivtsova pereulok, across the canal, and turn left onto ulitsa Grazhdanskaya. On the far right hand corner of ulitsa Przhevalskogo is **No 5**, one of the two possible locations of Raskolnikov's attic. Coincidentally, the building also bears marble plaques in Russian and German marking the waterline reached by the great flood of 7 November 1824, immortalised in Pushkin's poem, *The Bronze Horseman*. Unfortunately, the door to the stairwell is locked. Those who say that this is the place go further, saying that Rodya (the diminutive of Raskolnikov's first name, Rodyon) retrieved the murder weapon from a street-sweeper's storage bin inside the tunnel leading to the courtyard.

From that corner, turn south onto ulitsa Przhevalskogo (formerly Stolyarny pereulok, or 'S ... lane', from the book), where at **No 9**, you can enter the building of the second possible address (which I believe is the one, as in the first paragraph of the book it clearly says '... the cubicle sublet to him in S ... lane'). Walk through the tunnel, turn right and use entrance 2 (up the crumbling stone steps), and walk up four flights until the stairwell ceiling opens upward. Graffiti on the wall sometimes reads, 'Don't Kill, Rodya'. Rodya's flat would be the padlocked attic on the left hand side of the fifth floor.

Dostoevsky's Flats Back on Przhevalskogo, turn south again and walk the 50m to the corner of **ulitsa Kaznacheyskaya**. Dostoevsky lived in three flats on this street alone: from 1861-63 at **No 1**, far down and on the left at the Griboedova, and from 1864-67 at **No 7**, at the north-east corner of Przhevalskogo and Kaznacheyskaya. It was from this flat that he wrote *Crime and Punishment*. Dostoevsky spent one month

Dostoevsky's works, including *Crime and Punishment*, *The Idiot* and *The Brothers Karamazov*, have earned him a reputation as one of the world's greatest novelists.

living in the faded red building, **No 9**, before moving to No 7.

The Murder Route From whichever flat Raskolnikov lived, he walked out and down Przhevalskogo towards the canal. He crossed the **Kokushkin bridge**, where he would stand and gaze into the canal, deep in thought. Looking at the canal today you'd never guess it used to be very dirty (that was a joke).

Murderer yes, orienteering student no; the route to the pawn broker's house taken by Rodya is circuitous. After you cross the canal, head straight to ulitsa Sadovaya then turn right. Make your first right turn into ulitsa Rimskogo Korsakova. Cross Voznesensky prospekt, and continue past Bolshaya Podyacheskaya and Srednyaya Podyacheskaya; the pawn broker's building sits between there and the canal embankment.

For a good look at the building, cross the street and stand at the southern side of the Komsomolsky bridge. The entrance to the courtyard is a bit north on the embankment, **naberezhnaya Kanala Griboedova 104**. Enter the dank, pot-holed tunnel, and head straight for **entrance No 5** (flats 22-81).

The building's residents are very used to people entering the building to get a look. In fact, brass balls at the corners of the iron banisters are there specifically for visitors, and they end just after the third floor, where her flat (74) is on the right hand side. For you law enforcement types: after the murder, the suspect ran through the tunnel leading to **Srednyaya Podyacheskaya**.

Walk 3: From the Kazan Cathedral to Ploshchad Ostrovskogo

To start this walk, refer to Map 8. Time: about 2½ hours.

The Kazan Cathedral is a quintessential St Petersburg landmark due to its unique form (despite the fact that it's heavily based on St Peter's in Rome) and its absolute prime location. Almost equidistant from the Grand Hotel Europe and the former Duma to the east, the Church of the Resurrection of Christ to the north, the Bankovsky Most to the south and the Admiralty and the Hermitage to the west, it is a perfect starting point for this walk through the very heart of the city.

Directly across the street, **Dom Knigi** (literally, 'House of Books'), housed in the former Russian headquarters of the Singer Sewing Machine company, is definitely worth a browse, especially the map and poster sections upstairs. The view north from Nevsky prospekt to the **Church of the Resurrection of Christ** is spectacular, but if you missed Photo Opportunity 2 from Walk No 2, hold out a few more minutes and it gets even better. Begin the walk facing the Kazan Cathedral: cross to the left side of the building and walk south along naberezhnaya Kanala Griboedova; there may be a beer garden set up almost outside the side entrance to the **Museum of the History of Religion** housed inside the cathedral. Keep walking south along the canal until you reach the **Bankovsky Most** – one of St Petersburg's loveliest, suspended from chains

emerging from the mouths of golden-winged griffins – and cross this little footbridge. From the middle, turn north and *now*'s when to snap that picture of the cathedral, with Nevsky prospekt and the Italyansky bridge in the foreground.

Unless you want to get an education in economics (the school right in front of you) or buy a train ticket (the centre's just up the street to the left), let's keep going from here; turn left on the other side of the embankment and then make the first right turn onto Lomonosova ulitsa. This is, at this point, a quiet and somewhat dirty little street that serves as the rear end of one of the city's biggest shopping malls, which we'll get to shortly.

Make the first left turn onto ulitsa Dumskaya. On the left, at the corner of Dumskaya and Nevsky prospekt, is the former **Town Duma** (the pre-revolutionary municipal government's headquarters, 1799-1804), and the adjacent **Silver Stalls** (1784-87). The Duma's tall Western European-style clock tower is a landmark easily seen from most of Nevsky prospekt. In the centre of the street is a small building housing a theatre ticket office. In warmer months, there's an outdoor café in front (north) of the building serving beer, soft drinks and snacks. Across Nevsky is the **Grand Hotel Europe** and, further down ulitsa Mikhailovskaya, ploshchad Iskusstv with the Russian Museum and Maly Theatre (see Walk No 1).

Gostiny Dvor To your right is St Petersburg's answer to Moscow's GUM and any Western Kmart. There's an entrance on ulitsa Dumskaya, but the main entrance is around on Nevsky prospekt towards ulitsa Sadovaya. The stalls have varying quantities of varying supplies, but a walk through the ground floor is usually interesting enough of its own accord.

Passazh, Gostiny Dvor's more sophisticated cousin, is directly across Nevsky prospekt. At the turn of the century, Passazh (1846-48) was the arcade of choice for discerning Imperial Petersburgers, and recently it's become far easier to see why. As in

GUM, the main shopping area consists of stalls under a magnificent translucent arched ceiling with catwalks all around and balconies crossing here and there. The ground floor is worth a stroll, and the basement level has a fully fledged Western-style supermarket. From the main entrance on the ground floor (actually up a small flight of stairs), continue straight through to the rear of Passazh, through the exit and down the stairs; we're walking out to Italyanskaya ulitsa along the south-east corner of ploshchad Iskusstv, and north-east from there.

The Winter Stadium to the Engineer's Castle
Turn right onto Italyanskaya ulitsa, where you're likely to see stage trucks shuttling scenery to the nearby Musical Comedy and Komissarzhevskoy Drama theatres and lots of other loading/unloading activities, as well as track-suited gentlemen of dubious occupation barking into cellular phones. You'll pass through Manezhnaya ploshchad and its odd Winter Stadium. Make that left turn onto the 400m stretch of the divided Klenovaya alleya. Dead ahead is the Engineer's Castle (1797-1800), the evil-looking red-brick building built by the lunatic Tsar Paul I – in an attempt to insulate himself from assassination he went so far as to surround the place with moats (long since filled in). They didn't help anyway – he was killed by a group of highly placed civil and military officials in a coup in 1801.

Along the Fontanka
Standing on ulitsa Zamkovaya facing the castle, turn right and walk the short block to the Fontanka River. From here, if you look left, about 400m down towards the Neva is the Summer Garden, with its little Summer Palace of Peter the Great, tea house and statuary, worthy of a trip on its own but not included in this walk. Turn right and walk south along the river. At the next intersection is the St Petersburg Circus, the next block the Sheremetov Palace (with the Anna Akhmatova museum) and further south brings you to another great photo opportunity: The Anichkov bridge with its statues of four rearing stallions and

their trainers, and the fabulously lavish baroque Beloselsky-Belozersky Palace, a red building whose façades are supported by Atlases. If you want to take a break from this walk and feel like relaxing on the water, you're passing the river cruise pier right now; tickets are available from the little kiosk near the bridge.

Nevsky Prospekt to Ploshchad Ostrovskogo
Turn right back onto one of Nevsky prospekt's most thriving stretches. While there are many shops and boutiques between here and ulitsa Sadovaya, the hands-down landmark is Yeliseevsky Food Shop at Nevsky prospekt 58.

Just across the street is ploshchad Ostrovskogo, a Carlo Rossi designed park that is somehow both right on a bustling stretch of Nevsky prospekt and also quiet and peaceful, and a very good place to conclude this walk. There's a lovely statue in the centre of Catherine the Great surrounded by her lovers; this is, in turn, surrounded by street artists, chess and backgammon players and is swarming with tourists in summer.

As you face the statue, to the right is the Saltykov-Shchedrin Library, to the left is the Anichkov Palace and directly behind the statue is the enormous Pushkin Theatre (1828-32), with its Corinthian columns and relief of Apollo's horse-drawn chariot. Behind the theatre is ulitsa Zodchego Rossi, a perfectly proportioned street that's home to the Vaganova School of Choreography (where the Kirov trains its dancers); beyond that, the four-tiered Lomonosov bridge crosses the Fontanka.

ACTIVITIES
For classic entertainment and drinking and dancing venues, see the Entertainment section; for special events listings while you're in town, check The St Petersburg Times and Pulse.

Banya
Tired? Overworked? A good beating may be all you need, and St Petersburg's public banyas are as good a place as any to get

one! Here are a few of the better banyas (see the boxed aside for correct banya etiquette):

Kruglye Banya (☎ 550 09 85), Karbysheva ulitsa 29A (arrowed off Map 5, metro Ploshchad Muzhestva), has a large outdoor heated pool.

Banya 50 (☎ 233 50 92), ulitsa Malaya Posadskaya 28 (Map 5, metro Gorkovskaya), is a nice, clean and friendly place.

Nevskie Bani (☎ 311 14 00), ulitsa Marata 5/7 (Map 8, metro Mayakovskaya), the largest in town, is smack in the city centre.

Rowing Boat Rental

In summer, a lovely way to while away a day (or to keep the kids somewhat amused) is paddling through the canals and lakes on

---

A Russian Banya

Russians say there's a level of cleanliness that can only be attained through the rigorous action of a ritual Russian *banya*. A combination of dry sauna, steam bath, massage and plunges into ice-cold water, the banya is a weekly event that is as much a part of Russian life as, say, bowling in Bedrock. The word 'banya' has come to mean far more than its dictionary definition, which is 'bathhouse'.

Preparation begins at home, where thermos flasks are filled to their cork-plugged brims with specially brewed tea. These teas are peculiar to the banya; a mixture of jams, fruits, spices, tea and heaps of sugar. Armed with this brew, the bather heads out. (A couple of beers picked up along the way is not unheard-of either.)

Based on any number of scheduling concerns, people usually go to the banya on the same day each week and, with others there on the same day, a close circle is formed; the closest equivalent in the West would probably be your work-out buddies.

After a 'warm up' in the dry sauna (the word is the same in Russian, pronounced 'SA-oo-na'), where the temperature is in the low 100°s Celsius (lower 200°s Fahrenheit), you're ready for the *parilka* – the dreaded steam room.

The parilka will have a furnace that's heating rocks. Onto these rocks, bathers throw water, usually mixed with eucalyptus oil, with a long-handled ladle-like implement made specially for the purpose. When the room's got a good head of steam going, the bathers grab hold of bundles of dried birch leaves *(vennki)*, dip them in hot water and ... well ... beat each other with them. The beating (which isn't violent, and feels a lot better than it sounds) is said to rid your body of toxins.

As you might suspect, all that steam makes the air even hotter; bathers continue to throw water on until visibility is nil and the room is unbearably hot, at which point everyone runs out coughing. And as if the relatively cold air outside the parilka isn't enough of a shock to one's system, the next step is a plunge into the icy cold waters of the *basseyn* (pool), whose health benefits I've yet to work out (they're probably incredibly important).

After the plunge, it's out to the locker rooms wrapped up in sheets (available from the attendant or somewhere in the locker room), where the events of the world are discussed over the tea (or whatever). Then the process begins again; sessions can go on for two or three hours.

St Petersburg is teeming with public banyas; see the listings under Activities in this chapter for a few addresses. Baths are segregated by sex, and depending on the size of the place, there are either separate sections for men and women or the baths admit different sexes on different days. One more thing: alcohol affects you faster in a banya, so if you do partake, be careful and do it slowly. It's considered bad form to lose your lunch in a steam room!

Yelagin Island. See the section on Yelagin Island (under Kirovsky Islands), earlier.

There are also rowing boat rentals at the northern end of the moat around the Peter & Paul Fortress. Rates are about US$5 an hour.

Ice Skating

There's ice skating (with skate rental) at the Yubileyny Stadium (☎ 119 56 01), Dobrolyubova prospekt 18, Petrograd Side and at the Dvorets Sporta SKA (☎ 237 00 73), Zhdanovskaya naberezhnaya 2 (both Map 4, metro Sportivnaya). Both charge about US$7 an hour for skating and rental.

Skiing

Russians are avid cross-country skiers, and larger sporting goods shops carry skis and equipment, usually for about half the price you'd pay back home. Check *Luchshee V Sankt Peterburge* or *The Traveller's Yellow Pages* for sports shops. Very popular cross-country skiing destinations (for the day) are Toksovo and Tagalovo, small towns north of the city and reachable by elektrichka from Finland Station.

Expatriate Sports Events

Softball In summer, there are softball games every Saturday afternoon, attended by US Marines, heaps of American expats and even the odd Brit and German. Contact SPIBA (☎ 325 90 91, spiba@online.ru) for more information.

Frisbee There are great games of 'ultimate Frisbee' (a game played with teams on a field) every Sunday year-round at 3 pm in the field near Lesnaya metro station (though in winter it's sometimes held inside, sometimes in the snow); call George on ☎ 552 40 37 or email frisbee@neva.math.spb.ru for more information.

Hash House Harriers A 'drinking club with a running problem', the HHH started in Kuala Lumpur, Malaysia, and has since spread to British consulates all over the world. The runs are usually of 5km or less, followed by a 'down-down' chug-a-lug session during which you wear practically as much beer as you drink. It can be great fun in a football-hooligan sort of a way. They meet every Sunday at 2 pm – bring running gear. For more information contact Sarah Powell on ☎ 325 60 36, or fax inquiries to 315 64 34.

Working Out

The Grand Hotel Europe, Nevskij Palace and Astoria Hotels have health clubs that allow visitors. Prices average US$35 per day.

Backgammon players at ploshchad Ostrovskogo

Wedding pics by the *Aurora*

Chillin' with the gang

Tourist policeman: your friend in St Petersburg

GAI guy ticketing motorist

Roma woman and child

ROGER HAYNE

Interior, Peter & Paul Cathedral

GEORGI SHABLOVSKY

St Nicholas' Cathedral near Teatralnaya ploshchad

NICK SELBY

Smolny Cathedral

GEORGI SHABLOVSKY

Church of the Resurrection

GEORGI SHABLOVSKY

Peter & Paul Fortress

NICK SELBY

Artists near the Hermitage

Places to Stay

Since 1991, St Petersburg's accommodation scene has turned 180°; it's not just that big money moved in and built luxury places (which it did) but there are now two youth hostels, several B&B agencies, and a good stock of mid-range and cheap hotels. Even the former state-run places have begun performing hitherto unheard-of acts such as smiling, cleaning the rooms, charging on the basis of value and so on.

Since our last edition there's been a flurry of activity in the upper range, but the mid and lower ranges have remained pretty much the same. Prices have remained surprisingly stable and some have even come down a bit. But that does not by any means imply that St Petersburg accommodation is a bargain – it's reasonable, but more expensive than in the rest of the country outside Moscow.

Hostels charge from US$15 to US$19 for a bed. For a traditional hotel room, playing it straight (admitting you're a foreigner and using a Western passport), the rock-bottom price is about US$20/25 a single/double, but you'd have to stay out of the centre to find it.

There are, of course, ways to get into hotels for cheaper prices, but you'd need help from a Russian friend or, better, a Russian company. The dual-pricing system (see the boxed text in the Facts for the Visitor chapter) is firmly in place for hotels – Russians almost always pay less than foreigners, except in the highest of the top-end places.

One good tactic is to try booking accommodation through any of the Russian travel agencies in town – they always get better deals than the hotel's printed rack (ie walk-in) rates.

CAMPING

Camping is not a good idea. The only camping ground is far from the centre, dangerous and poorly equipped. I really don't recommend it – unless you're driving in from Finland and are so tired you can't possibly go a kilometre further. Skip the **Motel-Camping Olgino** (Map 3, ☎ 238 36 71), about 18km north-west of the centre at Primorskoe shosse 59. It's far away, inconvenient to public transport, and full of dangerous and heavy-drinking clientele. A taxi to the city will be at least US$20. Oh, yeah, tent sites are US$20.

HOSTELS

Russia's first (and to date its only) Hostelling International (HI) member hostel, the **HI St Petersburg Hostel** (Map 8, ☎ 329 80 18, fax 329 80 19, ryh@ryh.ru, www.ryh.ru) is located at 3-ya Sovetskaya ulitsa (metro Ploshchad Vosstania/Mayakovskogo). The hostel opened in 1992 and still has the cheapest rates in the city centre: US$19 per bed in rooms with three to six beds, US$24 per person in a double room, $18 for ISIC holders, $17 for HI members. All prices include breakfast. It's a five minute walk north-east of Moscow Station, and rooms are clean and comfortable. Staff are preternaturally friendly, and the hostel's visa support service is one of the best around (see the Facts for the Visitor chapter). They show videos downstairs daily, and you can send and receive email and faxes. In the evenings there's Internet access downstairs for US$3 per half hour.

Reserve by faxing 329 80 19 or through any HI hostel with IBN. It also accepts reservations for Holiday Hostel, Travellers Guest House in Moscow and Roza Vetrov in Novgorod.

The **Holiday Hostel** (Map 5, ☎/fax 542 73 64), ulitsa Mikhailova 1, 3rd floor, became St Petersburg's second Western-style youth hostel in 1994. Its location, just south of Finland Station, has its pros and cons. The pro is definitely the river view in summer – the rooftop café offers the classic panorama of the Peter & Paul Fortress against the backdrop of raised drawbridges. Among the disadvantages are that, aside from Finland Station and Kalinka Stockmann's food store, there's not much out this way, and that incessant shouting you hear is the families of inmates calling to loved ones being held at Kresty Prison, which is right next door (see the Things To See & Do chapter).

The hostel is clean and fun, staff are friendly and they try hard. It has two to five beds to a room; a bed is US$15 (US$19 if you get a double to yourself), and there's a US$10 fee for a visa invitation from them. From Finland Station (metro Ploshchad Lenina) make a left, walk to Mikhailova ulitsa, turn right and cross the street; the entrance to the yard is on the left (you'll see the big red-brick prison wall), the hostel's entrance is in the south-west corner of the courtyard.

Both the city's hostels have kitchens for guests' use.

STUDENT ACCOMMODATION

Unless you feel like spending upwards of US$300 per night, you can't get a much better location than that of the **Student Dormitory** (Map 8, ☎ 314 74 72), ulitsa Plekhanova 6, 120m behind the Kazan Cathedral, but this is an iffy proposition. Technically, you should be allowed to get into its clean, comfortable singles and doubles for US$12/14.50, but management runs from a bit unpredictable to downright dodgy, and availability is very tight, especially in summer. Calling first may help. If you try just showing up, be friendly.

HOTELS – BUDGET
City Centre

Two hotels told me that they charge foreigners the same rates as Russians, but I just can't believe it. Staff at the **Bolshoy Teatr Kukol Hotel** – yes, that does mean the 'Big Puppet Theatre Hotel' – (Map 7, ☎ 273 39 96), ulitsa Nekrasova 12, swear that you can stay in their clean if run-down singles/doubles for US$15/22.50. Please write and let us know if they charge more.

The other place is the **Hotel Rus** (Map 7, ☎ 273 46 83 or 272 66 54), ulitsa Artilleryskaya 1 (a one-block street near metro Chernyshevskaya). It's a large, Soviet-style place (guards may try to block your entry, staff are negligent), but it's popular and not far from the centre. Its rates are good value – US$50 for a single, US$70 for a double (with bath) and US$99 for a triple.

A bit farther out and seemingly under the same management, the **Hotel Neva** (Map 5, ☎ 278 05 04 or 273 25 63) is at ulitsa Chaykovskogo 17 near the former KGB headquarters. It has the same sort of rooms as the Rus, but the guards are less aggressive and staff negligibly more attentive – though their bar downstairs opens at 2 am and attracts some nefarious characters. Singles/doubles here are US$56/80.

Petrograd & Vyborg Sides

If there is a room to spare at the **Dvorets Molodyozhy** (Palace of Youth; Map 4, ☎ 234 32 78), ulitsa Professora Popova 47, it's only because it hasn't yet been rented out by some fly-by-night company as office space. It's in a very quiet location, but bus No 25 to Nevsky prospekt doesn't come by often, and it's a 25-minute walk to metro Petrogradskaya. It's big and Soviet-modern outside, plain inside. If you can get in, it has singles or doubles for US$29 not including breakfast. Double and triple rooms have attached showers (some baths). There is one pleasant restaurant and an OK gril-bar.

On the mainland, north of Kamenny Island, is the pleasant enough **Hotel Vyborgskaya** (Map 3, ☎ 246 91 41 or 246 23 19), Torzhkovskaya ulitsa 3. Its three buildings have singles/doubles/suites from US$34/51/65, some with own bath. There are two restaurants – and there's a branch of the excellent Russky Bliny just south of it (see Places to Eat). Nearby metro Chyornaya Rechka makes it convenient to the centre.

The **Hotel Sputnik** (Map 3, ☎ 552 56 32), prospekt Morisa Toreza 34, is in a quiet neighbourhood of apartment blocks, a 10 minute walk (or a short bus ride) north-west from Ploshchad Muzhestva metro. Foreigners get singles or doubles with attached bath, a restaurant with live music, and three *bufety* (snack bars). It's not a bad place, though it's quite far out and inconvenient thanks to the metro collapse – you'll have to take a Line 1 train to Lesnaya then the frequent shuttle bus or a taxi to ploshchad Muzhestva. Singles are US$44, doubles are US$58 and a 'half lyux' suite is US$70.

The crumbling *Hotel Karelia* (Map 5, ☎ 226 35 15/19), ulitsa Tukhachevskogo 27/2, is not good value and worth avoiding. Plain, quiet rooms with attached showers are US$48/66. The staff are pretty slack and the location – several kilometres from the centre – is lousy. It's a dreary 25-minute ride by trolleybus No 3 or 19 to metro Ploshchad Lenina.

South & East of the City Centre

The *Summer Hostel* (Map 3, ☎ 252 75 63; fax 252 40 19), ulitsa Baltiyskaya 26, is no longer a member of Russian Youth Hostels, and was closed when we visited. It might reopen, though, so check – last edition they had good, cheap rooms. From metro Narvskaya walk left (south), down prospekt Stachek away from the Narva Arch to ulitsa Baltiyskaya, where you turn left. The hostel is 300m ahead on the left-hand side.

There are two budget places south of the centre that aren't at all bad if you don't mind the hike to the city centre; the dumpy but surprisingly cheerful *Hotel Kievskaya* (Map 7, ☎ 166 04 56), Dnepropetrovskaya ulitsa 49, has singles or doubles for US$21, and the *Hotel Zarya* (Map 7, ☎ 166 83 98), a block away at Kurskaya ulitsa 40, has singles/doubles for US$28/47. They're in a boring neighbourhood on the Obvodny Canal, though transport is easy. Bus No 25 from the local bus terminal next door is a mini city-tour to Gostiny Dvor metro, Nevsky prospekt and Petrograd Side. Between nearby Ligovsky prospekt and metro Ploshchad Vosstania, take anything except bus No 14; the nearest stop is Obvodny Canal.

HOTELS – MID-RANGE
City Centre

The perfectly central *Hotel Oktyabrskaya* (Map 8, ☎ 277 63 30), Ligovsky prospekt 10, opposite Moscow Station, is a crumbling old place smack in ploshchad Vosstania. With comfortable but well-worn singles/doubles at US$59/123, it's no longer great value for money. There's talk of opening a tourist information centre in the lobby. The city's desperately trying to sell this property to a chain to turn it into a top-end place but for the moment it's still a mid-range option to be considered.

The *Hotel Moskva* (Map 7, ☎ 274 30 01 or 274 20 51), ploshchad Alexandra Nevskogo 2, just opposite the Alexandr Nevsky Monastery, is a large three-star place not far from the centre. But it comes second to the Hotel St Petersburg in everything except access (Ploshchad Alexandra Nevskogo metro is right under the hotel). Service is slacker, the lobby dimmer, rooms smaller (though comfortable and clean) and the feeling more institutional. For what you get, the rack rate of US$92/114 is a bit steep, but a lot of package tours and local travel agencies can book you into the Moskva for a considerably cheaper rate. Try for a room at the back where it's quieter.

Downstairs in the lobby there's a billiards room (US$7 an hour) with American and Russian versions of the game. The restaurants and cafés are so-so, with the exception of Salt & Pepper – see the Places to Eat chapter.

A newish and rather unheralded entry in this price range is the excellent *Matisov Domik* (Map 6, ☎ 219 54 45, fax 219 74 19), naberezhnaya reki Pryazhki 3/1, about 10 minutes walk west of the Mariinsky Theatre. This family-run place has super-clean and nice rooms, all with phone, TV, juices and soft drinks free from the room's mini bar and breakfast included. Singles/doubles cost US$67/104 for foreigners, but you may be able to talk the friendly staff down to the Russian rate of US$46/70. There is also a sauna for guest use (US$14 per person). From the Mariinsky, walk west

PLACES TO STAY

on Dekabristov ulitsa, past the Golden Dragon restaurant and up to the canal (the Blok House museum is on the north-east corner of the canal). Cross the canal and turn right and the hotel is 75m ahead on the left hand side of the road; enter the court-yard and it's on the right side.

The *Hotel Helen-Sovietskaya* (Map 6, ☎ 329 01 81), Lermontovsky prospekt 43, is only 3km south-west of the Hermitage, along the Fontanka River, but is poorly served by public transport. Rooms are about three-star standard and come with TV, telephone and bath; service is decent, and singles/doubles cost US$78/120. The nearest metro is Baltiyskaya, 750m south, or it's a US$4 taxi ride from the centre. Trolleybus Nos 3 and 8 follow Zagorodny prospekt to Nevsky prospekt; bus No 49 and tram No 1 go to the Mariinsky Theatre en route to ploshchad Truda.

Vyborg Side

The big three-star *Hotel St Petersburg* (Map 5, ☎ 542 90 31 or 542 95 60), Byro-govskaya naberezhnaya 4, opposite the Cruiser *Aurora*, has standard post-Intourist accommodation and facilities, with clean but dull rooms. The front rooms have amazing views over the Neva towards the Hermitage but also traffic noise if you open the windows. At US$77/97, it's not a bad deal, though the staff are *still* struggling to crawl out from under the rock of Intourist training. It has a good restaurant, a beer hall and even a concert hall downstairs.

The place just about burned down in 1991 after a Russian-made television set popped its cork and torched a couple of floors, but it's been renovated back to stan-dards. The extension may someday be finished.

On the down side, public transport is mediocre for a place so close to the centre. It's a 15 minute walk to the nearest metro, Ploshchad Lenina; and you may wait 20 minutes on Finlyandsky prospekt behind the hotel for the westbound tram No 6 or 63 to take you across the Sampsonevsky Bridge to metro Gorkovskaya. Tram No 63

continues to the Strelka. There are also buses and trams from ploshchad Lenina.

The *Hotel Okhtinskaya* (Map 5, ☎ 227 44 38), Bolsheokhtinskaya prospekt 4 (it's really on Sverdlovskaya naberezhnaya, about 200m south of the Nevsky Melody restaurant), is an under-publicised place just across the Neva from the Smolny. It's a fine business-class hotel with clean and modern rooms offering river views. Staff are pleas-ant and the dining rooms and the saunas are good. What's bad is its location, and because of that, the US$87/100 it charges seems a bit out of line.

Vasilevsky Island

The *Hotel Gavan* (Map 6, ☎ 356 85 04), Sredny prospekt 88, was under renovation when we visited; last time round its rooms were old and plain but clean. The neigh-bourhood is featureless aside from a small park. From the hotel, bus No 30 goes to the Hermitage and outer Nevsky prospekt; tram No 63 goes to the Hermitage and the Strelka.

South & East of the City Centre

The expensive *Hotel Deson-Ladoga* (Map 7, ☎ 528 52 00 or 528 52 01), prospekt Shaumyana 26, is a dreary block in a sea of dreary blocks, across the Neva from the Alexandr Nevsky Monastery.

Single and double rooms have attached showers, and include sauna and breakfast; they cost US$105/140, or a family single (actually a double room with a large bed) is US$120. It's one block east of metro Novocherkasskaya (take exit stairs No 8). The only bright spot in the neighbourhood is the Shvabsky Domik restaurant by the metro.

The *Hotel Neptune* (Map 7, ☎ 210 18 11), managed by Best Western, is in a pretty odd location, but its rooms are nice and clean and not outrageous at US$95 to US$140. It's at naberezhnaya Obvodnogo Kanala 93A, about a 10 minute walk from Avtovokzal (bus station) No 2, and 15 minutes from Avtovokzal No 1 and Warsaw and Baltic stations.

HOTELS – TOP END
City Centre

St Petersburg's luxury hotels are truly luxurious. The appearance of foreign-owned and operated hotels has resulted in a fundamental improvement in service levels in the city. The luxury hotels all offer heaps of amenities, including at the very least satellite television, telephone, health club, business centres, shops, newsstands, drinkable coffee, and a concierge desk to take the hassle out of buying tickets (this last amenity, to be sure, at a premium price). It says something (although I'm not sure what) that several of the top-end places have installed metal detectors at their entrances.

All the top-end hotels are in the city centre, and all accept major credit cards and offer several categories of rooms.

The *Hotel Astoria* (Map 6, ☎ 210 57 57, fax 315 96 68), ulitsa Bolshaya Morskaya 39, right in front of St Isaac's Cathedral, has been beautifully renovated; the original Astoria appears in its Art-Nouveau glory, and period furniture that wasn't stolen, looted or damaged can be seen in some of the more expensive rooms. The entrance is on Voznesensky prospekt.

The hotel is in two sections, new and old, and you'll have to walk outside to get to one wing from the other. The old wing's grand rooms and suites are large and luxurious, while the new wing's rooms are large and comfortable. Singles are US$170 to US$220, doubles US$210 to US$300, two-room suites US$370 to US$400, and three-room apartments (these are *nice*) US$600.

The hotel's restaurants are improving and are now a good option (see Places to Eat); the lobby bar is quite nice for business drinks.

The *Sheraton Nevskij Palace Hotel* (Map 8, ☎ 275 20 01, fax 301 73 23), Nevsky prospekt 57, is a fabulously renovated place, with about as much luxury as one can stand. All rooms are what you'd expect from any Sheraton luxury hotel.

Rack rates for singles are US$300, doubles US$375, including breakfast and VAT, though I booked on their website (www .sheraton.com) and was quoted US$185 for singles and doubles – a good deal for what you get. The nearest metro is Mayakovskaya, 200m east.

The hotel's restaurants are some of the best in town (see the Places to Eat chapter), and the service is excellent all around.

The *Grand Hotel Europe* (Map 8, ☎ 329 60 00, fax 329 60 01), Mikhailovskaya ulitsa 1/7, is perhaps the finest property in town if you go by architecture and location (it's certainly the most expensive!), but I found its service to be very poor. I've heard complaints about service from several guests of the hotel and personally experienced staff indifference in the lobby, restaurants and atrium bar. Too bad, because the rooms are nice (though smaller than you'd think), and the original and breathtaking Art-Nouveau interiors, along with a baroque façade designed by Rossi, have been completely restored to their turn-of-the-century glory.

Singles start from US$280, doubles US$320, suites are up to (now get this) US$2250. These prices, by the way, do *not* include breakfast (US$24!!) or 20% tax. In case you don't have your own limousine, Nevsky Prospekt metro is around the corner.

Inner Petrograd Side

On the corner of Kamennoostrovsky prospekt and the Karpovka River sits a building under perpetual construction that will someday be a top-end hotel, to be called the Royal Crown (Map 4). When it finally opens it will have a serene yet convenient location.

Vasilevsky Island

The *Hotelship Peterhof* (Map 4, ☎ 325 88 88, fax 325 88 89), moored off naberezhnaya Makarova, just north of the Tuchkov Bridge, is a Swiss-managed, Russian-staffed hotel-ship not inconvenient from the centre. It's about five blocks from metro Vasileostrovskaya, which is one stop from the Gostiny Dvor/Nevsky Prospekt metro stations.

The rooms aren't huge – in fact they're cabins – but they're very reasonably priced (singles/doubles are US$95/170 in high season, US$75/120 in low season). The ship has a good restaurant downstairs (it does 'theme nights', and its Italian food is darn good), a full bar and a great sundeck café upstairs (see Places to Eat). Staff are very courteous and helpful.

The *Pribaltiyskaya Hotel* (Map 6, ☎ 356 01 58, fax 356 44 96) is an Intourist-run behemoth on the Gulf of Finland, ulitsa Korablestroyteley 14. It's very popular with package-tour groups (perhaps you caught its movie debut in *The Russia House*) and has fair service and big, clean rooms (no singles) with stunning views of the Gulf of Finland if you're lucky (ask). The rack rate of US$194 for a double is laughable (no-one ever pays that), and it can be a very economical place to stay if you're here on a package.

The good news is that perhaps because its location is a bit inconvenient, it has a lot of extras – like a bowling alley (US$20 an hour), a business and conference centre, moneychangers and an in-house (though pricey) taxi service.

It's far away on the Gulf of Finland, at the windy end of Vasilevsky Island, half an hour from the city centre. From Nevsky prospekt, the fastest way is to metro Primorskaya, and then bus No 41 to the hotel.

South of the City Centre

Staying at Intourist's modern *Hotel Pulkovskaya* (Map 3, ☎ 264 51 22), 8km south of the centre at ploshchad Pobedy 1, has a couple of advantages. One is its proximity to the airport, 15 minutes away by bus No 13 (which stops right in front of the hotel). The other is that it is located close to the SKK stadium, site of conventions and trade shows. A taxi ride to the airport from here costs US$5 (don't take the in-house taxi service – walk a little north, away from the hotel, and flag one down on Moskovsky prospekt to avoid paying a 'tourist price'). No doubt the hotel's four-star rates (US$115/135) are to pay for all those Finnish lighting fixtures, but the rooms (all with bath) are comfortable and clean, service is good, and the restaurants and lobby bar are quite decent.

The hotel is about 750m south of metro Moskovskaya by the Defenders of Leningrad Monument; bus Nos 3 and 39-Э (not 39) go to ulitsa Bolshaya Morskaya (also known by its old name, ulitsa Gertsena) via Nevsky prospekt.

OTHER ACCOMMODATION
Homestays & Rentals

If you choose very carefully and aren't concerned about being far from the city centre, you may be able to find a homestay for as little as US$20 a double. The average, however, is US$35 to US$55 a couple.

There are several agencies advertising in the Russian and Western press that will find B&B accommodation for you.

The Host Families Association (HOFA; Map 5, ☎/fax 275 19 92, hofa@usa.net), ulitsa Tavricheskaya 5/25, originated at St Petersburg University and has been running a successful B&B booking service in St Petersburg for seven years. It places travellers with Russian families (generally academics and professionals) in their apartments around town. You'll get a private room and a shared bath, and breakfast is included. HOFA says that at least one member of the family will speak English. They have four programs, starting with basic B&B (US$30/50 single/double for a flat in the centre with discounts of US$5 per person per night after the seventh night). They charge US$30 for an invitation and registration.

You pay for the first two nights in advance by cheque (sent to a US address) or credit card, and the balance on arrival. They have branches in several Russian cities including Moscow, Yekaterinburg, Murmansk, Novgorod, Vladimir and Vladivostok, and in Riga, Tallinn and Vilnius.

In addition, from June to August the association rents flats in the centre from US$80 per night.

Private Flats

It's possible to stay in a private flat (for about US$10 to US$15 a night) by going with one of the older women who approach travellers arriving off major trains at Moscow Station, or finding a *kvartirnoe byuro* (listed in *The Traveller's Yellow Pages*), which is an agency that places short-term guests in private flats. You'll want to be sure that you can trust someone who approaches you at a station (many of them really are genuine folks just in need of some extra cash) and establish how far from the city centre their place is before accompanying them. It's better to actually see the place being offered before committing yourself to it.

I have heard of a number of people finding accommodation using this method, but I can't personally recommend it as I haven't done it myself.

2/2 w/exc Neva Vw, US$550

Have you ever shopped at a New York City or Hong Kong discount electronics store? And no matter what you bought, the experience left you with the mild sensation that somehow you just got ripped off in a major way? Such is the real estate market for foreigners in St Petersburg.

Prices for any long-term accommodation of European standard are stellar, with rents of over US$750 a month for a small one-bedroom flat the norm. One friend of mine pays US$1150 for a small two-bedroom. And another, who makes a bezillion dollars a year, has his company pay over US$3000 a month for his (admittedly nice) digs.

Most apartments come furnished. There are three standards: Russian, Good Russian (which the Russians claim is European) and European (which isn't really).

European means clean, wallpaper-free walls, good appliances, newly installed electrical outlets and the requisite steel door. Good Russian means floral wallpaper, newish appliances, reasonably comfortable furniture and doily-covered tables, creaking wooden floors and a spooky toilet. Russian means old appliances, a terrifying toilet and ghastly wallpaper and décor.

All but a select few apartments have filthy, dimly lit, frightening hallways and stairs, and creaking, shuddering, itty-bitty lifts that you should always think twice about entering.

Rentals are advertised in the *St Petersburg Times* – advertised prices are usually much lower than the real price (any ad claiming 'Nevsky prospekt two bed two bath US$550' is complete crap).

While agencies are the easiest (that's a relative term) way to find a pad, use them with caution. One well-established American realtor left town with heaps of his clients' cash. The legality of leases is iffy at best. Most foreigners living here have horror stories, but if your Russian's good you might do well. The best plan is to network – join SPIBA (St Petersburg International Business Association; see Tourist Offices & Information in the Facts for the Visitor chapter) and attend its meetings, hang out with expats and make as many contacts with established foreign residents as you can, then cross your fingers and hope for the best.

Because the market's so full of scoundrels, I can't recommend any specific agents (in the last edition of this book I probably would have sent you to the American guy who left town), but *Luchshee V Sankt Peterburg*, *The Traveller's Yellow Pages* and the *St Petersburg Times* are packed with realtor ads. The leading Western realty companies in town, who all charge an arm and at least half a leg, seem to be (but remember, this is not an endorsement) Pulford Enterprises (☎ 325 62 77), Atlantic Oncor (☎ 325 25 00) and Henry Chichester (☎ 325 90 05).

Good luck, and may the force be with you.

Places to Eat

Television news images of bread queues, meat shortages and empty shelves are as dated as Duran Duran, Betamax and power ties. In this edition, many of the smaller options that were listed last time simply because they existed last time in favour of more selective recommendations have been removed. There are small cafés and bistros throughout the city and the quality is generally very good to excellent, and good value for money. McDonald's, Carrols, Pizza Hut, KFC, Galileo and Grillmaster are foreign fast-food options with branches all around town, and excellent Russian chain fast-food places like Skazka, Europa, Koshki Dom and Russkaya Kukhnya are all terrific places to get dependably good Russian food at reasonable prices.

As a result, the food offered by the rest of the city's quick-snack and small bistro places has risen to a higher standard than ever before, so do experiment.

Restaurants in St Petersburg are civilised and plentiful. The old way of doing things (where a thug standing in a restaurant doorway asks a couple dressed for dinner, 'What do *you* want?!?') has mostly gone the way of the Five-Year Plan. You won't have to make reservations except on weekends and holidays, and if you're told there are no tables available, there probably aren't any. Going early – around 6 or 7 pm – increases your chances, as Russians usually dine later, from about 9 or 10 pm onwards.

There's no denying that an increase in price has come with the increase in quality; you can still eat cheaply at unpretentious cafés and Russian snack bars, but if you patronise the chic new eateries, bistros or cafés you'll pay Western prices, and the shock value of a bill from some of the city's finer restaurants is as worthy of a '*Mon Dieu!*' as any eatery that Paris has to offer.

But despite this, the wide range of choice can only be good news. Whatever you fancy – from Uzbek to Arabian, Chinese to Italian, Georgian to Japanese, Western European to good ol' Russian home cooking – it's here and in abundance.

Telephone numbers are listed here only if you'll need to reserve a table in advance, or if the establishment offers live music or entertainment so you can check what's on.

FOOD
Breakfast

Breakfast or *zavtrak* (*'ZAHF-truk'*) in hotels can range from a large help-yourself buffet spread to bread, butter, jam, tea and a boiled egg (or, worse, a pair of cold meatballs). Items you might find include:

Блины (*blee-NIH*)
  bliny or leavened buckwheat pancakes
Блинчики (*blinchiki*)
  bliny rolled around meat or cheese and browned
Каша (*kasha*)
  Russian-style buckwheat porridge
Сырники (*SEER-ni-ki*)
  fritters of cottage cheese, flour and milk
Творог (*tva-ROK*)
  cottage cheese
Яйцо (*yai-TSOH*)
  egg
Всмятку (*FSMYAT-ku*)
  soft-boiled
Крутое (*kru-TOY-eh*)
  hard-boiled
Омлет (*ahm-LYET*)
  omelette
Яичница (*yuh-EECH-nit-suh*)
  fried
Кефир (*kyi-FEER*)
  yoghurt-like sour milk, served as a drink

Bliny, kasha and syrniki can be delicious if topped with some combination of jam, sugar and the universal Russian condiment, sour cream, сметана (*'smye-TA-nuh'*).

Lunch & Dinner

Russians often like a fairly heavy early-afternoon meal, *obed* (*'ah-BYET'*), and a lighter evening meal, *uzhin ('OO-zhin')*, but a night-out supper can go on and on.

Meals (and menus) are divided into courses:

Закуски *(za-KU-ski)*
    zakuski (appetisers), often grouped into:
Холодные закуски *(kha-LOHD-ni-ye za-KU-ski)*
    cold zakuski, and
Горячие закуски *(gar-YA-chi-ye za-KU-ski)*
    hot zakuski
Первые блюда *(PER-vi-ye blYU-da)*
    first courses, usually soups
Вторые блюда *(fTAR-i-ye blYU-da)*
    second courses or 'main' dishes, also called
горячие блюда *(gar-YA-chi-ye blYU-da)*
    hot courses
Сладкие блюда *(SLAT-ki-ye blYU-da)*
    sweet courses or desserts
Мясные *(MYA-sni-ye)*
    meat
Рыбные *(RIB-ni-ye)*
    fish
Из птицы *(eez PTEET-si)*
    poultry
Овошные *(OH-vash-ni-ye)*
    vegetable

Appetisers The fancier appetisers rival main courses for price. Of course try the caviar, икра *('ee-KRA')*. The best is black (sturgeon) caviar, *ikra chyornaya*, also called *zernistaya*. Much cheaper and saltier is red (salmon) caviar, *ikra krasnaya*, also called *ketovaya*. Russians spread it on buttered toast or bliny and wash it down with a slug of ice-cold vodka. There's also ersatz caviar made entirely from aubergine or other vegetables.

A few other zakuski worth trying include:

Блины со сметаной *(blee-NIH sa-smi-TA-noy)*
    pancakes with sour cream
Грибы в сметане *(gree-BIH fsmi-TA-nyeh)* or
    Жульен из грибов *(hool-YEN eez gree-BOF)*
    mushrooms baked in sour cream, obscenely good
Рыба солёная *(RIH-buh sahl-YO-nuh-yuh)*
    salted fish
Сёмга копчёная *(SYOM-guh kahp-CHO-nuh)*
    smoked salmon

Salad, салат *('suh-LAHT')*, is an appetiser too. Most likely you will be offered one with tomatoes, из помидоров *('eez pa-mi-DOR-uf')*, or cucumbers, из огурцов *('eez a-goort-SOF')*, or the ubiquitous салат столичный *('suh-LAHT sta-LEECH-ni')*, comprised of vegetable and beef bits, potato and egg in sour cream and mayonnaise.

Soup Rich soups may be the pinnacle of Slavic cooking. There are dozens of varieties, often served with a dollop of sour cream. Most are made from meat stock. The Russian word sounds the same, суп.

Among the most common soups are:

Борщ *(borshch)*
    beetroot soup with vegetables and sometimes meat, usually served with smetana and hard-boiled egg
Лапша *(LAHP-shuh)*
    chicken noodle soup
Окрошка *(a-KROHSH-kuh)*
    cold or hot soup made from cucumbers, sour cream, potatoes, egg, meat and *kvas* (a beer-like drink)
Рассольник *(rah-SOL-nik)*
    soup of marinated cucumber and kidney
Солянка *(sahl-YAHNK-uh)*
    thick meat or fish soup with salted cucumbers and other vegetables
Уха *(OO-khuh)*
    fish soup with potatoes and vegetables
Харчо *(khar-CHOH)*
    garlicky mutton soup, Caucasian-style
Щи *(shchi)*
    cabbage or sauerkraut soup (many varieties)

Poultry & Meat Poultry is птица *('PTEET-suh')* – usually chicken, курица *('KOO-rit-suh')* or цыплёнок *('tsi-PLYOH-nuk')*. Meat is мясо *('MYA-suh'),* most commonly:

Говядина *(gav-YA-di-nuh)*
    beef
Свинина *(sfi-NEE-nuh)*
    pork

Cooking Styles Words you might spot on the menu are:

Варёный *(var-YOH-ni)*
    boiled
Жареный *(ZHAR-ih-ni)*
    roasted, baked or fried

Отварной *(aht-var-NOY)*
  poached or boiled
Печёный *(pi-CHOH-ni)*
  baked
Фри *(free)*
  fried

Poultry & Meat Dishes The list of possible dishes (and possible names) is huge, but following are some common ones:

Антрекот *(ahn-tri-KOHT)*
  entrecôte, boned sirloin steak
Бефстроганов *(byef-STRO-guh-nof)*
  beef stroganoff, beef slices in a rich sauce
Бифштекс *(bif-SHTEKS)*
  'steak', usually a glorified hamburger filling
Голубцы *(ga-loop-TSIH)*
  golubtsy, cabbage rolls stuffed with meat
Жаркое *(zhar-KOY-eh)*
  meat or poultry stewed in a clay pot; the commonest seems to be:
Жаркое по-домашнему *(... pa-da-MAHSH-ni-mu)*
  'home-style', with mushrooms, potatoes and vegetables
Котлета *(kaht-LYET-uh)*
  usually a croquette of ground meat
Котлета по-пожарски *(... pa-pa-ZHAR-ski)*
  minced chicken
Котлета по-киевски *(... pa-KEE-iv-ski)*
  chicken Kiev, fried boneless chicken breast stuffed with garlic butter (watch out, it squirts!)
Осетрина отварная *(a-si-TREE-nuh aht-VAR-nuh-yuh)*
  poached sturgeon
Осетрина с грибами *(a-si-TREE-nuh zgree-BUH-mi)*
  sturgeon with mushrooms
Пельмени *(pil-MYEN-i)*
  pelmeni – meat dumplings
Плов *(plov)*
  pilaf, rice with mutton bits, from Central Asia
Цыплёнок табака *(tsi-PLYOH-nuk tuh-buh-KAH)*
  chicken tabaka, grilled chicken Caucasian-style
Шашлык *(shashlyk)*
  skewered and grilled mutton or other meat, adapted from Central Asia and Transcaucasia

Fish Fish is рыба *('RIH-buh')*. Some common varieties are:

Осётр *(a-SYOTR)* or Осетрина *(a-si-TREE-nuh)* or Севрюга *(siv-RYU-guh)*
  sturgeon

Сёмга *(SYOM-guh)*
  salmon
Судак *(su-DAHK)*
  pike perch
Форель *(far-YEL)*
  trout

Vegetables Vegetables are овощи *('OH-va-shchi')*; greens are зелень *('ZYEH-lin')*. Any vegetable garnish is гарниры *('gar-NEE-ri')*. The most common vegetables include:

Горох *(ga-ROKH)*
  peas
Капуста *(kuh-POOS-tuh)*
  cabbage
Картошка *(kar-TOSH-kuh)* or Картофель *(kar-TOF-il)*
  potato
Морковь *(mar-KOF)*
  carrots
Огурец *(a-gur-YETS)*
  cucumber
Помидор *(pa-mi-DOR)*
  tomato
Свёкла *(SVYO-kluh)*
  beet, beetroot

Fruit Fruits are фрукты *('FROOK-ti')*. In the market (or in a restaurant if you're lucky) you might find:

Абрикос *(uh-bri-KOS)*
  apricot
Арбуз *(ar-BOOS)*
  watermelon
Виноград *(vi-na-GRAHT)*
  grapes
Груша *(GROO-shuh)*
  pear
Дыня *(DIN-yuh)*
  melon
Яблоко *(YA-bla-ko)*
  apple

Other Foods Stacks of bread, Хлеб *('khlep')*, are found on every table. The best is Russian 'black' bread, a vitamin-rich sour rye.

Russians are mad about wild mushrooms, грибы *('gree-BIH')*; in late summer and early autumn they troop into the woods with their buckets. Other items include:

Рис *(rees)*
   rice
Сыр *(seer)*
   cheese
Масло *(MAHS-la)*
   butter
Перец *(PYER-its)*
   pepper
Сахар *(SA-khar)*
   sugar
Соль *(sol)*
   salt

Desserts Perhaps most Russians are exhausted or drunk by dessert time, since this is the least imaginative course. Most likely you'll be offered ice cream, мороженое *('ma-ROH-zhi-nah-yuh')*. Other possibilities are:

Блинчики *(BLEEN-chi-ki)*
   pancakes with jam or other sweet filling
Кисель *(ki-SEL)*
   fruit jelly (jello to Yanks)
Компот *(kahm-POHT)*
   fruit in syrup (probably from a tin)
Оладьи *(a-LAH-dyi)*
   fritters topped with syrup
Пирожное *(pi-ROZH-na-ye)*
   pastries

Vegetarian Meals

St Petersburg is getting easier for vegetarians – the newer restaurants and even some of the older ones have caught on with salad bars and vegie dishes. Café Idiot and Troitsky Most (see Cafés later in the chapter) are dedicated vegetarian restaurants; the Idiot is one of the city's coolest places to hang out.

The new wave of chi-chi sandwich shops like Bon Jour and Minutka (formerly Subway) have begun offering all-vegie sandwiches, so in a pinch, head for one of these. The otherwise dreadful St Petersburg branch of Patio Pizza (which is great in Moscow) has a tremendously good all-you-can-eat salad bar for about US$8; Pizza Hut's salad bar is US$5.

If you're vegetarian, say so to restaurant staff early and often. You'll see a lot of tomato and cucumber salads, and will develop an eagle eye for the rare good fish and dairy dishes. Zakuski include quite a lot of meatless things like eggs, salted fish and mushrooms. If you spot овощи свежие, fresh (raw) vegetables, on the menu, you're in luck!

Main dishes are heavy on meat and poultry, vegetables are boiled to death and even the good vegetable and fish soups are usually made from meat stock.

Menus often have a category like овощные, молочные, яичные, мучные блюда (vegetable, milk, egg and flour dishes) – but don't get your hopes up. You may have to just run down the names of things you can eat, rather than relying on the waiter to think of something. In fact, be careful in following suggestions from the staff; some Russians consider items such as chicken and bacon to be 'non-meat' and suitable for vegetarians!

By the way, potatoes *(kartoshkuh, kartofel)* aren't filed under 'vegetable' in the Russian mind, so you must name them separately: 'potatoes and vegetables'.

I'm a vegetarian.
   Я вегетарианец. (masc; *ya vi-gi-ta-ri-AHN-yets*)
   Я вегетарианка. (fem; *ya vi-gi-ta-ri-AHN-ka*)
I cannot eat meat.
   Я не ем мясного. *(ya ni yem myis-NOH-va)*
without meat
   без мяса *(bis MYA-suh)*
only vegetables
   только овощи *(TOL-ka OH-va-shchi)*

Other Food-Related Terminology

Many restaurants in town will have menus in English.

waiter, waitress
   официант (masc; *ah-fit-si-AHNT*)
   официантка (fem; *ah-fit-si-AHNT-kuh*)
menu
   меню *(min-YU)*
hot
   горячий *(gar-YA-chi)*
cold
   холодный *(kha-LOHD-ni)*
another
   ещё *(yee-SHCHO)*
May we order?
   Можно заказать? *(MOZH-na zuh-kuh-ZAHT?)*

Please bring ...
  Принесите. пожалуйста ... *(pri-nyeh-SEE-tyeh, pa-ZHAHL-stuh ...)*
That's all.
  Всё. *(vsyo)*
Bon appetit!
  Приятного аппетита! *(pri-AHT-novuh ah-pih-TEET-ah!)*

When you're done you'll have to chase up the bill *('shchyot')*. If there's a service charge, noted on the menu by the words за обслуживание (for service), there's no need to tip further unless the service has been exceptional (see the Money section of the Facts for the Visitor chapter).

DRINKS

'Drinking is the joy of the Rus. We cannot live without it.' With these words Vladimir of Kiev, the father of the Russian state, is said to have rejected abstinent Islam on his people's behalf in the 10th century. And who wouldn't want to bend their minds now and then in those long, cold, dark winters? Russians sometimes drink vodka in moderation, but more often it's tipped down in swift shots, with a beer to follow, with the aim of getting legless.

The *average* Russian drinks more than 12L of pure alcohol a year – equivalent to over a bottle of vodka a week – and men drink much more than women.

There are dozens of pubs and bars in town, and more opening all the time. If it's a vodka that's being drunk, they'll want a man to down the shot – neat of course – in one (women are usually excused). This can be fun to start with as you toast international friendship etc, but vodka has a knack of creeping up on you from behind and if that happens just after you've started tucking into steak, chips and fried egg, the consequences can be appalling. A slice of heavily buttered bread before each shot, or a beer the morning after, are reckoned to be vodka antidotes.

Refusing a drink can be very difficult. Russians may continue insisting until they win you over, especially on some train rides. If you can't manage to stand firm,

take it in small gulps with copious thanks, while saying how you'd love to indulge but have to be up early in the morning etc. And if you're really not in the mood, the only tested and true method of warding off all offers (as well as making them feel quite awful) is to say 'Ya alkogolik' ('alko-golichka' for women) – 'I'm an alcoholic'.

Alcoholic Drinks

You can buy it everywhere. Kiosks, shops, bars, restaurants – you name it. Foreign brands as well as Russian are common, but be very suspicious of kiosk spirits. There's a lot of bad cheap stuff around that can make you ill, or worse. Only buy screw-top – never tin-top – bottles. Always check to see that the seal is not broken. Carefully taste any liquor you've bought at a kiosk to make sure it's really what it's supposed to be, and that it hasn't been diluted or tampered with. Err on the side of caution. People have been hospitalised after drinking tainted kiosk vodka – this is no joke.

In a restaurant you can order drinks by the bottle (which could be half a litre, three-quarters of a litre or one litre) or, for smaller quantities, by weight: 50g, equal to 50ml, for one shot, maybe 200g in a small flask for a few shots.

Vodka Vodka is distilled from wheat, rye or occasionally potatoes. The word comes from *voda* (water), and means something like 'a wee drop'. Its flavour (if any) comes from what's added after distillation. Pyati Zvyoz-dichnaya is a five-star brand said by the Russians to be the best. Two common 'plain' vodkas are Stolichnaya, which is slightly sweetened with sugar, and Moskovskaya, which has a touch of sodium bicarbonate. Tastier, more colourful and much rarer are Zolotoe Koltso (Golden Ring), Pertsovka (pepper vodka), Starka (with apple and pear leaves), Limonnaya (lemon vodka), and Okhotnichya (Hunter's), which has about a dozen ingredients, including peppers, juniper berries, ginger and cloves.

The more popular imports are Smirnoff (made in Connecticut, USA), Sweden's

Absolut (and all its varieties) and Finlandia, from a country that takes its vodka drinking *really* seriously. An export-quality, orange-flavoured Stolichnaya may be available as well – swoop it up, it's terrific.

Supermarket and liquor store prices range from around US$4.50 for a half-litre of Stolichnaya or Moskovskaya to US$18 for the most exotic ones.

Beer Ordinary Russian beer is hoppy. It's also not pasteurised, so after a couple of days those hops try to start a little hop-farm of their own right in the bottle – the date on the bottle is the date of production, not the sell-by date. Beer is safe for about three days after its production.

Probably the best of the brews is St Petersburg's Baltika, a fresh, slightly bitter Pilsner-style beer that's obscenely good, believe it or not, with a crushed clove of garlic added to it. Baltika is sold in shops and kiosks around town. There are several grades – you only want grades 3, 4 or 6.

Champagne, Wine & Brandy Soviet champagne (it's still called this – isn't it interesting that two of the things Russians hold most dear – their passports and champagne – *still*, in 1998, say 'Soviet'?) comes very dry *(bryut)*, dry *(sukhoe)*, semidry *(polusukhoe)*, semisweet *(polusladkoe)* and sweet *(sladkoe)*. Anything above dry is sweet enough to turn your mouth inside out. A 750g bottle is about US$10 in a restaurant and US$5 in a supermarket, kiosk or liquor store. Most other wine comes from outside the former USSR (Eastern European brands are the cheapest), though you can still find Georgian, Moldovan or Crimean wine.

Brandy is popular and it's all called *konyak*, though local varieties certainly aren't Cognac. The best non-Western konyak in Russia is Armenian (and simply labelled Konyak), and Five Star is fine.

Kvas & Mead *Kvas* is fermented rye bread water, dispensed on the street for under US$0.25 a glass from big wheeled tanks with 'kvas' printed on the side – and now it's available in bottles in supermarkets. It's mildly alcoholic, tastes not unlike ginger beer, and is cool and refreshing in summer.

Mead *(myod)*, brewed from honey, is a great winter warmer. It crops up here and there.

Alcohol-Related Terminology

Useful words include:

alcohol
   алкоголь *(al-ka-GOHL)*
glass
   стакан *(stuh-KAHN)*
bottle
   бутылка *(bu-TIL-kuh)*
50g
   пятьдесят грамм *(pit-dis-YAHT grahm)*
200g
   двести грамм *(DVYES-ti grahm)*
750g (three-quarter litre)
   семьсот пятьдесят грамм *(sim-SOT pit-dis-YAHT grahm)*
litre
   литр *(LEE-tr)*
vodka
   водка *(VOHT-kuh)*
Soviet champagne
   Советское шампанское *(sav-YET-ska-yuh sham-PAN-ska-yuh)*
very dry
   брют *(brYUT)*
dry
   сухое *(soo-kha-YEH)*
semidry
   полусухое *(pah-loo-soo-kha-YEH)*
semisweet
   полусладкое *(pah-loo-slat-kah-YEH)*
sweet
   сладкое *(SLAT-kah-yeh)*
wine
   вино *(vi-NOH)*
white wine
   белое вино *(BYEL-ah-yuh vi-NOH)*
red wine
   красное вино *(KRAHS-na-yuh vi-NOH)*
dry (wine)
   сухой *(soo-KHOY)*
sweet (wine)
   сладкий *(SLAT-ky)*
brandy
   коньяк *(ka-NYAK)*
beer
   пиво *(PEE-vah)*
beer bar
   пивной бар *(piv-NOY bar)*

kvas
    квас (*kvahs*)
mead
    мёд *(myoht)*
takeaway
    с собой (*sa-BOY*)
To your health!
    За ваше здоровье! (*za VA-sheh zda-ROH-vyeh!*)

Nonalcoholic Drinks

All the major Western soft drinks are available in Russia. Pepsi Cola, which was ubiquitous in the Soviet Union after Pepsico cut the world's best deal ever (they traded Pepsi for Stolichnaya vodka!), watched in horror as Coca-Cola deftly swatted the monopoly and fast became Russia's most popular soft drink.

Water & Mineral Water Stick to mineral water, which is omnipresent and cheap (see the Health section in the Facts for the Visitor chapter for more on tap water, which you shouldn't drink at all). BonAkva (from the Coca-Cola bottling company) is club soda. Saint Springs is bottled high quality, uncarbonated Russian mineral water.

Tea & Coffee The traditional Russian tea-making method is to brew an extremely strong pot, pour small shots of it into glasses and fill the glasses with hot water from the *samovar*, an urn with an inner tube filled with hot charcoal. The pot is kept warm on top of the samovar. Modern samovars have electric elements, like a kettle, instead of the charcoal tube. Putting jam (instead of sugar) in tea is quite common.

Coffee comes in small cups and these days is usually good. Cappucino and espresso are now common, even in Russian-run places. Almost any café, restaurant or *bufet*, and some bakery shops, will offer tea or coffee or both.

Sok, Napitok & Limonad *Sok* is juice, of a kind, usually sweetened, flavoured and heavily diluted. It never resembles the original fruit, but a jugful with a meal often goes down a treat. *Napitok* means beverage but in practice it's often a fancy sok, maybe with some real fruit thrown in. *Limonad* is a fizzy drink apparently made from industrial waste and tasting like mouthwash.

Other Nonalcoholic Drinks Jugs of *kefir*, liquid yoghurt, are served as a breakfast drink. Milk is common and sold cheaply in dairy shops *(molochnaya)* – but is sometimes unpasteurised.

Nonalcoholic Drinks Terminology

water
    вода (*va-DAH*)
boiled water
    кипяток (*ki-pya-TOHK*)
mineral water
    минеральная вода (*mi-ni-RAL-nuh-yuh va-DAH*)
soda water
    газированная вода (*ga-zi-ROH-va-nuh-yuh va-DAH*)
coffee
    кофе (*KOF-yeh*)
tea
    чай (*chai*)
with sugar
    с сахаром (*s SAKH-ar-am*)
with jam
    с вареньем (*s far-YEN-yim*)
juice
    сок (*sohk*)
apple juice
    яблочный сок (*YAHB-luch-ny sohk*)
orange juice
    апельсиновый сок (*ah-pil-SIN-ah-vy sohk*)
grape juice
    виноградный сок (*vi-na-GRAD-ny sohk*)
beverage
    напиток (*na-PEET-ak*)
lemonade
    лимонад (*li-ma-NAHD*)
soft drink
    безалкогольный напиток (*biz-al-ka-GOHL-ni nuh-PEE-tuk*)
milk
    молоко (*ma-la-KOH*)

FAST-FOOD OUTLETS

Practically every street in the city centre has several places where you can grab a bite of something. This list is not by any means complete, though it does cover the major bases and will help you to keep your stomach quiet until dinner time.

In addition to these places, the standard Russian *blinnayi* (pancake houses), *bistros* (fancy cafés), *kafe morozhenoe* (ice-cream restaurants), *kafeterii* (cafeterias), *stolovayi* (canteens) and *bufety* (stand-up snack bars) are all over the place, and these days most of them have what they say they have! Nevsky prospekt, for example, has something every 100m or so, and it's really a question of what you're *craving* as opposed to what you *can* have.

Russian Fast-Food Outlets

Several excellent Russian fast food places and chains have opened in the last year and all offer great value for money. The best are *Skazka* (Map 8), Nevsky prospekt No 27 and No 127, serving Russian bliny (pancakes) served with a variety of fillings including mushrooms and cabbage for US$1.10 and honey for US$0.90; *Vassa* (Map 6), 12-ya Krasnoarmeyskaya ulitsa 14, with quick snacks and small meals; *Koshki Dom*, a 24-hour chain (with with locations including ulitsa Vosstania 2 and Liteyny prospekt 23) doing fantastic salads (US$2.10 to US$2.75), Russian specialities (like potatoes in meat sauce for US$2, chicken shashlik for US$4.25) and soups for US$2.50; and *Russkaya Kukhnya* (Map 6), Admiralteysky prospekt 8, another place with excellent Russian fast food where meals come in under US$5.

Other offerings in the centre include the fabulous *Pyshki-Pyshechnaya* doughnut shop (Map 8), next to the DLT department store on ulitsa Bolshaya Konyushennaya. It's been around for decades and still serves up great sugar-coated plain doughnuts for next to nothing and drinkable coffee for less. Inside DLT itself, on the 2nd floor in the south wing, the *kafe* serves up some good coffee, small pizzas, sandwiches and hot dogs.

Springtime Shwarma Bistro (Map 7), Radishcheva ulitsa 20, at the corner of Nekrasova ulitsa, four long blocks east of Liteyny prospekt, has cheap and good Middle Eastern food, like gyro or felafel for under US$3, and heaps of vegetarian entries.

And an old favourite, *Russky Bliny* (Map 5), ulitsa Furmanova 13 (Furmanova runs parallel to and on the west of the Fontanka River), does great bliny in a cosy setting for incredibly cheap prices – US$3.50 for a minced chicken pancake is as high as things go. It's only open for lunch and an early dinner, Monday to Friday from 11 am to 6 pm.

Petrograd Side If you're peckish at Petrogradskaya metro, there's a very decent *Schwarma* place (Map 4) just across the street, with good, filling sandwiches for US$1. Adjacent to metro Petrogradskaya in Dom Mod (see the Shopping chapter) is *2 + 2*, which has sandwiches, salads, pizzas and other snacks. Fifty metres north of the metro is one of St Petersburg's McDonald's, and 50m south is a Carrols (see Foreign Fast-Food Outlets, below).

Foreign Fast-Food Outlets

All the foreign fast-food places in town sell their standard wares – they taste the same here as everywhere else – at prices a bit higher than in the US but somewhat lower than in Western Europe, and offer good value for money. That said, it would be a shame if you travelled all the way to Russia to have Egg McMuffins for breakfast, a three-piece KFC bucket for lunch and a Big Carolina burger for dinner. For God's sake get out and explore the Russian options. Or consider staying home and watching TV, and sending the money you would have spent on your trip to Nick Selby, Calle San Hiscio 3, Plaza del Perulero, 11380 Tarifa, Cádiz, Spain.

'McDonald's is here!' wrote one jubilant traveller, and I'm not sure whether this is a good thing. There are now several *McDonald's* restaurants in St Petersburg, and they're very crowded. Locations (and these are sure to multiply over time) include Bolshaya Morskaya ulitsa 11, near the Hotel Astoria; Kamennoostrovsky prospekt 39, Petrograd side (Map 4); Sennaya ploshchad 4 (Map 6);

the nicest yet, the church-like building at Sredny prospekt 29 opposite the Vasileostrovskaya metro station (Map 4); Moskovsky prospekt 195a, opposite Moskovskaya metro, and 45a Zagorodny prospekt, near Pushkinskaya metro.

Other burger joints in town include the Finnish *Carrols*, which does pretty much the same stuff as McDonald's: the original is at ulitsa Vosstaniya 5 very convenient to the HI St Petersburg Hostel (Map 8); other locations around town include Nevsky prospekt 45 (Map 8); ulitsa Marata 2; inside Gostiny Dvor; and Kamennoostrovsky prospekt 31, Petrograd Side (Map 4).

The Germans beat all *schnell*-food hamburger joints to town in 1994 when they opened the city's first *Grillmaster* (Map 8), Nevsky prospekt 46. Crowds still fight to get at the jumbo burgers, hot dogs and chicken fillet sandwiches, and they also do pretty awesome roast chicken and *schweinshaxn* – oh-so-lovely roasted pig thigh. They have a second location on the southeast corner of Nevsky prospekt and ulitsa Marata, opposite the city's newest fast-food offerings, *KFC* (Kentucky Fried Chicken), Nevsky prospekt 96 and the second branch of *Pizza Hut* (all Map 8).

Americans from the Subway company opened a wonderful sandwich shop at Nevsky prospekt 20 in 1994, and their Russian partners screwed them out of their investment and chased them from the country. The Russians reopened the place – with the same menu – as *Minutka*, but a court ruling ordered it turned back over to Subway. The Russians are still fighting, so it may be called either when you visit. Either way, they do submarine-style sandwiches with the works. Six-inch sandwiches include vegies and cheese at US$3 and roast beef at US$5.

CAFÉS

These are anything from a step up from fast food to pleasant places for a hot meal, with service approaching that of a restaurant.

Nevsky 27 (Map 8) is a stand-up café/bakery/pastry shop right near the Grand Hotel Europe, with decent coffee and dirt-cheap pastries.

The *California Grill* (Map 7, ☎ 274 24 22), Nevsky prospekt 176, is a cheery addition to the scene here, with American food, good Cobb and Caesar salads, and killer burritos, fajitas, philly steak sandwiches and Reubens, great mud pie, cheesecake ... and then there's beer, wine and drinks and their huge-screen satellite TV. They're open 24 hours, and have live music on weekends and parties for major sporting events. Meals will cost you US$10 plus drinks.

The coolest new entry is *Café Idiot* (Map 6, ☎ 315 16 75), naberezhnaya reki Moyki 82. All the food is vegetarian (US$7 to US$12), and the atmosphere is excellent – kitschy garage-sale furniture, funky lamps and tables, and there are several rooms including one that's non-smoking. Add Louis Armstrong, Marlene Dietrich and Ella Fitzgerald on the stereo (or live jazz on weekends), bookshelves packed with used books and magazines (read them there or buy them), chess, backgammon and checkers sets, a good Sunday brunch and enormous mugs of cappucino and this place is *the* place to be.

For a treat before or after the Church of the Resurrection of Christ, hit *Kafe St Petersburg* (Map 7) across the Griboedova Canal – an incredibly popular place with great food for very reasonable prices. You may have to queue amongst all the foreign students trying to grab a portion of the splendid baked mushrooms in cream sauce for about US$3. They do great borshch as well. In summer they have a very nice shaded outdoor seating area.

We list *Kafe Literaturnoe* (Map 8) because it's in so many other guidebooks you might wander in thinking it's a good place. It may have had its day back in Pushkin's time (his last meal was eaten here) but today the Lit Caf is nothing more than a highly priced tourist trap.

Bahlsen – Le Café (Map 8) at Nevsky prospekt 142, just east of ploshchad Vosstania, is an inexpensive stand-up café, serving hot dogs, pizzas and snacks. It's open from

View to the Strelka, the eastern point of Vasilevsky Island

Cruiser *Aurora*

Masterpiece or mockery? Peter the Great statue

Narva Arch

NICK SELBY

Town Duma & new sponsor

NICK SELBY

Cigarette marketing bunny on skates

NICK SELBY

Grand Hotel Europe

NICK SELBY

The not-so-attractive side of St Petersburg

NICK SELBY

Typically clear parking regulations

noon to midnight and takes most credit cards.

Petrograd Side

Bistro Samson (Map 4), Kamennoostrovsky prospekt 16 at Avstriyskaya ploshchad, has good, large, hot meals from US$2.50 to US$3; tasty, if small, salads from US$1 to US$1.75 and beer and champagne.

Troitsky Most (Map 5), Malaya Posadskaya ulitsa 2, near metro Gorkovskaya and no longer a Hare Krishna café, is a vegetarian place that has excellent salads and soups from US$0.75 to US$2, and it's open 24 hours.

Along or just off Bolshoy prospekt are several snack places, including *Shau Lin* (Map 4), Bolshoya Pushkarskaya 30 (entrance on Shamsheva ulitsa), with Chinese food that looks and smells excellent. There is also *Galeo* (Map 4), Bolshoy prospekt 56, just north of ulitsa Gatchinskaya, with cheap burgers, chicken and salads. Way down at the south-west end of Bolshoy prospekt next to Pirosmani Restaurant is the *Pirosmani* pavement café (Map 4), doing lavash bread, pastries, hot dogs and hamburgers. They were renovating when we visited but should re-open.

Up near the Hotel Druzhba, the *Kafe* (Map 4) at Kamennoostrovsky prospekt 54 (actually under a sign that says Druzhba), is very cheap and has good coffee and hot chocolate. It's open from 7 am to 8 pm (closed between 1 and 2 pm).

Bistro Laima (Map 4), Bolshoy prospekt 88/1, has perfectly serviceable food in a pleasant setting. Beef and chicken dishes cost up to US$6.50. The nearest metro is Petrogradskaya. There's a second branch right next to the Chayka bar at the corner of Nevsky prospekt and naberezhnaya kanala Griboedova.

Vasilevsky Side

The tiny *Sirin Bar & Restaurant* (Map 6) at 1-ya Liniya 16 has surprisingly good and cheap Russian food, including chicken dishes. It's open from 11 am to midnight. *Kafe Grilette* (Map 4) at 1-ya Liniya 40 has

ice cream and hot sandwiches for about US$1.50. *Kafe Nika (De Koninck)* (Map 6), Bolshoy prospekt 8, is yet another café to sport this Belgian beer logo. Some substantial café food is served here, like a pork grill (US$5) and a beef grill (US$7). It's a nice place.

The *Sun Deck Kafe* at the Hotelship Peterhof (Map 4) is, in summer anyway, a pleasant deck-top café serving hot and cold snacks, sandwiches, drinks etc at Swiss prices. It's on board the hotel-ship, moored along naberezhnaya Makarova just northwest of Tuchkov Bridge.

Ice Cream

In addition to foreign packaged ice-cream offerings, two rather good Russian ice-cream bars are available throughout town; Mitya and Dasha. They're roughly – and I mean that literally – comparable to Mars and Snickers ice cream and are definitely worth trying.

St Petersburg's ice-cream stands are everywhere – especially in well-touristed areas.

Baskin Robbins (Map 8), Nevsky prospekt 79, is just one of the US ice-cream parlour chain's locations in St Petersburg (it also has a branch out by the Planetarium behind the Peter & Paul Fortress, and kiosks here and there) and it's spreading throughout the country. Killer ice creams are about US$1.25 per scoop.

Gino Ginelli's (Map 8) is an Italian ice and ice-cream place next to the Chayka bar that also does microwaved pizza and burgers. It's open from 10 am to 1 am, at naberezhnaya kanala Griboedova 14.

In the Smolny region, *Sladkoezhka* (Map 5), on the south-western corner of Chernyshevskogo prospekt and Zakharevskaya ulitsa, is a totally slick ice-cream café and pastry shop serving good cappucino.

There's also a good *Kafe Morozhenoe* (Map 4) just west of the Buddist datsan north of Yelagin island.

RESTAURANTS

Almost all restaurants in town accept Visa, MasterCard and American Express. Higher-end ones also accept Diner's Club and JCB.

Russian

Soviet Inexplicably, the *Restoran Nevsky* (Map 8, ☎ 311 30 93), Nevsky prospekt 71, above metro Mayakovskaya, is still around, doing its best to keep up the traditions of the Communist Dining Experience. The fact that it's lasted this long means something, but I'm not sure what. It has several theme rooms to choose from.

Mid-Range *Sunduk* (Map 5), ulitsa Furshtadskaya 42, has a wonderful and eclectic atmosphere and sandwiches and soups from US$1 to US$3, full meals from US$4, salads from US$2 and English-speaking staff. It's a wonderful and as yet undiscovered spot, with a full bar and draught Grolsch beer.

Syurpriz (Map 7) is in fact *syurpriz*ingly good – with a café to the left (see Pizza) and full restaurant to the right. It's a modern place with friendly service at Nevsky prospekt 113. The shrimp and beef dishes are

---

Home Delivery

Having food delivered to a flat or hotel room is still generally the stuff of which expatriates' dreams are made, but there are a couple of places that'll do it: *US Subs* (☎ 314 03 65) delivers good if overpriced (around US$5 to US$7) submarine sandwiches anywhere in the centre free of charge from 10 am to 5 pm weekdays. And if money's no object, give the folks at *Fujiyama* a shout for sushi delivery (see Japanese, under Asian).

---

good, though they cost US$12 and US$15 respectively.

Kafe Tet-a-Tet (Map 4, ☎ 232 75 48), Bolshoy prospekt 65, Petrograd Side, has been round for aeons, and still offers a quiet, cosy place for just what the name suggests. The food's fine, and there's a pianist tinkling away while you dine – worth it on a date.

Staraya Derevnaya (Map 4, ☎ 431 00 00), ulitsa Savushkina 72, is a first-rate family-run traditional Russian restaurant (the nearest metro is Chyornaya Rechka, from where you can take tram No 2, 31 or 37). Service is great and the staff speak English, and because it's small, it's very intimate and cosy – make reservations. On weekend evenings, there's musical entertainment in the form of traditional Russian ballads. Main courses are priced from US$9 to US$18, starters from US$5 to US$10.

For location and service, nothing in this category comes close to touching *Austeria* (☎ 238 42 62), in the Peter & Paul Fortress; dine outside and count on excellent Neva views, solid Russian food and live music nightly. Meals run from US$15 to US$25.

Restaurant St Petersburg (Map 7, ☎ 314 49 47), opposite the Church of the Resurrection of Christ on the Griboedova Canal, has a nice setting, and at dinner (from US$20 to US$30), an over-the-top floor show occurs in which Peter the Great flounces about the place.

Speaking of floor shows, *Troyka* (Map 7, ☎ 113 53 43), has a variety show so execrable it's worth the US$50 set price. There's Russian food, pseudo-exotic dancers and big hats. It's in the basement at Zagorodny prospekt 27 (in the same building as the Jazz Philharmonic Hall), about equidistant from the Pushkinskaya and Vladimirskaya metro stations.

Top End The *Senat Bar* (Map 6, ☎ 314 92 53), Galernaya ulitsa 1-3, is a first-class Russian place with an odd but interesting interior designed by local artists and a beautiful vaulted ceiling. The food is good (at about US$25 for a main course), and beer-lovers will appreciate the extensive beer list. It's open from 11 am to 5 am.

The heavily advertised *Kalinka* (Map 4, ☎ 213 37 18), Syezdovskaya liniya 9 on Vasilevsky Island, has a beautiful atmosphere and fine food and service, but it's so packed with tourists we'd say it's worth skipping.

Caucasian & Central Asian

There's a decent Armenian restaurant, the *Nairy* (Map 6, ☎ 314 80 93), on ulitsa Dekabristov 6, near metro Sadovaya/Sennaya Ploshchad, open from 11 am to midnight.

Metekhi (Map 7, ☎ 272 33 61), Belinskogo ulitsa 3 near the Belinskogo Bridge, is still going strong with Georgian specialities at reasonable prices. Main courses are priced from US$5 to US$9, starters from US$2 to US$6. It offers good vegie dishes and fine service. The closest metro is Gostiny Dvor.

Kafe Tbilisi (Map 4, ☎ 230 93 91), Sytninskaya ulitsa 10, St Petersburg's first co-operative, has reopened and does fine Georgian food – though since reopening in 1998 it's received mixed reviews. Definitely try the home-made cheese, and its lavash and khachipuri breads.

1001 Nights (Map 5, ☎ 312 22 65), Millionnaya ulitsa 21/6, is an Uzbek place near the Hermitage that has okay Central Asian food and a prime location; it's set to be taken over by the folks who run La Strada (see Pizza, later in this chapter) and completely revamped, so stay tuned.

Kavkaz Restaurant (Map 7, ☎ 221 43 09), Stakhanovtsev ulitsa 5, does the city's best Caucasian and Georgian food, and if you're lucky they'll have real kindzamaruli Georgian wine. Don't order main courses, but just get one of each of the excellent appetisers (the khachipuri is to *die* for) and you'll get out for under US$20 a person (including wine). They've also got live Georgan music, and are open 24 hours in summer. Metro station Novocherkasskaya is close by.

Pirosmani Restaurant (Map 4, ☎ 235 46 66) at Bolshoy prospekt 14, Petrograd Side, has excellent Georgian food in a unique setting. It's not advisable to go if you're subject to hallucinogenic episodes – the rear wall of the restaurant is psychedelically sculpted in what's billed as a tribute to the Georgian artist's work, and there are rivers flowing through the restaurant. It serves dependable Georgian food; an average meal will cost you US$20. It's not convenient to public transport: from metro Petrogradskaya take any trolleybus south along Bolshoy prospekt.

Asian

St Petersburg's Asian offerings are on par with London's.

Korean The *Korean House* (Map 6, ☎ 259 93 33), Izmailovsky prospekt 2, near Tekhnologichesky Institut, serves up what may be the best Korean food in Eastern Europe. There are signs in both English and Russian on the street, but the entrance itself is not very conspicuous – go through the building's entrance and on the right you'll see the Korean House sign. The food is awesome, with a decidedly heavy hand with the garlic and spices, and the staff – still the same after five years – are incredibly friendly. Specialities are Korean-style beef (marinated and cooked at the table), marinated carrots, and kim chi. They also do darn good cold and hot noodle soups and dishes for both vegetarians and carnivores. Main courses run from US$5 to US$9.

Another Korean place very popular with Asian tourists for both its food and its fun karaoke is *Restaurant Arirang* (Map 7, ☎ 274 04 66), 8-ya Sovetskaya ulitsa 20. The main courses are expensive – around US$30 – but they come with free salads, appetisers and other starters that make the whole meal worth the price.

Chinese *Akvarium Restaurant* (Map 4, ☎ 237 06 47), Kamennoostrovsky prospekt 10, does exceptionally good Asian food, all prepared by Singaporean chefs. They don't deliver, but they do offer a take-away service, and everything on the menu is good value for money – count on spending US$10 to US$14 for a main course.

Restaurant Kharbin (Map 7, ☎ 272 65 08), ulitsa Zhukovskogo 34 in the basement, has wonderful service and dependably good Chinese food, including excellent fried eggplant in soy sauce with ginger for US$8, super Szechuan tofu for US$10 and awesome dumplings for US$2.25.

Golden Dragon (Map 6, ☎ 232 26 43), ulitsa Dekabristov 62, is conveniently close to the Mariinsky (as well as to the Matisov Domik hotel). It has good Chinese meals served by friendly staff for under US$15 per person.

The *Red Rose* (Map 4, ☎ 346 33 43), Kamennoostrovsky prospekt 44/46 on the south side of the Karpovka Canal, opened recently, and they're promoting the fact that they brought their chef over from Hong Kong. It looks promising.

Chopsticks (☎ 119 60 00), at the Grand Hotel Europe (Map 8), has good Chinese food in a stylish setting, but it's pricey and portions could be bigger. Main courses are priced from US$10 to US$30, and it's open from 1 to 11 pm. It's at the entrance closest to Nevsky prospekt – the restaurant to the right as you enter.

A reader wrote to us and recommended *Kitayski* restaurant (Map 6), on the west side of 1-ya Linia on Vasilevsky Island, just south of Bolshoy prospekt.

Japanese There are several Japanese places in town preparing sushi and Japanese specialities and, generally speaking, the farther from the city centre the better the food is. In the centre it's outrageously expensive, and not always good. Most sushi bars brought over Japanese chefs to train the Russians that are here now – it's surprising how many Japanese visitors scoff down the products of a *gaijin* sushi chef – go figure.

The best bet is probably *Fujiyama* (Map 4, ☎ 234 49 22), Kamennoostrovsky prospekt 54, Petrograd Side. It's a very comfortable place with two-piece sushi portions from US$3 to US$5; five-piece sashimi plates from US$13 to US$16 and rolls from US$8 to US$12. They also deliver sushi anywhere in town.

Everyone in town recommends *Shogun* (Map 7, ☎ 275 32 97), Vosstania ulitsa 26, which has beautiful interiors, private shuttered rooms and absolutely lovely staff; main courses range from US$9 to US$18, but when I visited it was a little under par.

The third best is the outrageously expensive *Sakura* (Map 8, ☎ 315 94 74), naberezhnaya kanala Griboedova 12, which is hugely popular more for its location than for its food.

Indian

Tandoor (Map 6, ☎ 312 38 86), Voznesensky prospekt 2, just off Isaakilevskaya ploshchad, is the most central (but not the best – see below) Indian place in town, with a full – albeit Russianised – Indian menu (about US$7 for starters and US$10 to US$20 per main meal) and a limited wine list. The only drawback I found was a tendency to undercook chicken dishes – specify that you want yours well done. It has a number of vegetarian items on the menu, as well as a good selection of traditional Indian breads and desserts.

Given a choice, I'd choose its less convenient competitor on Vasilevsky Island, *Swagat* (Map 6, ☎ 217 21 11), Bolshoy prospekt 91, every time. All diners are instantly transformed into Homer Simpson-like characters, reduced to slumping in their

Welcome to Kindly Fussy Bangaman

Creative English is a worldwide phenomenon; Japanese T-shirts or Indian shop signs written in it have been the subject of articles ad nauseam.

But there's a charm to the English spoken in Russia that must be mentioned. Often – especially with names that go on forever – it's a hangover from Soviet days: the 'Leningrad Order of Lenin Metropolitan Subway System Named After VI Lenin' springs to mind.

Sometimes it's the Russian compunction when speaking the English to pepper the sentences with the articles so missing in the Russian: 'Tomorrow I am going to the Moscow,' said one friend, whom we all dubbed 'The Daniel'.

But Russian English is at its best when trying to be showy, especially in advertising. 'Two crumpled eggs served from the frying,' is how one menu temptingly described an omelette (it gave the translating credit to a 'Dr of Philology').

Pizza Pronto holds that it has a 'Comfortably and cozy atmosphere! Real hospitality of the personal!'

Restaurant Austeria's ad claims it's 'probably the oldest resturant in the city and because of it "Austeria" suggesting you the traditional Russian cooking. Big choice at drinks and foods, not high price sure making "Austeria" a wonderfull places for lunch and dinner.'

'Bank MANATEP St Petersburg,' we're told, 'Invites to collaborate artificial personos and offers a wide range of banking services.'

Safety instructions are usually good for a laugh; the 'Rules of the Lift' in the lifts of the Pribaltiyskaya Hotel warn that 'the cabin arriving at the floor produces both the light and sound signals; the light signal indicates further direction of the cabin but the direction of the cabin cannot be changed by pushing the buttons.'

Runner up for best Russian English appeared in the magazine *St Petersburg Today*. This is the introductory paragraph under the headline 'Our Advice' – not one word has been omitted:

'How is it possible then to know in which direction the numbers increase? Turn left of the building Number 20 and go straight. There is your building Number 40. Accordingly, if you are standing on the opposite side of the street, right side to the building, the beginning of the street is behind your back.'

But the winner in town is this sign in the window of Pivnoy Klub, a small beer bar in central St Pete, which promises the following:

'Only here country primitive kitchen all in the nature fire welcome to kindly fussy Bangaman.'

I collect these things, so if you find any more of them in your travels, please send them to me at nselby@lonelyplanet.com. I'm always on the lookout for a few new fussy Bangamans.

PLACES TO EAT

---

seats as plate after plate of stupendous Indian food gets placed in front of them ('Mmmmmm garlic ... Mmmmm tandoor chicken ...'); fabulous main courses like mixed kebabs cost US$15 and murg joshina – chicken in a spicy tomato sauce – US$9. Service is great and there's live sitar music nightly.

Pizza

While nothing approaches the Pizza Nirvana that *is* New York City, St Petersburg now has some good pizza places, though there are still lots of places serving shite. A hard and fast rule on pizza here and everywhere else on earth: if it's Finnish, forget it.

The best pizza in town is at the beautiful *La Strada* (Map 8, ☎ 312 47 00), Bolshoya Konyushennaya ulitsa 27, which has hugely attentive staff, a large, spacious area with an enormous skylight and an open kitchen area where you can watch the cooks prepare the pizzas. Get the quatro stagioni with capers, onions, olives and garlic. Portions are huge. Pizzas start at US$9 but average US$12, small salads are US$7 to US$10, and there are good baked potato dishes for about the same.

St Petersburg has two *Pizza Hut* restaurants; the original (Map 8, ☎ 315 77 06), naberezhnaya reki Moyki 71/76, and the latest addition (Map 8, ☎ 327 26 42), Nevsky prospekt 96, both do countless varieties of pizza (large pan margarita US$8.50, large pan vegetarian US$13.50 or to go the other way, the meat feast is US$15), sell beer, wine and cappuccino, and have salad bars (US$5). The Nevsky location also does pizza by the slice (thank you!) from US$1 to US$2.

The worst pizza from an expensive restaurant in town is at *Patio Pizza* (Map 7, ☎ 271 31 77), Nevsky prospekt 182. While it's great in Moscow, here it charges about US$11 for thin-crusted, poorly sauced, badly topped and under-cooked 'pizza' complete with vile service (they gave me grief when I dared to request that it be cooked longer). But they have an excellent all-you-can-eat salad bar (US$8).

Two dependable Russian-run pizza places are *Pizzeria Verona* (Map 7), Suvorovsky prospekt 43, and the eminently-named *Pizzeria* (Map 7), Rubinshteyna ulitsa 30. *Syurpriz Kafe* next to Syurpriz restaurant (Map 7), east of ploshchad Vosstania at Nevsky prospekt 113, serves up fine little pizzas for around US$5 and other snacky things. It also has Tuborg draught beer.

European

European food is clearly the most crowded entry in the St Petersburg restaurant scene, and the most expensive. These days you get very good value for the admittedly high prices, and it's worth investigating the options: even if you're on a limited budget

St Petersburg has enough places to make a one-night splurge something to remember.

This category includes restaurants that specialise in a broad range of European rather than national cuisines; see later in the chapter for listings of French, Italian, German and Yugoslavian restaurants.

Mid-Range *Nikolai* (Map 6, ☎ 311 14 02), in the House of Architects (Dom Arkitektora) at Bolshaya Morskaya 52, does its best to serve up European and even Brazilian food. It has a nice layout, and its main courses average US$10 to US$15. It's popular with tourists and there's a good floor show.

Dinner at the Sheraton Nevskij Palace Hotel's *Imperial Restaurant* (Map 8), where guests also have their breakfast, is a superb buffet affair, with continental and international specialities and live music on most evenings. Here is where it also holds its blow-out Sunday jazz brunches (US$40). On the 2nd floor, the *Admiralty Restaurant* has fine Russian and seafood specialities, in a sort of 'Ahhhr, matey' setting, with ship models from the St Petersburg naval museum. Main courses are priced from US$30 to US$50, starters from US$10 to US$21 and salads from US$15 to US$15.

In its first year, *Sadko's* (Map 8, ☎ 329 60 00) at the Grand Hotel Europe was so popular that it became unmanageable (it charged in roubles but looked and felt like a Western bar). It seemed that every business deal – dirty or otherwise – involving foreigners that went down in town was discussed here, and speculators used to hop from table to table to schmooze. In 1992, when it turned to hard currency in an attempt to flush out the riffraff, it was such a big deal that it was written up in *Newsweek*. Today, Sadko's is a huge, Texan-inspired barn of a bar, still popular but by no means what it was. It serves decent though pricey food (burger and fries US$15, starters US$7 to US$14) and it has a great beer selection (US$4 to US$9), but its 'speciality cocktails' – like a piddle of whisky at the bottom of a cup of coffee – are out of line at US$10. It has good live bands on weekends, when the place really starts jumping. It's open till midnight. They also do a jazz brunch on Sunday.

Domenico's (Map 8, ☎ 272 57 17), Nevsky prospekt 70, between the Fontanka River and Rubinshteyna ulitsa, is a popular restaurant and more popular disco; food is rich but good: steak, a speciality, is US$19, pasta dishes are US$10 to US$14.

Svir (Map 4, ☎ 325 88 88) is the Hotelship Peterhof's restaurant, and it's quite a nice place to spend an evening. The dining room is on the lower level of the ship, moored off naberezhnaya Makarova just west of the Tuchkov Bridge at the north-east end of Vasilevsky Island, so there's a nice Neva view, and the food and service are both very good. It runs food festivals (rotating monthly) during which it highlights specific cuisines. Main courses cost from US$15 to US$30, starters from US$7 to US$14. The Sun Deck Kafe (see Cafés earlier in the chapter) is excellent in summer for late-night drinks.

Nevsky Melody (Map 5, ☎ 227 15 96), Sverdlovskaya naberezhnaya 62, is a pleasant enough restaurant that's been around for ages; it offers good food at reasonable prices (and a 10% discount for ISIC holders), but it's in the middle of nowhere. There's a casino and nightclub here too.

Top End See the boxed text for information on the Old Customs House, which I vote St Petersburg's best.

The rooftop *Landskrona* at the Sheraton Nevskij Palace Hotel (Map 8) is thought by many to be St Petersburg's finest restaurant. The Italian specialities are served in a gorgeous setting, and there's dancing and live music; in summer, an open-air terrace offers panoramic views of the city. Main courses are priced just a bit higher than in the Admiralty (see mid-range, above). In all of these restaurants the service is impeccable.

For a look at St Pete's nouveaux riches and to observe how they live and dine, hit the reportedly excellent *Taleon Club* (Map 8, ☎ 315 76 45), naberezhnaya reki Moyki 59,

restored to turn-of-the-century elegance. How's this for class: upstairs there's a casino for the boys and a hairdresser for the gals as after-dinner entertainment.

The Grand Hotel Europe's flagship, *Restaurant Europe* (Map 8, ☎ 329 60 00), has the most beautiful setting in town, if not the country. This extravagantly luxurious place, with its stained-glass ceilings and luminous history (you want celebrities, we got celebrities, from the King of Siam to Krushchev to Buzz Aldrin to Michael Caine ... the list goes on and on!), serves spectacular food at celestial prices – so celestial, in fact, they're hidden from women (the 'Ladies' Menu' contains no prices): figure on starters from US$18 to US$28, soups from US$10 to US$12, meat dishes from US$38 to US$95 and some excellent German lobster with crayfish ragout and caviar sauce for US$45. It also serves a heavenly Sunday jazz brunch (US$45) from noon to 3 pm. If someone well off is taking you out to dinner, this is the place to have them take you. It's open for breakfast (around US$20) from 7 to 10 am and for dinner from 6 to 11 pm.

Obscene Dvorianskoye Gnezdo (Map 6, ☎ 312 32 05), ulitsa Dekabristov 21, is the most expensive (expect to pay US$60 to US$80 or more per person) place in town, with a menu of European and Russian specialities. Bill Clinton ate here when he stopped into St Petersburg, but I don't have his expense account so I couldn't tell you if it's worth the price. Madeleine Albright seemed happy. The atmosphere, I can say, is spectacular; posh, elegant but not overdone. And Charles, who runs the place, is the kind of guy who remembers what you ordered and who you were with when you came in 10 years ago. If you want to spend a packet on good food, excellent wine and sensational service, this is the place to do it.

French

Bistro Le Francais (Map 6, ☎ 210 96 22 or 315 24 65), ulitsa Galernaya 20, is just that – the genuine French chef greets guests with a jaunty '*Bonjour*' – but *sans* surly maître d' pretending not to speak English. It has very nice, very rich specialities priced from US$12 to US$25. There's a nice bar here too.

Italian

Rossi's (Map 8, ☎ 329 60 00) is the Grand Hotel Europe's casually elegant dining option, gone Italian just last year; it has a more relaxed atmosphere than the Restaurant Europe, but hasn't let its hair down so low that it's become similar to Sadko's (see earlier). With excellent food and service, it's good for a business lunch. Its main courses are priced from US$20 to US$35, starters from US$9 to US$15.

Milano (Map 8, ☎ 314 73 48), Karavannaya ulitsa 8, has dependably good Italian food (though it may be going downhill – their Italian chef recently left – stay tuned), and good service; dinner costs about US$40 to US$50 per person.

German

Schvabsky Domik (Map 7, ☎ 528 22 11), Novocherkassky prospekt 28 at metro Novocherkasskaya, was one of the earliest joint-venture restaurants in town. The Bavarian décor is still pushing the hokey barrier but it's fun, and the food – schnitzel, sauerkraut, sausage and roast pork – is good. The excellent German beer is reason to go in and of itself.

Yugoslav

I asked one of St Petersburg's leading restaurateurs which (other than his) place was the best top-end place in town and he disagreed with my choice (see boxed text for information on The Old Customs House) and said his fave was ***Drago Restaurant*** (Map 4, ☎ 430 69 84), Primorsky prospekt 15, near metro Chyornaya Rechka. It's a Yugoslavian restaurant which specialises in barbequed beef and has live music every night.

Steak Houses

Montreal Steak (Map 7, ☎ 310 92 56), Apraksin pereulok 22, at the corner of

Best Splurge

For the best value top-end meal in town – taking into account atmosphere, service, food and value for money – I vote *Staraya Tamozhnaya* (The Old Customs House; Map 6, ☎ 327 89 80), Tamozhenny pereulok 1 on the Strelka. The atmosphere is simply delightful, with vaulted brick ceilings, excellent live jazz, fantastic service and wonderful food. Nothing outrageous, just large portions of very well prepared Russian and European specialities from US$18 to US$30. There's always a vegetarian offering from US$14 to US$18, a good wine list (and a good house red), and once again that wonderful service really makes it. The potatoes au gratin are smothered with an avalanche of cheese, and mixed with garlic; the entrecôte a succulent pleasure, the steaks thick and tender. The only drawback was the Caesar salad, which was neither.

naberezhnaya reki Fontanki, does excellent thick steaks at high but not outrageous prices. Its central location makes it a better choice than its south-of-the-centre competitor ***Daddy's Steak Room*** (Map 6, ☎ 298 95 52), Moskovsky prospekt 73 (just next to metro Frunzenskaya), which was St Petersburg's first Western-style steakhouse. You can get a good, large steak, garlic potatoes and a couple of trips to the salad bar for about US$25.

Mexican

All I'll say about the only Mexican place in town when I visited is that its name is appropriate – ***La Cucaracha*** (Map 7), naberezhnaya reki Fontanki 39. But there will likely be a St Petersburg branch of the American Mexican food chain ***Señor Pepe's*** – it's all finished, they brought their staff over from Cuba and Mexico along with two enormous tortilla presses, and installed adobe interiors and nice tiled floors. It hadn't opened when I was researching, but it looks promising. It's on ulitsa Lomonosova between ulitsa Sadovaya and the Fontanka.

Hotel Restaurants

Most hotels in town worth their ilk have restaurants or cafés.

The reasonably priced *Salt & Pepper* is popular with the expat crowd. It's in the Hotel Moskva (Map 7), has a nice atmosphere, friendly staff and it's very convenient if you're staying in the hotel or visiting the Alexandr Nevsky Lavra.

I never thought I'd say this but the restaurants at the Astoria Hotel are seriously coming up in the world; the *Winter Garden* (Map 6, ☎ 210 558 15) does a terrific set-price lunch with a main course, salad and dessert buffet for US$22, and its Sunday brunch (US$40) is great too.

SELF-CATERING

Self-catering is now not only possible but plausible. The city has seen an explosion in food shops, and Western-style supermarkets are popping up all over the place. Teeming with fresh meats, cheese, vegetables, tinned goods, frozen prepared foods (like pizza, some dinners and even fresh-frozen prawns) and usually booze, in many of these places you'd swear you'd been transported back home to a Safeway or Coles. There are dozens of 24-hour grocery shops in several areas of the city, several along Nevsky prospekt alone, and a good one for quick snacks at ploshchad Vosstania, just east of Moscow Station.

Food Shops & Supermarkets

The biggest supermarket in the city centre is called – surprise – *Supermarket*, in the basement of Passazh shopping centre (Map 8), open from 9 am to 9 pm.

Yeliseevsky Food Shop (Map 8), on Nevsky prospekt opposite ploshchad Ostrovskogo, is Russia's most beautiful, if not most famous, food shop. A turn-of-the-century rich-people's food court, the place has now been mostly restored to its pre-Soviet Art-Nouveau splendour, with huge stained-glass windows and chandeliers.

Meat, chicken and fish are found through the right-hand entrance, while Western and high-end Russian packaged and bulk dry goods are to the left.

Out at the Petrograd Side, *Babylon Super* (Map 4), Maly prospekt 54, has a terrific selection of exotic (for Russia) fresh vegies, like fresh ginger root and avocado, as well as frozen vegies and a French-inspired bakery that makes awesome pastries and wonderful breads several times daily. It also has lots of wines and beers. It takes Visa, MasterCard, American Express and Eurocard. And while you're out there on the Petrograd side, check out the florist at Kamennoostrovsky prospekt 5 (Map 5). It sells flowers, plants and, oh yes, a full line of Mercedes Benz sedans. It's open daily from 9 am to 7 pm.

The *Kalinka Stockmann's* (Map 5), behind the Hotel St Petersburg at Finlyandsky prospekt 1, is a smaller affair, with good Finnish milk supplies. It's a good place to buy decadent Western luxuries – like fresh meats and poultry – to cook up at the nearby Holiday Hostel. It also sells some international newspapers and magazines.

And if you're in that Finnish-food mode, head for one of *Spar Market*'s two locations: Slavy prospekt 30 (way out in southern nowhere; take metro Moskovskaya then trolleybus No 27 or 29 east – it's just past the Kupichinsky department store), and at the much more central, but smaller, prospekt Stachek 1 (Map 3, metro Narvskaya) location, at which there is also a small café serving very nice pastries and coffee for about US$1.50.

Markets

With the advent of widespread supermarket and 24-hour store trading, St Petersburg's markets (*rynky*; singular *rynok*) no longer cause St Petersburgers to drop their jaws to pavement level and drool in envy, but they're still fascinating places to visit and fabulous sources of fresh produce, meats and other food.

The markets are held daily in buildings large enough to house small football fields, and food and produce from all over the former Soviet Union can be had, including exotic fruits and vegetables that you may never have seen before (and sometimes wish you never had!). Most of the markets also feature fresh meats, as in so fresh they're still in the process of being hacked off the carcass. Markets are also a good place to pick up honey and honey products (try before you buy – it's free), cottage cheese, heavy cream and sometimes even flowers.

Two of the liveliest and most central (and most expensive) are the **Kuznechny** (Map 7) on Kuznechny pereulok, two minutes walk from Vladimirskaya metro, and the **Maltsevsky** (Map 7) at ulitsa Nekrasova 52 (metro Ploshchad Vosstania). Some others are the **Sytny** (Map 4) at Sytninskaya ploshchad 3/5 (metro Gorkovskaya, behind Alexandrovsky park and up towards Kafe Tbilisi); the scary **Torzhkovsky** (Map 3) at Torzhkovskaya ulitsa 20 (metro Chyornaya Rechka); the **Kondratevsky** (Map 5) at Polyustrovsky prospekt 45 (metro Ploshchad Lenina, then tram No 6 or 19, bus No 100, 107, 136 or 137 or any trolleybus except No 8). The Kondratevsky has a fur (and shamefully cruel pet) market out the back, where you can buy great hats. Other markets include the **Sennoy** (Map 6)

at Moskovsky prospekt 4; and the more inexpensive **Vasileostrovsky** (Map 6) at Bolshoy prospekt 18 on Vasilevsky Island (metro Vasileostrovskaya).

Bakeries

Even in the old days the standard Russian *bulochnaya* (bakery) turned out some terrific rich, sour brown bread. There are bread shops in every neighbourhood (almost always marked by a sign that just says булочная, but sometimes just Хлеб) as well as speciality bakers. **Wendy's Baltic Bread** (Map 7), at the corner of 8-ya Sovetskaya ulitsa and Grechesky prospekt (a five minute walk from the HI St Petersburg Hostel), has great cakes, tortes, eclairs, croissants filled with ham and cheese, baguettes, hot cross buns and other wonderful baked specialities.

Karavay Bakery (Map 5), opposite the City Children's Park, has great bread, cakes and buns; it's at Tavricheskaya ulitsa 33 and is open from 8 am to 7 pm. **Nevsky 27** (Map 8), across from the Grand Hotel Europe, also does good bread, and is open from 8 am to 1 pm and from 2 to 7 pm. The **Bahlsen Bakery** (Map 8), Nevsky prospekt 142, does good bread and cakes. It's open Monday to Saturday from 8 am to 8 pm.

Entertainment

St Petersburg is the entertainment equal of many Western cities, and government agencies here no longer require you to like opera or ballet. Sure, the classical entertainment in the city is among the best on the planet – ballet, opera, music and theatre – but there's a new world of rock clubs, jazz joints and discos that has St Petersburg nightlife soaring to heights never before witnessed in Russia.

However, due to the precarious nature of everything here, clubs come and go faster than in other places. Both *Pulse* and the Friday *St Petersburg Times* have comprehensive weekly club and pub listings, as well as names and addresses of new clubs and venues. For other listings, being able to decipher Cyrillic is a huge advantage. St Petersburg has listings magazines in Russian, such as *To Da Vsyo (This and That)*.

A huge amount of information, including some about rock and sporting events, is published on posters. Check what's-on charts in hotel service bureaus, at concierge desks and in the central ticket kiosks (they can be identified by the words *teatralnaya kassa*, Театральная касса; or just *teatr*, Театр). For performances listed on posters look for words like Продажа, *prodazha* (sale), and билети, *bileti* (tickets).

CLASSICAL MUSIC, BALLET & OPERA

September to early summer is the main performing season – the cultural scene goes into neutral for the rest of the summer, with companies away on tour. An exception is the last 10 days of June, when St Petersburg stages the White Nights Dance Festival, with events ranging from folk to ballet. Extra events of variable quality are also mounted through the summer tourist season at halls like the ***Lensovieta Culture Palace*** (Map 8) at Kamennoostrovsky prospekt 42 (metro Petrogradskaya) and the ***Oktyabrsky Concert Hall*** (Map 7) at Ligovsky prospekt 6 (metro Ploshchad Vosstania).

Tickets

According to a hateful law introduced in October 1997, foreigners officially pay six times the Russian rate, to a maximum of US$48.50. This unforgivable situation is worsened by the fact that ticket-takers in some theatres actually enforce the law – if you show up for an opera at the Maly Theatre with Russian tickets, they'll be confiscated and you'll only be seated after you pay the difference between them and your foreigner tickets (curiously, it seems easier to get away with Russian tickets at the Mariinsky!). Students officially studying in Russia (with a Russian student ID, *not* an ISIC, which is useless for these purposes) and foreigners working here receive a 'discount', but still pay more than the Russian price.

There are a couple of ways around this, none foolproof. The easiest is to buy the absolute cheapest ticket you can and simply move down to the good seats at intermission – this hardly ever fails. Shop around – if one ticket office tells you that you must pay the foreigner price, head to another (there are heaps along Nevsky prospekt). In a pinch, ask a Russian in line to buy them for you.

Face-value tickets are sold at the venues themselves (usually from 11 am to 3 pm and 4 to 6 pm, and best bought in advance) or through the combined booking offices. Apart from the Kirov Ballet (it's still called that, even though the theatre is now the Mariinsky), the dearest tickets are rarely more than US$10. In 1998, tickets paid by Russians to performances at the Mariinsky Theatre ranged from US$1.20 to US$15, depending on performance and seat.

The best booking office at which to buy tickets is the Teatralnaya kassa (Map 8, ☎ 314 93 85) at Nevsky prospekt 42, in the middle of Dumskaya ulitsa on the western side of Gostiny Dvor. You can get tickets for everything here, including the Kirov, but they sell out quickly.

Concierge desks at the better hotels will be only too pleased to sell you Mariinsky tickets from US$65 to US$85. They do, however, get some of the best seats in the house, so if you've got a limited amount of time, you may be happy to pay their price.

Touts, who hang around in front of the venue before a performance, will almost certainly be selling Russian tickets. If you want to buy a ticket from one of them, go along to the venue an hour or so before the performance. A standard tout price you shouldn't feel fleeced paying (even though you're probably being fleeced) is US$40 to US$50, but you risk being fined and having to pay that same US$40 to US$50 again once you're inside. And when you get the ticket, make sure it's for the date and section you want: first floor is the *parter*; the mezzanine is the *beletazh*; and the balcony is the *balkon* or *yarus*.

Sometimes people sell tickets from tables in pedestrian subways; check the underpasses at Nevsky Prospekt and Gostiny Dvor metros.

Wherever you decide to buy your tickets, good seats will go fast! Most theatres and concert halls are closed on Monday. There are usually matinees on Sunday and sometimes on Saturday.

Classical Music

The St Petersburg Philharmonica's Symphony Orchestra is particularly renowned. It has two concert halls: the **Bolshoy Zal** (Big Hall, Map 8, ☎ 311 73 33) on ploshchad Iskusstv; and the **Maly Zal imeni M I Glinki** (Small Hall, not to be confused with the Maly Theatre, the Maly Dramatic Theatre or the Glinka Capella; Map 8, ☎ 312 45 85) nearby at Nevsky prospekt 30. The **Glinka Capella** (Akademicheskaya Khorovaya Kapella imeni M I Glinki, Map 8, ☎ 314 10 58), naberezhnaya reki Moyki 20, also has high standards, focusing on choral, chamber and organ concerts. Other venues include **Smolny Cathedral** (Map 5, ☎ 271 91 82), which usually features choral works, and the **Peterburgsky Concert Hall** at ploshchad Lenina 1.

Ballet & Opera

St Petersburg was the birthplace of Russian ballet back in 1738; the Kirov Ballet (www.kirovballet.com) premiered Tchaikovsky's *Sleeping Beauty* and *Nutcracker Suite*, and nurtured Nijinsky, Pavlova, Nureyev, Makarova and Baryshnikov. But the Kirov went through some difficult times in the early to mid-1980s, as a talent drain, lack of funding and ever more apathetic players dragged down the quality.

Today, under director Valery Gergiev, the Kirov is blowing away Moscow's Bolshoy. Gergiev, who simultaneously runs the Kirov, guest conducts at the New York Metropolitan Opera and still manages to hold down the gig of principal conductor at the Rotterdam Philharmonic Orchestra, has brought a commercial rebirth, an artistic renaissance and a serious boost in morale to the Kirov that's infectious. Don't miss it.

The Kirov Opera can also be a treat, though it's occasionally truly awful. Both are at the **Mariinsky Theatre** (Map 6) at Teatralnaya ploshchad 1. Russian and international classics are in the repertoire, and about five

Anna Pavlova studied with the Imperial School of Ballet at the Mariinsky Theatre from age 10.

ballets and five operas are performed each month. The operas are performed in Russian.

The companies tend to go away on tour for about two months in the summer and unpredictably the rest of the year. The ballet's home shows are nearly always booked out; ticket sales from the theatre usually start 20 days in advance. Be sure it's the Kirov company itself, and not the Russian Ballet, that you're paying to see; sometimes visiting ensembles perform here too.

Cheaper and easier-to-get-into ballet and opera performances are staged at the *Maly Theatre* (Peterburgsky Gosudarstvenny Akademichesky Maly Teatr Opery i Baleta imeni M P Mussorgskogo) at ploshchad Iskusstv 1. The Small Theatre stages more contemporary works than the Kirov and standards are respectable. The *Conservatory*, on Teatralnaya ploshchad, also stages some operas.

THEATRE

Tickets for theatrical venues in town are available from the same sources as those for classical music – see Tickets under Ballet, Opera & Classical Music for more information.

The premier drama theatre is the *Pushkin* (Map 8), at ploshchad Ostrovskogo 2, which stages (in Russian) the likes of Shakespeare, Aristophanes and even Arthur 'Aeroport' Hailey as well as home-grown plays. The *Lensoviet Theatre* (Map 8), at Vladimirsky prospekt 12, and the *Gorky Bolshoy Dramatic Theatre* (Map 7), at naberezhnaya reki Fontanki 65, are the other top mainstream drama theatres.

For experimental fare, try the *Maly Dramatic Theatre* (Map 8) at Rubinshteyna ulitsa 18 or the *Music hall* (Map 4, ☎ 232 68 21) at Alexandrovsky Park 4. Music-hall variety shows are staged here and at the *Teatr Estrady* (Map 8, ☎ 314 70 60) at Bolshaya Konyushennaya ulitsa 27. The *Teatr Mironova* (Map 4, ☎ 346 16 79), Bolshoy prospekt 75, Petrograd Side, on the corner of Kamennoostrovsky prospekt, has an excellent variety of Russian comedies and musicals.

CIRCUS & PUPPETS

The *St Petersburg State Circus* (Map 7, ☎ 210 46 49) has a permanent building at naberezhnaya reki Fontanki 3, half a kilometre south of the Summer Garden. There are shows on Tuesday, Wednesday and Friday at 7 pm and on Saturday and Sunday at 3 and 7 pm. It's closed Monday and Thursday. The season runs from September to June. Tickets bought here cost from US$0.60 to US$3, although the foreigners' price is US$10.

For puppets, the main venue is the *Bolshoy Teatr Kukol* (Map 7, ☎ 272 88 08), at Nekrasova ulitsa 10, with shows on Saturday and Sunday at 11.30 am and 2 pm; tickets for everyone (Russian or not, kid or not) cost about US$1. The *Teatr Kukol-Marionetok* (Map 8, ☎ 311 19 00), at Nevsky prospekt 52, has, as the name suggests, puppet and marionette shows on a varying schedule.

PUBS, BARS & BEER GARDENS

There are tons of bars in town.

City Centre

One of the coolest is the *Corner Bar* (Map 7) on the south-west corner of ulitsa Bolshaya Konyushennaya and the Moika River. It's a popular expat hang-out and a great little local – good drinks, excellent service, tables outside in summer, snacks and satellite television playing all major sporting events. There's also a good bar at the *Café Idiot* (Map 6) and a great one at the *California Grill* (Map 7), with live rock and rockabilly, and sometimes jazz (see Cafés in the Places to Eat chapter for more information).

The *Tribunal Bar* (Map 6), Senatskaya ploshchad 1, opposite the Bronze Horseman, was a great and fun place before they went for the down and dirty crowd – they started dressing their waitresses in next to nothing and advertising the place with them covered in whipped cream and chocolate sauce. Friends (male ones) say it's still a great place to hang out. Right next door there's a cool *Billiards Bar*, with American and Russian pool tables and beer.

A St Petersburg Pub Crawl

St Petersburg's pub scene has a decidedly 'British Isles' tone, with Irish and English pubs holding the most prominent positions in expats' hearts. There are a couple of other noteworthy entries: the Belgians have been making great inroads with beer distribution if not actual pub management; and the Swedes over at the Grand Hotel Europe have run one of the most successful of St Petersburg pubs with Sadko's since the place re-opened in late 1991.

Because of the far-flung nature of the pub crawl, taxis and the metro play a key role in getting from some pubs to others. Once you're in the centre, you can easily walk between places. Purists: while beer from many nations is the focus here, all the following places serve Russian vodka. For drivers and other non-drinkers, there is a full line of soft drinks, coffee, tea and fruit juices. If you skip the nightclub, you can get away with all this for around US$50.

The Brits

While the *London Club* (Map 4) aspires to what sounds to me the worst of all worlds – namely British-Russian cuisine (overboiled meat and underdone toast I guess) – it's kind of fun. It's got the standard doorman in Beefeater get-up, a model of Big Ben inside and over 100 kinds of beer, billiards, live music and a dance floor. It's inconvenient, so go here first. From metro Chyornaya Rechka, walk north about 200m across the canal (Chyornaya rechka, or 'Black River'), then turn right and the very comfortable, convincingly English pub is 400m ahead, at naberezhnaya Chyornaya rechka 41 on the corner of ulitsa Grafova.

The Belgians

Finish up your pint and walk back to metro Chyornaya Rechka; take the metro two stops towards the centre to Gorkovskaya station. Across the street is the *Grand Café Antwerpen* (Map 5). It's really a restaurant, but it does have a very nice and very chic bar: turn right as you enter, bear left and the bar is near the back. Service is repugnant, but the reason you're here is the draft Belgian beer and bottles of Duvell – don't linger too long (you may notice that no-one else does).

The Fighting Irish: Part One

The battle of the Irish pubs has been raging for a while now and no expat is neutral on the subject. The relative newcomer, the *Shamrock* (Map 6), is a short taxi ride from metro Gorkovskaya at Teatralnaya ploshchad, perfectly located just across the street from the Mariinsky Theatre. Here, in this cosy, vault-ceilinged hang-out, you can enjoy a pint of Guinness. Remember that taste: Shamrock management claims that their Black Stuff comes direct from Dublin, while 'other' pubs use 'English muck'. Don't be put off by these allegations; that 'other' pub would be Mollies Irish Bar which is a great and popular place (see later for directions).

Around the corner on Galernaya ulitsa, next door to Bistro Le Francais (which also has a pleasant bar; see the Places to Eat chapter), is the *Krokodil Klub* (Map 6), packed with stuffed iguanas, terracotta and serving good wines and beer.

After I researched, the enormous *Tinkoff Restaurant* (☎ 314 84 85) opened at ulitsa Plekhanova, just south of Nevsky prospekt. Expat friends tell me it's a great place with good microbrewed beers (wheat, pilsener and others) and pizzas. There are few goons and lots of beautiful people.

Mollies Irish Bar (Map 7, ☎ 319 97 68), Rubinshteyna ulitsa 36, first brought the Black Stuff to the city on the Neva: draught

The Swedes
From Teatralnaya ploshchad, get a taxi to the south-west corner of ulitsa Bolshaya Konyushennaya and the Moyka River, where the *Corner Bar* (Map 7) has fast become a great hang-out. Have a beer here, then walk on over to the Grand Hotel Europe, where at the corner of Mikhailovskaya and Nevsky prospekt is a staple of St Petersburg nightlife, *Sadko's* (Map 8). There's live music and lots of young people – foreign and Russian, businesspeople and students. It's also probably a good idea to get some protein at this point; the food here is good although it gets a bit pricey. Service is very friendly.

Good Old-Fashioned Russians
Two great Russian bars are very close by at Apraksin Dvor 14, behind Gostiny Dvor, and it's good to get here early as they close at 11 pm. *Money Honey Saloon*, downstairs, does live rock and rockabilly and *City Club*, upstairs, has a good dance floor and pool tables (both Map 7).

The Finns
What would drinking in Russia be without Finns? A lot less crowded for one thing. From metro Mayakovskaya, cross Nevsky prospekt and turn left (west) back towards the Admiralty. Behind No 86, almost directly opposite the Sheraton Nevskij Palace Hotel, is a courtyard *Beer Garden* (Map 8); it's a lovely place to sit on a summer evening, but don't drink too much of that Lapin Kulta – it's given everyone I know a headache. They also do grilled shashlyk.

The Irish Again
Cross Nevsky, turn right and make your second left onto Rubinshteyna ulitsa. Two and a half long blocks down on the left-hand side of the street is *Mollies Irish Bar* (Map 7), a bastion of civility and civilisation. It's worth hanging out here for a while – it was once the city's most popular watering hole, and there's a happy hour (hours change) when drinks are half-price. That's when I ran into Ireland's Minister of Education. Smart lady.

Still Standing?
If you're still on your feet you should probably be using them, so from Mollies turn right onto Rubinshteyna back towards Nevsky prospekt. Almost directly across the street is your final destination, *Domenico's* (Map 8), one of St Petersburg's most popular nightclubs. The place gets packed on weekend nights, and as the evening progresses it's easy to forget where you are. If you do get lost, the HI St Petersburg Hostel, Sheraton Nevskij Palace Hotel and Grand Hotel Europe are very close by and would be happy to set you up with a bed for the night.

Guinness pints are US$5 and lagers US$4. It's still popular for its classic pub décor and friendly service. It serves pub food – sandwiches for about US$6 to US$8, soups for US$4. You never know who might turn up – one night I met Ireland's Minister of Education!

The cool and cavernous *Shamrock* (Map 6, ☎ 219 46 25), ulitsa Dekabristov 27, opposite the Mariinsky Theatre, is another excellent Irish pub with a great atmosphere and similar prices to Mollies. Just down the street is the *Klub*, which has American pool tables.

Fish Fabrique (Map 8), in a flat on the 4th floor at ulitsa Pushkinskaya 10, gets an interesting crowd of artists and Berlin-loving types; pre-faded splendour, some live music and theme nights.

The Beer Garden (Map 8), behind Afrodite restaurant (Nevsky prospekt 86), is in a secluded courtyard with music, beer and snacks.

If you're wondering how the *John Bull Pub* (Map 8), Nevsky prospekt 79 near metro Mayakovskaya, managed to get an entire English pub to St Petersburg, the answer is: on a truck. The whole kit and caboodle. Thankfully, they don't only serve John Bull – you can get Guinness and other beers as well and it's a fun place to sit after a long day of walking up and down Nevsky.

On the weekend, *Sadko's* (☎ 329 60 00) huge bar gets packed, people generally have a great time and one can glean why it's one of the most popular places in town. It's located inside the Grand Hotel Europe (Map 8) and has live bands on Friday and Saturday nights, a huge selection of booze and beer, snacks, and full meals in the adjacent restaurant.

The *Marine Bar* (☎ 274 86 89) at the US Consulate (Map 5), ulitsa Furshtadtskaya 15, isn't really open to the public, but it does have movie nights, barbecues, Friday night get-togethers etc that are open to citizens of most countries by invitation only. The bar itself is kind of cool, and there's also a pool table. You'll have to check at the consulate to see if anything's happening, and you will need to be invited by one of the marines – don't just show up.

Warsteiner Forum (Map 8), on ploshchad Vosstania, isn't very popular, but it's a nice place with good German beer and schnitzel. Beers cost about US$5, and the schnitzel is US$12; its 'peasant breakfast' (sausage, eggs, toast) is US$7, and a plate of sausages is a mean US$9. It's open from noon to 2 am.

The Bierstube in the Sheraton Nevskij Palace Hotel (Map 8) is pretty much what you'd expect: waitresses in dirndl, an Austrian setting, snacks and good but expensive beer. Draughts (0.5L) are US$6. It's open from 10 am (for those in need of a *Frühschoppen*) to 11 pm.

The Grand Hotel Europe's *Lobby Bar* (Map 8) is a very civilised place, best visited if you have an expense account. It has beer for US$7 to US$10 a bottle, and mixed drinks get expensive! It also serves coffee, espresso and cappuccino. There's piano entertainment in the evenings, and you can walk through the archway into the library to read a newspaper.

On any given night, *Chayka* (Map 8), naberezhnaya kanala Griboedova 14, near the corner of Nevsky prospekt, is filled with foreign businesspeople, German tour groups singing *Schunkellieder* and swarms of prostitutes who'll sidle up to you at the bar and say something coolly seductive like, 'I want peanuts. Buy me beer.' Worth avoiding if you're picking up the tab.

There are several *beer gardens* in the centre: one opposite the Grand Hotel Europe, between the former Town Duma and Gostiny Dvor, and one in front of the Lutheran church. Both have draught and bottled beers for about US$4 and US$2.50, respectively.

Chyornaya Rechka

London Club (Map 4) is a really cool place, with over 100 kinds of beer, billiards, live music and a dance floor – see the boxed text 'A St Petersburg Pub Crawl' for more information. Teeny *Xali Gali* (Map 3), Lenskoe Shossee 15, one block west of metro Chyornaya Rechka, has a biker-bar atmosphere and attitude, topless waitresses and huge crowds of tourists and locals. Conveniently, there's a sex-toy shop across the street.

Petrograd Side

See the boxed text 'A St Petersburg Pub Crawl' for more information on *Grand Café Antwerpen* (Map 5), a restaurant with a bar serving good Belgian beer.

A Final Word on Beer

The queues you see early in the morning at places around town – at the corner of naberezhnaya reki Fontanki and ploshchad Lomonosova, for example – are folks waiting to fill up their jars at *The Odd Stray Beer Cart*, a dying but fine tradition that

Metro station statue

NICK SELBY

Triptych part 1: 'Glory to the Soviet People'

NICK SELBY

Triptych part 2: Middle of square

NICK SELBY

Triptych part 3: 'If You Smell Gas, Dial 09!'

The Grand Cascade, Petrodvorets

The Grand Palace, Petrodvorets

SS Peter & Paul Cathedral

Tree-lined lane, Petrodvorets

The Grand Cascade, Petrodvorets

should be experienced at least once during a stay in St Petersburg. The beer is fresh and usually ... well, it won't kill you. Bring your own jar.

NIGHTCLUBS & DISCOS

Check the *St Petersburg Times* and *Pulse* for listings as they both list all clubs and discos in town – with everything changing so rapidly in the city, there will be new places, and some closures, by the time you read this.

The Western influence has taken its toll here; most new clubs are decidedly Western, and many import DJs from cities renowned for their nightlife – Paris and New York come to mind – and sometimes from more unlikely places like Ouagodougou, Lagos and London. St Petersburg's raves are all-night affairs replete with laser shows, naked people, the works, usually in a converted theatre or sporting complex, where thousands of young Russians and a smattering of foreigners party to acid-house and trance. There's usually a high enough door fee to keep the riffraff out. Check the radio for ads or ask Russian friends. Most nightclubs charge a small entry fee, between US$5 and US$10, but many are free.

There's good Latin music at *Marstall* (Map 8), naberezhnaya kanala Griboedova 5, from Monday to Thursday, and 1970s and 80s music on the weekends. If topless dancers slinking on poles above your head bother you, then it's best to leave before they start at around 11 pm. Needless to say, it's popular with foreign men, but fun for all before 11 pm. No charge for foreigners.

Domenico's (Map 8), Nevsky prospekt 70, between the Fontanka River and Rubin-shteyna ulitsa, is a classy disco and nightclub popular with expats and Russians alike.

City Club (Map 7), Apraksin Dvor 14, right upstairs from Money Honey Saloon (see the boxed text 'A St Petersburg Pub Crawl'), has a good dance floor and pool tables. The only problem is it has to close at 11 pm because of its residential location.

Valhall (Map 8), Nevsky prospekt 22/24, a Viking-theme bar, is a trip. Staff are dressed in bad opera costumes, and there's live

blues, rockabilly and disco after midnight. It has a good beer-drinking atmosphere.

Speaking of theme bars, are you a Beatles fan? Well, Beatles lunatic? Then head for *Liverpool* (Map 8), ulitsa Mayakovskogo 16, a basement place that plays only Fab Four, is packed with Beatles memorabilia and features a young, heavily smoking crowd. Fun for a while.

Billing itself as an art bar, *Manhattan Club* (Map 7), naberezhnaya reki Fontanki 90, has good live blues and is a totally relaxed, attitude-free place to hang out. You can dance how you want, act how you want, but it sometimes gets a little too packed with Nouveaux Bohemian Wannabes.

The cavernous *Metro Club* (Map 7), Ligovsky prospekt 174, is hugely popular with techno-loving students (and non-students). Flash your ISIC card and receive a 10% discount on the entrance fee.

Though the slapstick comedy at the *Chaplin Club* (Map 5), ulitsa Chaykovsko-go 59, is mainly in Russian, foreigners will still understand a lot of it – it's even worth the US$7 cover fee.

Nevsky Melody (Map 5) would be more popular if it were closer to the centre; it's out on Sverdlovskaya naberezhnaya, opposite the Smolny Cathedral and across the Bolshoy Okhtinsky bridge. If you don't mind shelling out a lot, it's an interesting place to spend an evening and they also give ISIC discounts! It has a disco downstairs, along with a casino, and there are erotic shows at about 1 am. It's open from 10 pm to 4 or 5 am.

And while we're out in the middle of nowhere, *Candyman* (Map 3, ☎ 521 14 10), Kosygina prospekt 17, is an astonishingly popular disco considering its inconvenient location and heavy mafia scene. But there's good top-40 dance music and sometimes top Russian acts performing live, so check what's on when you're here in any of the listings magazines. From metro Ladozhskaya take bus No 21 or trolleybus No 22 two stops.

Gay & Lesbian

Pickings are thin, but improving all the time, though there's still no lesbian bar in town.

Back rooms, called *chyornaya komnata* (black room), are not very common, and are frowned upon by gay-rights activists because their legality is iffy at best.

69 Club (Map 6, ☎ 259 51 63), 2-ya Krasnoarmeyskaya ulitsa 6, is the city's premiere gay nightclub, complete with drag queens and striptease shows from 2 am – free entry.

Jungle (Map 4), ulitsa Blokhina 8, Petrograd Side, is another gay disco, with house and techno music and a wild crowd.

Two other gay places in town include **The Mayak** (Map 6), ulitsa Galernaya 33, a weekend disco with a US$6 entry fee; and the very small **U Pegas** (Map 5) on ulitsa Mokhovaya 15.

ROCK VENUES

St Petersburg can lay a strong claim to being the Russian rock capital, having produced in the 1980s top bands like Akvarium, Alisa, Kino, DDT, AVIA, Televizor and Populyarnaya Mekhanika. And now that the government is no longer involved in the creative process, the rock scene is far less bleak than it used to be. It's not Amsterdam or London yet, but there are increasingly more venues in which to let off steam. Check the *St Petersburg Times* or *Pulse* for listings of who's in town. And see the Pubs, Bars & Beer Gardens and Discos & Nightclubs sections earlier for venues.

JAZZ VENUES

The excellent **JFC Jazz Club** (Map 5), Shpalernaya ulitsa 33, is probably the best in the city. A little New York-style jazz club, it's got a fun crowd, lot of expats, great beer and atmosphere, and really good jazz bands from Russia and around the world. There's also blues on some nights.

The famous **Jazz Philharmonic Hall** (Map 7), Zagorodny prospekt 27, has two bands – a straight jazz and a Dixieland – plus guests doing mainstream and modern jazz, all hosted by co-founder David Goloshchyokin, who runs about being seen. It's a 10 minute walk to the south-west of metro Dostoevskaya.

Also in that neighbourhood, the clubbier **Kvadrat Jazz Club** (Map 7), Pravdy ulitsa 10, does traditional and mainstream jazz. From metro Dostoevskaya, head for Bolshaya Moskovskaya and take it south-west until it turns into Pravdy.

There's more live jazz on weekends at **Café Idiot** (Map 6), naberezhnaya reki Moyki 82, and occasionally at the **California Grill** (Map 7), Nevsky prospekt 176.

CINEMA & VIDEO

Most of the cinemas in St Petersburg play US or other foreign movies that have been heinously translated and dubbed using a single male voice (the man is called a *lektor*) for all characters, which is especially amusing during love scenes. Cinemas charge about US$1 for entry and films run continuously from about 1 to 10 pm. One great exception to the lektor rule is the **Crystal Palace** (Map 8, ☎ 272 23 82), Nevsky prospekt 72, which has regular screenings of recent-ish foreign films in the original language for around US$5 – check the *St Petersburg Times* for details.

When you tire of trying to pick out the English from beneath the lektor's voice, you can either attend a video screening or rent an English-language video.

The HI St Petersburg hostel screens free movies nightly. Westpost (see Post in the Facts for the Visitor chapter) rents combination VCR/TVs for US$25 for a weekend, US$45 a week, and has a selection of over 1100 videos in English. Membership costs US$10 and tape rentals run from US$2 to US$3 daily.

GAMBLING

Casinos have popped up all over town in the past few years. Mainly these are sleazeball magnets, but there are a couple of more civilised places where you can try your luck (though I think that staying home and flushing dollar bills down the toilet one at a time is just as exciting and perhaps less expensive). Casinos advertise in all the local tourist information sheets and the *St Petersburg Times*.

SPECTATOR SPORTS

Zenit, St Petersburg's rather pathetic football team, loses consistently to all comers at the 100,000-seat *Kirov Stadium* (Map 4), located at the western end of Krestovsky Island. If you do go, consider that the team's wretched state is one price paid for the collapse of the Soviet Union: they used to be better, but at the fall of the Iron Curtain, all the good players headed west.

Shopping

No-one comes here specifically for the shopping, but a lot of people leave with their wallets a lot lighter, now that St Petersburg has almost everything you'd want – often cheaper than at home.

Most St Petersburg shops are open from 11 am to 7 or 8 pm, but Western-style shops, *beryozki* (the network of privatised shops which were operated by Intourist as hard-currency-only enterprises under the Soviets) and department stores give you an extra hour or two at both ends. Virtually everything shuts for lunch from 2 to 3 pm and some places also close all day Sunday.

WHAT TO BUY
Souvenirs

Souvenir stands set up shop around all major tourist attractions, especially at the Hermitage and in front of the Peter & Paul Fortress. If you're into *matryoshka* dolls, military hats and Russian-language T-shirts and the like, the best place to buy them is at the Souvenir Fair (Map 7) just north and across the canal from the Church of the Resurrection of Christ. Prices are reasonable, the selection is enormous and the hawks speak perfect English. The latest matryoshka dolls depict the usual – Yeltsin, Gorbachev, Clinton – and some new twists: Spike Lee, Michael Jordan, Arantxa Sanchez Vicario ... you name it.

Arts & Antiques

There are dozens of art and antique shops throughout the city, but only some of them – generally the more expensive ones – will walk you through the customs clearing procedures. See the Customs section in the Facts for the Visitor chapter for complete details on what you can take out of the country and how to do it.

Gallery Central in St Petersburg is ulitsa Pushkinskaya 10 (Map 8), where heaps of galleries share a building with Timur Novikov's Museum of the New Academy of Fine Arts (☎ 315 28 32). The galleries have everything from paintings and sculpture to digital works, and usually you'll see lots of deep people stoned out of their brains and philosophising against a backdrop of some of the best art in Russia today. (See Arts in the Facts About St Petersburg chapter for more background information.)

Palitra (Map 7, ☎ 277 12 16) is a gallery owned and operated by St Petersburg artists. It's at the end of Stary Nevsky, at No 166, and is open Tuesday to Saturday from 11 am to 7 pm. It also serves coffee.

There's modern art for sale at Staraya Derevnaya restaurant and at Café Idiot – see the Places to Eat chapter for more information.

The Center of Graphic Arts at the Union of Artists (Map 6, ☎ 224 06 22) displays some excellent artworks, though prices here are higher and the artists give a cut to the union. It's at ulitsa Bolshaya Morskaya 38, near Isaakilevskaya ploshchad, and is open Tuesday to Sunday from 1 to 7 pm.

Ananov at the Grand Hotel Europe (Map 8, ☎ 329 60 00) has that Fabergé egg you've been planning to buy to add elegance to the study; its prices are high enough to ensure that you'll have no problems clearing customs on the way out. It's open from 11 am to 8 pm.

There's an artists' market for tourists on both sides of Nevsky prospekt, near the Nevsky Prospekt metro station entrance at ulitsa Mikhailovskaya. On the southern side of the street portrait artists sit beneath the arches. Opposite, the space just west of the Grand Hotel Europe's Sadko's restaurant is reserved for 'painting' and other locally produced 'art'.

Na Liteynom antiquarian bookshop (Map 8, ☎ 275 38 73), in the courtyard at Liteyny prospekt 61, has a good selection of old books, as well as a small antique collection. It's open daily except Sunday from 11 am to 7 pm.

China

There are great deals on fine china at the Lomonosova China Factory (Lomonosova Farforvy Zavod, Map 3), prospekt Obukhovskoy oborodny 151, open Monday to Saturday from 10 am to 7 pm. In the little factory outlet shop, you can choose anything from the company catalogue at prices lower than in the department stores. I saw teapots for US$7, serving dishes for about US$15 and an absolutely lovely set of four plates for about US$50. Take a Line 4 metro to Lomonosovskaya metro; from here turn left (east), walk under the bridge to the embankment then left (north) – the factory's ahead. The shop is inside the main door and to the right, not around the corner on the embankment as the sign outside would seem to indicate.

Ninja Stuff

Swords, guns, knives and martial arts equipment? Well, if you're at Springtime Schwarma Bistro it couldn't hurt to walk two doors down to ulitsa Nekrasova 37 to peep inside Soldat Udachi (Map 7), which sells all that and more.

Books

Café Idiot (see the Places to Eat chapter) has shelves and shelves of books for purchasing or reading there. So far there are no real Western-style bookshops, but the Russian-run stores are getting better all the time. Start at Dom Knigi (Map 8), the biggest bookshop in town, which has some books in Western languages plus books on Russian-language courses, science and engineering, school texts and, upstairs, maps and postcards. It's on the corner of naberezhnaya kanala Griboedova and Nevsky prospekt in the pre-Revolutionary St Petersburg headquarters of the Singer Sewing Machine company.

Grouped near the corner of Nevsky prospekt and ulitsa Bolshaya Morskaya you'll find four bookshops facing each other. Iskusstv, on the south-west corner, is tiny but has a good collection of art books. Of the four, the one next door to Iskusstv is the cheapest, and it features some Western-

language books, Euro-Cart maps and some stationery. It's also got a tacky souvenir shop. Across Nevsky and west of the corner, the art bookshop is pretty much a rip-off, while on the eastern side, Staraya Knigi has a good collection of old books (including, perhaps, some second-hand novels in English) and other ... er ... old stuff.

Nevsky prospekt is lined from top to bottom with smaller book and map shops (there's another good one at Nevsky prospekt 141), and there are various others around the city. Pedestrian subways are rife with book-stalls.

The HI St Petersburg Hostel sells internationally and locally produced travel guides, including Lonely Planet guides.

Music & Video Cassettes

Musik Shock is a high-quality chain of CD shops selling licensed copies of international pop, rock, jazz and classical music, and a huge selection of up-to-date Russian music as well; the most central branch is at ulitsa Vosstania 13 (Map 8).

Copyright? Huh? Russia is the world's largest market for bootlegged music (that's right, bigger than Asia), and you can find bootlegged music cassettes and both bootlegged and licensed CDs at kiosks around the city. Usually labelled in Russian or bad English, the tapes are of varying quality.

Mir Muzika (Map 5) at ulitsa Furshtadtskaya 42 has a good selection of CDs at US prices (about US$7 to US$12).

Russians have been ahead of the curve in their adherence to ABBA, Tom Jones and the meaningful ballads of Mr Julio Iglesias, and you'll find these kitschy treasures around town, priced from US$8 to US$15; Melodia (Map 4, ☎ 232 11 39) is still around at Bolshoy prospekt 47 (Petrograd Side), and stocks CDs and LPs of mainly Russian musicians. Russian CDs are US$10; CDs by Western artists US$12 to US$15; LPs US$1.50 to US$3.

Software

Speaking of copyright violation, the market for bootlegged computer software is huge in

St Petersburg. Bootlegged software is illegal and Lonely Planet recommends that you do not buy it.

WHERE TO SHOP
Nevsky Prospekt

Russia's most famous avenue, Nevsky prospekt, is St Petersburg's grandest shopping street; as things are renovated and restored and new businesses open and old ones shape up, the strip between the Admiralty and Moscow Station is rapidly becoming the chic thoroughfare it was at the turn of the 20th century.

There are a couple of good pharmacies along Nevsky prospekt, and other shops along Nevsky include:

Art Books, No 20, sells maps and has an exchange office.
Nike, No 34
Reebok, No 75
Barbie, No 63, has a Birthday Fun Barbie for US$66, and a relatively cheap Miami Ken for US$10.50, as well as toys, Lego etc.
Original Levi's, No 102, has just that, at Western European prices.
Grafika T, above Passazh, has absolutely everything in office supplies.
Yves Rocher, No 61, sells perfumes and cosmetics.
Wella, No 54, offers hair-care products and swish hairdressers.

Western Speciality Shops

Throughout the city, Western-owned shops (or shops appearing to be Western) pop up now and then, the most obvious examples being those along Nevsky prospekt. There are many more opening every day: Bally's mind-blowingly expensive accessories and trinkets shop (sports jacket – US$500), at Bolshoy prospekt 46 (Petrograd Side), comes to mind. Nina Ricci does French cosmetics at Liteyny prospekt 24; Diesel and Marco Pizzo at the Petrogradskaya metro sell, respectively, jeans, sweaters and casual wear and (decent) shoes; and just across the Karpovka, Rifle Jeans sells a great selection of out-of-season stock.

There's a 24 hour Super Babylon food shop at Maly prospekt 16.

Department Stores

The city is dotted with department stores; service and supplies are better than ever and it's great fun to join the thronging crowds in the big ones. Gostiny Dvor (Map 8) on Nevsky prospekt between ulitsa Dumskaya and Sadovaya ulitsa is St Petersburg's answer to Moscow's GUM, though its selection and service just aren't up to those of its big brother across the street, Passazh (Map 8). Both of these stores are covered in the Things to See & Do chapter.

DLT (Map 8) at Bolshaya Konyushennaya ulitsa 21/23 began as a children's department store but now has a great supply of everything. It's still the best place to start looking for imported and Russian-made toys and games, children's clothing etc. It also has a great selection of sporting goods at the back of the store.

Dom Mod (Map 4), Kamennoostrovsky prospekt 37 above the Petrogradskaya metro station, is a newly renovated collection of small but flash shops selling fashions and accessories.

All the department stores in the city have money-changing offices, and many let out space to Western firms like Wrangler and Littlewoods, which sell a variety of Western goods (though, usually, not the best).

Kiosk Cities

Throughout the city, usually (though not always) adjacent to metro stations, dozens of kiosks group en masse selling generally the same stuff – counterfeit clothing from China, Finnish juice drinks, Western beer, cheap vodka, blue liquors, bootleg video cassettes and Western cigarettes (the average price for a pack of 20 Marlboro or Winston in 1998 was US$1.20, L&M US$0.85). Some, like the ones near Chernyshevskaya, Ploshchad Muzhestva and Ploshchad Vosstania metros, are reliable suppliers of staple items, music cassettes and other goods, while others, like the one at metro Primorskaya, are just a blight on the landscape. The City of St Petersburg has passed regulations forcing kiosks to conform to aesthetic standards, so the kiosk cities are getting marginally prettier.

Sennaya ploshchad is the most bustling marketplace in the centre of the city, and there are opportunities to buy everything from bootleg CDs and a wonderful selection of flowers, fruits and vegies to doing business with the highly trustworthy gents wearing signs that say they offer gold and icons.

Be *extremely* careful when buying alcohol in kiosks: make certain that the cap is an untampered screw-top (never the foil seal), and taste carefully before taking a full drink; err on the side of caution.

Markets

Markets are mainly for food, but the Kondratevsky fur market (see, unfortunately, the Places to Eat chapter) has some good buys. Always check the inside for mismatched fur, poor stitching etc.

Excursions

Between 25 and 45km from central St Petersburg lie five splendid old tsarist palaces surrounded by lovely parks, all fine outings from the city. The time to see Petrodvorets (`petradvahr-YETS'`), also known as Petergof, on the coast is in the summer, when its famous fountains are flowing and it can be reached by hydrofoil from St Petersburg. Pushkin has another glorious palace, and Pavlovsk has probably the loveliest park. These last two, lying close together south of the city, can be combined in one trip. Then there's Lomonosov (formerly known as Oranienbaum), beyond Petrodvorets and Gatchina, further south than Pushkin and Pavlovsk. All except Lomonosov suffered varying degrees of damage in WWII and some are still being restored.

All of these obscenely lavish estates are open to the public and easily accessible by inexpensive public transport. The tours that leave from in front of the Kazan Cathedral on Nevsky prospekt are good; book your tickets with the person with the megaphone.

Tickets can also be booked at the excursion booth – use Davran Travel Agency – just outside the west end of Gostiny Dvor on ulitsa Dumskaya. They charge between US$6.50 and US$15 for a tour of Novgorod, Petrodvorets, Pushkin/Pavlovsk, Kronstadt or Lomonosov, including transport.

The most frequently visited places are Petrodvorets, Pushkin and Pavlovsk. It's a good idea to take your own snacks to the palaces; most of them only have minimal (none, in the case of Lomonosov) offerings, though Petrodvorets has a couple of good cafés.

For longer hauls, visitors to Petrozavodsk can get a quick ferry to the open-air museum on Kizhi Island, featuring the dazzling 220-gabled Cathedral of the Transfiguration. And an overnight trip to the monastery and pleasant little town at Valaam can make a very rewarding experience that not many take the time to enjoy.

PETRODVORETS (Petergof)
ПЕТРОДВОРЕЦ (Петергоф)

Peter the Great had a cabin 29km west of St Petersburg on the Gulf of Finland, to oversee construction of his Kronstadt naval base. He liked it so much there that he built a villa, Monplaisir, and then a whole series of palaces across an estate originally called Petergof (a direct Russian transliteration of the German 'Peterhof', meaning Peter's Court). From 1944 the Soviets called the place Petrodvorets (Peter's Palace), and attempts from 1992 to rename it Petergof have met with difficulties – Russians are as likely to call it the former as the latter, though most signs now say Petergof.

Whatever you call it, it's set within a spectacular ensemble of gravity-powered fountains that are now the site's main attraction. This lavish 'Russian Versailles' is probably the most impressive of St Petersburg's suburban palaces, and certainly the most popular.

Petrodvorets was completely trashed by the Germans in WWII and is largely a reconstruction from photos, drawings and anecdotes.

There will almost always be something closed while you are there because, inexplicably, each site has its own closing days: Grand Palace, Monday and the last Tuesday of the month; Marly, Tuesday and last Wednesday; Monplaisir, Hermitage and Catherine Building, Wednesday and last Thursday; Cottage, Friday and last Thursday. The estate is open from 9 am to 10 pm daily, while the museums are open from 11 am to 8 pm from the end of May to the end of September. The Lower Park and Alexandria Park are open every day.

Because of the confounded opening hours, it's only possible to take in all the museums and palaces in a single day during weekends, when, naturally, the place is swarming with visitors. All the attractions charge separate admissions, and some will hit you for a small photo or video fee (usually US$2/5), but I got away without paying last time. Admission to the grounds is payable at the cash booth on the jetty or outside the gate leading to the Grand Cascade.

Grand Cascade

The uncontested centrepiece is the Grand Cascade and Water Avenue, a symphony of fountains and canals partly engineered by Peter himself. The central statue of **Samson** tearing open a lion's jaws celebrates, as so many things in St Petersburg do, Peter's victory over the Swedes. All the fountains (over 140 of them) run on gravity-pressured water.

Other fountains are functional, and the trick fountains triggered by hidden switches (hidden, that is, by hordes of kids jumping on them) are designed to squirt passers-by. Normally the fountains play from 11 am to 8 pm daily from May to September.

Grand Palace

Between the cascade and the formal Upper Garden is the Bolshoy dvorets (Grand Palace). Peter's modest project, finished just before his death, was grossly enlarged by Rastrelli for Empress Elizabeth and later redecorated for Catherine the Great. It's now a vast museum of lavish rooms and galleries – a monument above all to the craft of reconstruction (which is still going on). Anything not nailed down was removed and hidden before the Germans arrived, so the paintings, furniture and chandeliers are original.

Highlights include the **Chesma Hall**, full of huge paintings, all by the same German artist, of Russia's destruction of the Turkish fleet at Çesma in 1770. Of some 20 rooms, the last, without a trace of Catherine, is the finest – Peter's simple, beautiful study, apparently the only room to survive the Germans. It has 14 fantastic carved-wood panels, of which six reconstructions (in lighter wood) are no less impressive; each took 1½ years to do. Peter the Great still looks like the tsar with the best taste.

This palace should not be missed and is best viewed with a guide. You'll need to join a tour group to enter (US$4.50/2.25 for foreigners/students, US$1.60/0.75 for Russians – but I got the Russian price just by asking for '*odin bilet, pazhalsta*' – 'one ticket, please'). Tickets are sold inside, near the lobby where you pick up your *tapochki* (slippers you wear over your shoes to avoid damaging the wooden floors).

Monplaisir

Peter's outwardly more humble villa, with study and galleries facing the sea, remained his favourite and it's not hard to see why: wood-panelled, snug and elegant, peaceful even when there's a crowd – which there used to be all the time, what with Peter's mandatory partying (`misbehaving' guests were required to gulp down huge quantities of wine). The main hall has marble floors and a richly painted ceiling; the kitchen is Dutch style, a little study is Chinese. Admission for foreigners/Russians is US$3/0.75.

To the left is an annexe called the Catherine Building because Catherine the Great was living here – establishing an alibi? – when her husband Peter III was overthrown. Catherine Building admission is US$3/0.75. Tickets are sold at the east side of the building.

Lower Park & Other Pavilions

Along the gulf is the Lower Park, with more fountains big and small, elegant and silly (watch out for more trick fountains), and more pavilions.

Near the shore, and finished soon after the Grand Palace, is a two-storey pink-and-white box called the **Hermitage**, which features the ultimate in private dining on the second floor. Special elevators hoist a fully laid table into the imperial presence, thereby eliminating any hindrance by servants. The elevators are circular and directly in front of each diner, whose plate would be lowered, replenished and replaced. Admission for foreigners/Russians is US$2/0.50.

Further west is **Marly**, another of Peter's mini-palaces and guesthouses. To the east an old **Orangery** – which would appear to be a rest home for Russian tourists – houses the Historical Museum of Wax Figures, containing 49 figures of big-wigged Russians (from Peter I to Nicholas II) from the 18th and 19th centuries. Admission to the museum is US$2/0.50. Get tickets in the small shack outside. It's open daily from 11 am to 6 pm.

Petergof Palace Pharmacy

This peculiar tourist attraction is a renovated old-style apothecary with drawers full of medicinal plants – it looks (and smells) like the real thing. The staff will whip up a herb drink for you, and if your Russian's good enough you can talk to them about your ingrown whatsit. They've also got a fair selection of Western remedies, like Panadol. The Pharmacy is open from 8 am to 8 pm (closed Saturday). It's just east of the Upper Garden.

Alexandria Park

Even on summer weekends, the rambling, overgrown Alexandria Park is peaceful and empty, and ideal for a leisurely walk. It was built for Tsar Nicholas I (and named after his tsarina) and it looks like his heart wasn't in his royal work. Besides a mock-Gothic chapel, its diversions include the **Farmer's Palace** (1831), which vaguely resembles a stone farmstead and is currently in ruins, and the **Cottage** (1829), which is modelled on an English country cottage.

Now a museum, the Cottage's rooms – neo-Gothic, rococo or Art Nouveau depending on later renovations – are full of imperial bric-a-brac and hundreds of works by minor Russian artists. In the boudoir is a clock with 66 faces, one for each pre-1917 province.

On the way back, what looks like a Gothic college campus was once the imperial stables and is now a retirement home (for humans, we suspect).

Petrodvorets Town

Outside the grounds is Petrodvorets town. Don't overlook the five-domed **SS Peter & Paul Cathedral** across the road, built in traditional style at the turn of the century. If you're around at 9.45 am and 4.45 pm you'll hear the church bells play a lovely tune. The cathedral holds evening services at 5 pm, and closes at 6 or 7 pm except on holidays, when night services are held.

Six kilometres east of Petrodvorets is **Strelna**, another estate with parklands and two palaces built for Peter (later enlarged for Empress Elizabeth by Rastrelli).

Places to Eat

Just across from the pharmacy, the *Kafe Trapeza* is a nice, cosy place doing veal with fried potatoes and chicken Kiev for about US$6. The *Galereya Kafe*, in the back of the Grand Palace, is a stylish place serving very good salads and light lunches from US$2 to US$4, and beer for about US$2. It's open from 10 am to 8 pm (closed Monday). The round pavilion near the boat landing has an adequate café, gril-bar and canteen, open from noon to 6 pm (closed Saturday).

Getting There & Away

Suburban trains take 40 minutes from Baltic Station to Novy Petrodvorets (not Stary Petrodvorets), departing every 30 to 60 minutes until early evening. Tickets are less than US$0.50. From Novy Petrodvorets Station, take any bus but No 357 to the fifth stop (the fourth is a church), which takes about 10 minutes; ask for '*fontana*'. As you enter, arrowed signs direct you to the lower park, Monplaisir, Marly and the booking office.

You can avoid the queues by taking a coach tour, but be sure to check what you'll see besides the grounds. An individual excursion with guide and rental car is a complete waste of money.

By road it's about an hour from St Petersburg; there's plenty of street parking outside the grounds. For about US$35 to US$40 you can get an official taxi to take you there, wait for you and bring you back; alternatively, you can negotiate with any other taxi for a bit more.

From May to September, a fine alternative is the *Meteor* hydrofoil from the

Hermitage Landing in front of St Petersburg's Hermitage, which goes every 20 to 30 minutes from 9.30 am to at least 7 pm. A ferry, which is much slower, leaves every 20 to 40 minutes from Morskaya pristan (Sea Landing) near Tuchkov Bridge on naberezhnaya Makarova, Vasilevsky Island. The trip takes half an hour and costs US$9, plus the park entry fee, payable on the way out from St Petersburg.

To tour the grounds with the locals, queue at the ticket kiosks and join a tour narrated in Russian.

LOMONOSOV
ЛОМОНОСОВ

While Peter was building Monplaisir, his right-hand man, Alexandr Menshikov, began his own palace, Oranienbaum, 12km farther down the coast. Menshikov never saw the finished product; following Peter's death and Menshikov's exile, the estate served briefly as a hospital and then passed to Tsar Peter III, who didn't much like ruling Russia and spent a lot of time at Oranienbaum. After doing away with him, his wife Catherine (the Great) made it her private pleasure ground.

Oranienbaum was not occupied by the Nazis. After WWII it was for some reason renamed after the scientist-poet Mikhail Lomonosov and now doubles as museum and public park, with boat rentals and carnival rides alongside the remaining buildings.

The park is open from 9 am to 10 pm all year, while the opening hours for the palace-museums vary (see below).

Things to See
Biggest of all, with semicircular galleries and lower garden, is Menshikov's **Grand Palace** (☎ 423 16 27), which is *still* mostly under restoration, though three halls are currently open to visitors (Wednesday to Monday from 11 am to 5 pm, closed Tuesday and the last Monday of the month). Admission is US$1 for foreigners, US$0.75 for Russians, US$0.50 for all students. A canal once linked the palace to the gulf. Beyond the pond is **Peterstadt**, Peter III's boxy toy palace, with

rich, uncomfortable-looking interiors and some Chinese-style lacquer-on-wood paintings. It's approached through the **Gate of Honour**, which is all that remains of a toy fortress where he amused himself drilling his soldiers.

Most worth seeing is Catherine's over-the-top **Chinese Palace**, baroque outside and extravagantly rococo inside, a private retreat designed by Italian Antonio Rinaldi with painted ceilings, fine inlaid-wood floors and walls, and decoration probably unequalled in any of the other St Petersburg palaces. The most blindingly sumptuous is the **Large Chinese Room**, designed in the 'Oriental' style of the day. The house, though restored, is not a reconstruction but the real thing. The nearby kitchen house has a small exhibition of furnishings. The Chinese Palace is open Monday and Wednesday, Thursday and Friday from 11 am to 6 pm, and Saturday and Sunday from 10 am to 6 pm (closed Tuesday and the last Monday of the month).

The building that looks like a blue-and-white wedding cake is the **Coasting-Hill Pavilion**, the launching pad for Catherine's private roller coaster, a multistorey wooden slide down which courtiers would fly on little carts or toboggans. The slide is gone but the pavilion's extravagant inner rooms are worth a look. Tickets are sold inside the main entrance (US$5 for foreigners, US$2.10 for Russians) to the Porcelain Room and the White Room.

Perhaps Lomonosov's best feature is the several kilometres of quiet paths through pine woods and sombre gardens, with relatively small crowds – a rarity on the Russian tourist trail.

Getting There & Away
The suburban train from Baltic Station to Petrodvorets continues to Lomonosov; a ticket is US$0.75. Get off at Oranienbaum-I (not II) Station, an hour from St Petersburg. From the station, walk past a church and then cross prospekt Yunogo Lenintsa to the park entrance, a small stone gatehouse by a Lenin statue.

From May to September, hydrofoils come here from the Morskaya landing at naberezhnaya Makarova (near the Hotel-ship Peterhof) and the Tuchkov Bridge on Vasilevsky Island every 30 minutes, from about 7.30 am to at least 6 pm, for US$11. The route is Morskaya, Kronstadt, Lomonosov, Morskaya.

PUSHKIN & PAVLOVSK
ПУШКИН И ПАВЛОВСК

The sumptuous palaces and big, beautiful parks at Pushkin and Pavlovsk, 25km and 29km south of St Petersburg, can be combined in a day's visit, but since they're both good places to relax, you might want to take them more slowly.

Pushkin's palaces and parks were created under Empress Elizabeth and Catherine the Great between 1744 and 1796. The centre-piece is the vast 1752-56 baroque Catherine Palace (Yekaterininsky dvorets), designed by Rastrelli and named after Elizabeth's mother, Peter the Great's second wife. Pushkin used to be called Tsarskoe Selo (Tsar's Village), then Detskoe Selo (Children's Village) after the revolution, but was renamed in 1937 after Russia's favourite poet, who once studied here. The country's first railway opened in 1837 to carry the royal family between here and St Petersburg.

Pavlovsk's park of woodland, rivers, lakes, little valleys, avenues, classical statues and temples is one of the most exquisite in Russia, while its Great Palace (Bolshoy dvorets) is a classical contrast to the Catherine Palace. Palace and park were originally designed by Charles Cameron between 1781 and 1786 on Catherine the Great's orders for her son, the future Paul I.

Information

At both places, getting into the parks and lesser exhibitions is little or no problem, but tickets for the two main palaces are zealously guarded by stern babushkas who, like their comrades in the Hermitage, can smell Reeboks at 500m: expect to pay the foreigner price (US$7/5, as opposed to US$2/0.75) unless your Russian is good.

The town of Pushkin was named after the famous writer on the 100th anniversary of his death.

Russian-language tours (lose the group and wander freely amidst the luxury) run at set times between noon and 5 pm, and tickets for these are sold from 10 am until they run out, which they may do in an hour or two on busy days. If you're keen to see the inside of a palace, you can avoid disappointment by taking one of the excursions from St Petersburg (see the introduction to this chapter) – separate trips for the two places are usually available, each lasting about four hours. You could make your own way back to the city if you wanted to stay on afterwards.

The interior of the Catherine Palace is the more sumptuous, if you have to choose between the two. Count the breasts on the ceiling and see if you come up with an even number.

The parks are open every day. The Catherine Palace is open from 11 am to 6 pm in summer and until 5 pm in winter, closed on Tuesday and the last Monday of the month. The Great Palace at Pavlovsk is open from 10 am to 5 pm and closed on Friday and the last Tuesday of the month.

Catherine Palace

As at the Winter Palace, Catherine the Great had many of Rastrelli's original interiors remodelled in classical style. Charles Cameron, reputedly an aristocratic Scot but probably a London builder's son with a flair for long-term acting, was her chief re-designer. The palace was used in varying degrees by different tsars until 1917, but was ruined by the Germans in WWII. So far, most of Rastrelli's wonderful exterior and 20-odd rooms of the interior, including the Amber Room, have been restored with no mean skill – compare the results with the photographs of the devastation left by the Germans and you will be suitably impressed. The palace is 300m long, with the golden domes of its **chapel** rising at its northern end, and outbuildings enclosing a courtyard on its western side. The visitors' entrance and ticket office are in the middle of the courtyard side.

All the rooms on show are upstairs. Visits normally start with the white State Staircase, an 1860 addition. South of here, only two rooms, both by Rastrelli, have been restored: the Gentlemen-in-Waiting's Dining Room (Kavalerskaya stolovaya) and, beyond, the **Great Hall** (Bolshoy zal), which is the largest room in the palace, all light and glitter from its windows, mirrors and gilded woodcarvings.

North of the State Staircase on the courtyard side come the State Dining Room, then the Crimson and Green Pilaster Rooms, and then the Portrait Room and the **Amber Room** (Yantarnaya komnata). This last room was decorated by Rastrelli with gilded wood-carvings, mirrors, agate and jasper mosaics, and exquisitely engraved amber panels given to Peter the Great by the King of Prussia in 1716. But its treasures were plundered by the Nazis and went missing in Kaliningrad (then Königsberg) in 1945. Next is the large, sumptuous Picture Hall (Kartinny zal).

Most of the northern end is Cameron's early classical work. The elegant proportions of the Green Dining Room (Zelyonaya stolovaya) on the courtyard side are typical. Also on the courtyard side are three rooms with fabulous patterned silk wall-coverings: the Blue Drawing Room (Golubaya gosti-naya), the Chinese Blue Drawing Room (Kitayskaya golubaya gostinaya) – a se-verely classical design enlivened by the

18th century fashion for Oriental motifs, all re-created since WWII from photos – and the Choir Anteroom (Predkhornaya), whose gold silk, woven with swans and pheasants, is the original from the 18th century. The anteroom leads into the Choir (Khory) itself and the chapel, designed by Rastrelli – both are painted blue and gold. On the park side, next to the Chinese Blue Drawing Room, is an elegant monarchical bedroom.

On the ground floor beneath the chapel are rooms used for temporary exhibitions, entered from the road outside, across which is the entrance to a branch of the Pushkin Museum. It has more than 20 rooms, and the only way to get in is to queue for a guided tour – it's mainly for enthusiasts of poetic paraphernalia and 19th century Russia!

Pushkin Parks

Around the south of the Catherine Palace extends the lovely Catherine Park (Yeka-terininsky park). The main entrance is on Komsomolskaya ulitsa in front of the palace.

The park's inner, formal section runs down terraces in front of the palace to Ras-trelli's blue-and-white **Hermitage** building. Just off the south-east corner of the palace, Cameron's Cold Baths building, containing his extravagant **Agate Rooms** (Agatovye komnaty), is sometimes open. The **Cameron Gallery** next door, with a display of 18th and 19th century costumes and carriages, is open daily except Tuesday. Its upper arcade was built so Catherine the Great could enjoy the views. Between the gallery and the palace, notice the south-pointing ramp which Cameron added for the ageing empress to walk down into the park.

The park's outer section focuses on the **Great Pond**, where you can rent a boat in summer. This section is dotted with an in-triguing array of structures ranging from the **'Pyramid'**, where Catherine the Great buried her favourite dogs, to the **Chinese Pavilion** (or Creaking Summerhouse), the **Marble Bridge** (copied from one at Wilton, England) and the **Ruined Tower**, which was built ready-ruined in keeping with a 1770s romantic fashion – maybe an 18th century empress's equivalent of pre-faded jeans!

A short distance north of the Catherine Palace along ulitsa Vasenko, the classical **Alexander Palace** (Alexandrovsky dvorets) was built by Quarenghi in 1792-96 for the future Alexander I. It's the least touristed palace, so in some ways the most pleasant, and now open after an aeons-long renovation (US$4/2 for foreigners/students, US$1/0.75 for Russians). The overgrown and empty Alexander Park (free) extends on three sides of the palace and adjoins the Catherine Park in the south.

Akhmatova Museum

A 90-something year old Anna Akhmatova fan named Sergey Dmitryvich Umnikov runs a small Akhmatova museum (☎ 470 44 05) from his home at Akhmatovskaya ulitsa 25, flat 21, but you'll need to call him in advance (in Russian) and make an appointment – it was closed when I visited, but said to be fascinating.

Another small Akhmatova museum in Pushkin is in the Music Gymnasium (☎ 466 19 64), Leontevskaya ulitsa 17, right next to Pushkin Gostiny Dvor (bus No 370 from the train station stops right there), open Monday to Friday from 10 am to 6 pm during the academic year and by special arrangement in the summer. There are special celebrations on Akhmatova's birthday, 23 June.

Pavlovsk Great Palace

Cameron's original palace was a three-storey domed square with single-storey wings curving only halfway round the existing courtyard. Paul loathed his mother, and he and his wife, Maria Fyodorovna, wanted a more restrained, more French approach to building than Cameron's. The Scot was replaced by his assistant Vincenzo Brenna, who disproportionately enlarged the wings and, along with other noted architect/designers like Quarenghi and Rossi, completed the inside. The palace was a royal residence until 1917; it was burnt down in WWII but was fully restored by 1970.

The finest rooms are on the middle floor of the square central block. Cameron designed the round Italian Hall beneath the dome, and the Grecian Hall to its west, though the lovely green fluted columns were added by Brenna. Flanking these are two private suites mainly designed by Brenna: Paul's along the north side of the block, and Maria Fyodorovna's (set to re-open just after we went to press) on the south. The insane, military-obsessed Paul's Hall of War – he's also responsible for the Engineers' Castle in St Petersburg – contrasts with Maria's Hall of Peace, which is decorated with musical instruments and flowers. Cameron's Egyptian Vestibule is on the ground floor at the foot of the stairs.

On the middle floor of the south block are Paul's Throne Room and the Hall of the Maltese Knights of St John, of whom he was the Grand Master. Also in the palace is an exhibition on 19th century Russian interiors, for which tickets are sold separately.

Getting There & Away

Take one of the frequent suburban trains from the Vitebsk Station in St Petersburg. They usually go from platform 1, 2 or 3, and you can get tickets from the cash desk. They go to Detskoe Selo Station (zone 3, US$0.25) for Pushkin, and to Pavlovsk Station (zone 4, US$0.35) for Pavlovsk. It's about half an hour to either place. If you're *really* cheap you can save US$0.10 by taking a Line 2 metro to the southern terminus at Kupchino and taking the elektrichka from there.

A five minute ride on bus No 370, 371 or 378 from outside Detskoe Selo Station takes you to within two minutes walk of Pushkin's Catherine Palace. From Pavlovsk Station, you can reach the Great Palace by bus No 370, 383, 383A or 493 (five to 10 minutes), or by entering the park across the road from the station and walking 1.5 to 2km across it to the palace. Walking at least one way across the park is a good idea. Bus No 370 also runs to and from Pushkin (two blocks from the Catherine Palace), so it's easy to get between Pavlovsk and Pushkin.

GATCHINA
ГАТЧИНА

Catherine the Great's lover Grigory Orlov had a palace and park created at Gatchina, 48km south of St Petersburg, between 1776 and 1782. Later, Paul I moved here from Pavlovsk to remodel it as a medieval castle with drawbridges and battlements – there's a statue of Paul right in front.

Post-WWII renovation is still going on (the place looks like the Soviet warehouse it once was), but about half the place is up and running as a museum of firearms and weaponry from the 17th to the 19th centuries. It's open Tuesday to Sunday from 10 am to 6 pm (closed Monday and the last Tuesday of the month). Admission is US$3.25 for foreigners, US$1.50 for Russians.

In the lovely palace park is the **Birch House**, an imperial joke that looks like a stack of logs from outside, but opens up (whenever they feel like opening it – it was padlocked when I visited) to reveal a suite of palatial rooms lined with mirrors. There's also Black Lake, with a **priory** on its shore, and White Lake, with a **Temple of Venus** on its Island of Love.

Getting There & Away

Frequent trains go to Gatchina from St Petersburg's Baltic Station. There aren't regular group coach trips to Gatchina: a car and guide from the St Petersburg Travel Company costs around US$100 for up to three people, for about four hours including the drive there and back.

VALAAM
ВАЛААМ

The Valaam Archipelago, which consists of Valaam Island and about 50 smaller ones, sits in north-western Lake Ladoga (`LAH-da-ga') south of south-western Karelia and north of St Petersburg. Access is somewhat difficult but a visit is worthwhile. The main attractions here are the unique14th century **Valaam Transfiguration Monastery** (Spaso-Preobrazhenskii Valaamsky monastyr), its

cathedral and buildings, and the pleasant town that surrounds it.

There is some dispute about the identity of the first settlers – some sources say that they were 10th century monks – but most agree that the monastery was first settled in the late 14th century as a fortress against Swedish invaders, who managed to destroy it completely in 1611. Rebuilt with money from Peter the Great, the monastery doubled as a prison.

Many of the monks and much of the monastery's treasure were moved to Finland, which controlled the territory from 1918 to 1940, when it fell back into Soviet hands. The Soviet authorities closed the monastery, took whatever was left and built what they referred to as an 'urban-type settlement' here.

Today the buildings are protected architectural landmarks, but neglect has taken its toll. Many of the buildings are decrepit and in need of immediate repair. Concerned people are trying hard, but in many cases arguments about how to proceed with the restoration have impeded progress, and lack of funding compounds the difficulties.

There are about 600 residents on the main island, including army service personnel, restoration workers, guides and clergy, most of whom get around in horse-drawn carriages or motorboats.

The most common way to get here and, once here, to get around is on tour boats which leave from St Petersburg at night, arrive in the morning, do about a six-hour tour of the islands, and then head back, arriving in St Petersburg the following morning. You can also get here from Karelia – a rather interesting adventure: see Lonely Planet's *Russia, Ukraine & Belarus* for more information.

Getting There & Away

Cruise ships frequently leave the St Petersburg River Terminal (☎ 262 02 39 or 262 13 18), prospekt Obukhovskoy oborony 195, near metro Proletarskaya, from May to September, but on uncertain schedules. Itustour (☎ 164 99 56), Ligovsky prospekt 64 in St

Petersburg, is the best source of tickets and information – Jana there speaks English and is quite helpful.

Cruises last two nights and two days and cost from US$115 to US$165 per person. If you add Kizhi, the trip becomes one of four nights and five days and costs from US$306 to US$330 including full board.

KIZHI ISLAND
КИЖИ ОСТРОВ

An old pagan ritual site, Kizhi Island, 55km north-east of the Karelian city of Petrozavodsk across Lake Onega, made a natural 'parish' for 12th century Russian colonists, though none of the earliest churches remain.

Its centrepiece is the fairy-tale **Cathedral of the Transfiguration** (Preobrazhensky sobor, 1714), with a chorus of 22 domes, gables and ingenious decorations to keep water off the walls. Even so, it's now so rickety that the interior's closed, and in spite of UNESCO protection nobody can agree on how to restore it. Next door is the nine-domed **Church of the Intercession** (Pokrovskaya tserkov, 1764). The icons from the cathedral are on display here and in the Petrozavodsk Fine Arts Museum.

The other buildings in the collection were brought from the region around Lake Onega. Rich and poor 19th century peasant houses are nicely restored inside. The little 14th century **Church of the Resurrection of Lazarus** may be the oldest wooden building in Russia. The **Chapel of the Archangel Michael** has an exhibit on Christianity in Karelia, and music students from Petrozavodsk play its bells in the summer.

There are more wooden churches outside the 'museum', and a hamlet with houses like the ones inside, but occupied. From the landing it's 3km north to another village and 5km to the end of the island. The silence, fresh air and views on a sunny day are reason enough to come here (but beware of poisonous snakes in the more remote parts).

The whole collection of buildings on the island makes up the museum. The ticket price is steep for foreigners (though we paid the Russian price simply by saying '*odin bilet, pazhalsta*', meaning 'one ticket, please') at US$9.50; Russians pay about US$0.50, and Russian students pay less than US$0.05. Karelian residents enter free.

A restaurant is near the landing, but it seems to want to sell drinks more than food. Just opposite the pier is a small kiosk cluster, including an 'art shop' selling heinously overpriced souvenirs, and a café that has some snacks. There's a map of the museum and island 50m south-east of the kiosk cluster.

Getting There & Away
Trains leave Moscow Station in St Petersburg nightly at 9.50 pm (US$41/38 2nd class for adults/students) for Petrozavodsk, from where hydrofoils leave three times daily for Kizhi Island. Cruise ships from St Petersburg stop here as part of the St Petersburg-Valaam-Kizhi circuit (for more information, see the Getting There & Away section of Valaam above). You can only go during 'navigation season', which is from mid-May to mid-November.

Language

Just about everyone in Russia speaks Russian, though there are also dozens of other languages spoken by ethnic minorities. Russian and most of the other languages are written in variants of the Cyrillic alphabet. It's easy to find English-speakers in the big cities but not so easy in small towns (sometimes not even in tourist hotels).

Russian grammar may be daunting, but your travels will be far more interesting if you at least take the time to learn the Cyrillic alphabet, so that you can read maps and street signs.

Since most of what's in this section is aimed at spoken situations, Cyrillic forms are mostly accompanied with phonetic translations rather than direct transliterations.

BOOKS

A good teach-yourself set (a book and two tapes) is the BBC's *Get By in Russian*. Another good book and cassette set for beginners is *Colloquial Russian* by Svetlana le Fleming and Susan E Kay. The paperback *Penguin Russian Course* is good for more devoted learners. When you go, take along Lonely Planet's detailed and useful *Russian Phrasebook* and a small dictionary such as the *Pocket Oxford Russian Dictionary*.

Two recent books are worthy of mention. The 4kg *Random House Russian-English Dictionary of Idioms* by Sophia Lubensky is a must for any serious student of Russian. Developed over 12 years, originally to help spies (it was undertaken by the US National Cryptologic School, Department of Defense), it contains over 7500 idioms and set expressions not found in traditional Russian-English dictionaries. It's not much fun for beginners – all the Russian listings are in Cyrillic, and no literal (only idiomatic) translations are given. Also note that the meanings and spellings are in American English.

Russian Proverbs by Chris Skillen and Vladimir Lubarov is a lovely little hardcover with a selection of the most charming Russian proverbs – from 'it's madness to bring a samovar to Tula' to 'a bad peace is better than a good fight'. It lists both Russian and English and has very nice illustrations throughout (though a couple are in the wrong place!).

CYRILLIC ALPHABET

The Cyrillic alphabet resembles Greek with some extra characters. Each language that uses Cyrillic has a slight variant.

Pronunciation

The sounds of **a**, **o**, **e** and **я** are 'weaker' when the stress in the word does not fall on them – in во,ла (*voda*, water) the stress falls on the second syllable, so it's pronounced *vo-DA*, with the unstressed pronunciation for **o** and the stressed pronunciation for **a**. The vowel **й** only follows other vowels in so-called diphthongs (vowel combinations), eg **ой** *'oy'*, **ей** *'ey, yey'*. Russians usually print **ё** *'yo'* without the dots, a source of confusion in pronunciation.

The 'voiced' (when the vocal cords vibrate) consonants **б**, **в**, **г**, **д**, **ж** and **з** are not voiced at the end of words (eg х,леб, bread, is pronounced *khlyep*) or before voiceless consonants. The **г** in the common adjective endings **-его** and **-ого** is pronounced *'v'*; 'Mayakovskogo', for example, is pronounced *Maya-KOV-skuvuh*.

Two letters have no sound but are used to modify others. A consonant followed by the 'soft sign' **ь** is spoken with the tongue flat against the palate, as if followed by the faint beginnings of a 'y'. The rare 'hard sign' **ъ** after a consonant indicates a slight pause before the next vowel.

Transliteration

There's no ideal system for going from Cyrillic to Roman letters; the more faithful

LANGUAGE

Russian Cyrillic Alphabet

Cyrillic	Roman	Pronunciation
А, а	a	as the 'a' in 'father' (stressed); as the 'a' in 'about' (unstressed)
Б, б	b	as the 'b' in 'but'
В, в	v	as the 'v' in 'van'
Г, г	g	as the 'g' in 'god'
Д, д	d	as the 'd' in 'dog'
Е, е	ye	as the 'ye' in 'yet' (stressed); as the 'ye' in 'yeast' (unstressed)
Ё, ё	yo	as the 'yo' in 'yore'
Ж, ж	zh	as the 's' in 'measure'
З, з	z	as the 'z' in 'zoo'
И, и	i	as the 'ee' in 'meet'
Й, й	y	as the 'y' in 'boy'
К, к	k	as the 'k' in 'kind'
Л, л	l	as the 'l' in 'lamp'
М, м	m	as the 'm' in 'mad'
Н, н	n	as the 'n' in 'not'
О, о	o	as the 'o' in 'more' (stressed); as the 'a' in 'about' (unstressed)
П, п	p	as the 'p' in 'pig'
Р, р	r	as the 'r' in 'rub' (but rolled)
С, с	s	as the 's' in 'sing'
Т, т	t	as the 't' in 'ten'
У, у	u	as the 'oo' in 'fool'
Ф, ф	f	as the 'f' in 'fan'
Х, х	kh	as the 'ch' in 'Bach'
Ц, ц	ts	as the 'ts' in 'bits'
Ч, ч	ch	as the 'ch' in 'chin'
Ш, ш	sh	as the 'sh' in 'shop'
Щ, щ	shch	as the 'shch' in 'fresh chips'
ъ		'hard' sign
Ы, ы	y	as the 'i' in 'ill'
ь		'soft' sign
Э, э	e	as the 'e' in 'end'
Ю, ю	yu	as 'you'
Я, я	ya	as the 'ya' in 'yard'

a system is to pronunciation, the more complicated it becomes. This book uses the simple US Library of Congress System I,

good for deciphering printed words and rendering proper names in familiar form.

In this system Cyrillic е (pronounced 'ye') is written as Roman e except at the start of words where it's ye (eg Yeltsin). The combination кс becomes x. At the end of words certain pairs get special forms: -ия is written -ia, -ье -ie, -ьи -yi. Russian names are simplified by making final -ый and -ий into plain -y.

In a few cases exceptions are made for common usage. The names of 18th to 19th century Russian rulers are anglicised – eg Peter the Great not *Pyotr*, Tsar Nicholas not *Nikolay*. For names ending in -чёв we write -chev not -chyov (eg Gorbachev); similarly for -шёв and -щёв. Other familiar exceptions – which would all be spelled differently if we stuck adamantly to the system – are *rouble, nyet, soviet, Baikal, perestroika, Tchaikovsky*, even *Intourist*. Note, though, that while we spell the composer's name Tchaikovsky, we spell things named after him (eg *ulitsa Chaykovskogo*) under our system.

Capital letters in the transliterations indicate where the stress falls in a word.

USEFUL WORDS & PHRASES
Basics
Two words you're sure to use are Здравствуйте *(ZDRAST-vooy-tyeh)*, the universal 'hello', and Пожалуйста *(pa-ZHAHL-stuh)*, the multipurpose word for 'please' (commonly included in all polite requests), 'you're welcome', 'pardon me', 'after you' and more.

Yes.
    Да. *(da)*
No.
    Нет. *(nyet)*
Thank you (very much).
    Спасибо (большое).
    (spuh-SEE-ba (bal-SHOY-uh))
Pardon me.
    Простите, пожалуйста.
    (pra-STEE-tyeh, pa-ZHAHL-stuh)
Can you help me?
    Помогите мне?
    (pa-ma-GEET-yeh mnyeh?)

No problem/Never mind.
Ничего. *(ni-che-VOH)* (lit: nothing)
Good/OK.
Хорошо. *(kha-ra-SHOH)*

Greetings

Hi. (casual, to friends)
Привет. *(preev-YET)*
Good morning.
Доброе утро. *(DOH-bra-yuh OO-tra)*
Good afternoon.
Добрый день. *(DOH-bri dyen)*
Good evening.
Добрый вечер. *(DOH-bri VYEH-chir)*
Goodbye.
До свидания. *(das-fi-DA-nya)*
Goodbye. (casual)
Пока. *(pah-KAH)*

Meeting People

When introducing yourself use your first
name, or first and last. Russians often
address each other by first name plus
patronymic, a middle name based on their
father's first name – eg Natalya Borisovna
(Natalya, daughter of Boris), Pavel Niko-
layevich (Pavel, son of Nikolay).

What's your name?
Как вас зовут? *(kahk vahs za-VOOT?)*
My name is ...
Меня зовут ... *(min-YA za-VOOT ...)*
Pleased to meet you.
Очень приятно. *(OH-chin pree-YAHT-na)*
How are you?
Как дела? *(kak dyi-LAH?)*
Where are you from?
Откуда вы? *(aht-KUH-dah vi?)*
I'm from ...
Я из ... *(ya iz ...)*

Australia
Австралия *(uf-STRAH-li-uh)*
Canada
Канада *(ka-NA-duh)*
France
Франция *(FRAHN-tsi-yuh)*
Germany
Германия *(gehr-MAH-ni-yuh)*

Great Britain
Великобритания *(vi-LEE-ka-bri-TA-ni-uh)*
Ireland
Ирландия *(eer-LAHN-di-yuh)*
New Zealand
Новая Зеландия *(NOH-vuh-yuh zyeh-LAHN-di-yuh)*
USA, America
США/Америка *(seh sheh ah/uh-MYEH-ri-kuh)*

Language Difficulties

I don't speak Russian.
Я не говорю по-русски. *(ya nye ga-var-YU pa-RU-ski)*
I don't understand.
Я не понимаю. *(ya nye pah-ni-MAH-yu)*
Do you speak English?
Вы говорите по-английски? *(vih ga-var-EE-tyeh pa-an-GLEE-ski?)*
Could you write it down, please?
Запишите, пожалуйста? *(zuh-pi-SHEE-tyeh, pa-ZHAHL-stuh?)*

Getting Around

How do I get to ...?
Как мне попасть в ...? *(kak mnye pa-PAST' v ...?)*
Where is ...?
Где ...? *(gdye ...?)*
When does it leave?
Когда отлетает? *(kug-DA aht-li-TA-yit?)*
Are you getting off?
Выходите? *(vih-KHA-di-tyeh)*

cashier/ticket office
касса *(KAH-suh)*
transport map
схема транспорта *(SKHEM-uh trahns-POR-tuh)*
ticket/s
билет(ы) *(bee-LYET/-i)*
metro token/s
жетон(ы) *(zhi-TOHN/-i)*
one-way
в один конец, единый *(vah-DYIN ka-NYETS, ye-DYIN-i)*
return
туда и обратно *(tu-DA ee a-BRAHT-na)*

bus
  автобус *(uf-TOH-boos)*
trolleybus
  троллейбус *(trahl-YEY-boos)*
tram
  трамвай *(trum-VAI)*
bus stop
  остановка *(ah-sta-NOV-kuh)*
train
  поезд *(PO-yest)*
train station
  железнодорожный вокзал *(zhi-LYEZ-nuh da-ROHZH-ni vahg-ZAHL)*
taxi
  такси *(tahk-SEE)*

Accommodation

How much is a room?
  Сколько стоит номер? *(SKOL-ka STO-eet NOHM-yer?)*
Do you have a cheaper room?
  У вас дешевле номер? *(u vahs dye-SHYEV-lye NOHM-yer?)*

hotel
  гостиница *(gus-TEE-nit-suh)*
room
  номер *(NOHM-yer)*
key
  ключ *(klyooch)*
blanket
  одеяло *(ah-di-YAH-la)*

The ... isn't working.
  ... не работает. *(... ni ruh-BOH-tuh-yit)*

tap/faucet
  кран *(krahn)*
heating
  отопление *(a-ta-PLEN-i-yeh)*
hot water
  горячая вода *(ga-RYA-chaya va-DA)*
light
  свет *(sfyet)*
electricity
  электричество *(eh-lik-TREE-chist-va)*

Around Town

Note that house numbers are not always in sequence on opposite sides of the street.

Signs

ВХОД/ВЫХОД	ENTRANCE/EXIT
МЕСТ НЕТ	NO VACANCY
СПРАВКИ	INFORMATION
ОТКРЫТ	OPEN
ЗАКРЫТ	CLOSED
КАССА	CASHIER/ TICKET OFFICE
БОЛЬНИЦА	HOSPITAL
МИЛИЦИЯ	POLICE
ТУАЛЕТ	TOILET
МУЖСКОЙ (М)	MEN
ЖЕНСКИЙ (Ж)	WOMEN

Russian addresses are written back-to-front; see Post & Communications in the Facts for the Visitor chapter.

Where is ...?
  Где ...? *(gdyeh ...?)*
Is it nearby?
  Близко? *(BLIS-ka?)*
Is it far?
  Далеко? *(da lye-KO?)*
I'm lost.
  Я заблудился *(ya zuh-blu-DEEL-suh)* (m)
  Я заблудилась *(ya zuh-blu-DEE-lus)* (f)

avenue
  проспект (просп.) *(pra-SPYEKT)*
boulevard
  бульвар *(bool-VAHR)*
church
  церковь *(TSER-kuf)*
circus
  цирк *(tsirk)*
highway
  шоссе *(sha-SEH)*
hospital
  больница *(BOHL-nit-suh)*
lane
  переулок (пер.) *(pi-ri-OO-lahk)*
museum
  музей *(mu-ZYEY)*
square/plaza
  площадь (пл.) *(PLOH-shchut)*

street
у.лица (у.л.) *(OO-leet-suh)*
theatre
театр *(ti-ATR)*

Directions
north
север *(SYEH-vir)*
south
юг *(yook)*
east
восток *(va-STOK)*
west
запад *(ZAH-puht)*
to/on the left
налево *(nuh-LYEH-va)*
to/on the right
направо *(nuh-PRAH-va)*
straight on
прямо *(PRYAH-ma)*
here
тут *(toot)*
there
там *(tahm)*

May I take a photo?
Фотографировать можно?
(fa-ta-gruh-FEE-ra-vut MOZH-na?)

Bank, Post & Telecommunications
bank
банк *(bahnk)*
currency exchange
обмен валюты *(ahb-MYEHN vahl-YU-tuh)*
small change
размен *(ruz-MYEN)*
travellers cheques
дорожные чеки *(da-ROHZH-nih-yeh CHEH-ki)*

post office
почтамт *(pahch-TAHMT)*
postcard
открытка *(aht-KRIT-kuh)*
stamp
марка *(MAR-kuh)*

telephone
телефон *(ti-li-FOHN)*

intercity telephone office
междугородный телефонный пункт
(mizh-du-gahr-OHD-ni ti-li-FOHN-i punkt)
international telephone office
международный телефонный пункт
(mizh-du-nah-ROHD-ni ti-li-FOHN-i punkt)
fax
факс or телефакс *(fahx or ti-li-FAHX)*

Food
For a longer list of words and phrases
related to ordering meals, and specific
foods, dishes and drinks, see Places to Eat.

What is this?
Что это? *(shto E-ta?)*
I'd like ...
Я возму ... *(ya vaz-MU ...)*

breakfast
завтрак *(ZAHF-truk)*
lunch
обед *(a-BYET)*
dinner/supper
ужин *(OO-zhin)*
restaurant
ресторан *(ri-sta-RAHN)*
café
кафе *(ka-FYEH)*
canteen
столовая *(sta-LO-vuh-yuh)*
snack bar
буфет *(bu-FYET)*

Shopping
Do you have ...?
У вас ...? *(u VAHS ...?)*
How much is it?
Сколько стоит? *(SKOL-ka STO-eet?)*

bookshop
книжный магазин
(KNEEZH-ni muh-guh-ZYIN)
department store
универсальный магазин
(u-ni-vir-SAHL-ni muh-guh-ZYIN)
market
рынок *(RIH-nuk)*
newsstand
союзпечать or газетный киоск
(sa-YOOZ-pi-chat or gazetnyi kiosk)

pharmacy
  аптека *(up-TYEK-a)*
souvenirs
  сувениры *(su-vin-EER-i)*

Time

Round hours are fairly easy, except that
there are three different ways of saying the
Russian equivalent of 'o'clock', depending
on the hour. Thus one o'clock is *ah-DYIN
chahs* (or simply *chahs*), two o'clock is *dva
chuh-SAH* (and similarly for three and four
o'clock) and five o'clock is *pyaht chuh-
SOF* (and similarly up to 20). For
in-between times the standard formula
gives brain-twisters like 'without-25-five'
for 4.35. You'll be understood if you say the
hour followed by the minutes: eg 9.20 is
девять-двадцать *(DYEV-yut DVAHD-sut)*.
For minutes under 10 insert zero, ноль
(nohl): eg 2.08 is два-ноль-восемь *(dva
nohl VOH-sem)*. Timetables use a 24-hour
clock: eg 3 pm is пятнадцать часов *(pyit-
NAHT-sut chuh-SOF)*.

What time is it?
  Который час? *(ka-TOR-i chahs?)*
At what time?
  В котором часу? *(fka-TOR-um chuh-
  SOO?)*
local time
  местное время *(MYEST-na-yuh VREM-
  yuh)*
Moscow time
  московское время *(muh-SKOF-skuh-
  yeh VREM-yuh)*
hour
  час *(chahs)*
minute
  минута *(mi-NOOT-uh)*
am/in the morning
  утра *(oo-TRA)*
pm/in the afternoon
  дня *(dnya)*
in the evening
  вечера *(VYEH-chi-ruh)*

Days & Dates

Dates are given day-month-year, with the
month usually in Roman numerals. Days of
the week are often represented by numbers
in timetables; Monday is 1.

When?
  Когда? *(kahg-DA?)*
today
  сегодня *(si-VOHD-nyuh)*
yesterday
  вчера *(fchi-RA)*
tomorrow
  завтра *(ZAHF-truh)*
day after tomorrow
  послезавтра *(pa-sli-ZAHF-truh)*

Monday
  понедельник *(pa-ni-DEL-nik)*
Tuesday
  вторник *(FTOR-nik)*
Wednesday
  среда *(sri-DA)*
Thursday
  четверг *(chit-VERK)*
Friday
  пятница *(PYAT-nit-suh)*
Saturday
  суббота *(su-BOHT-uh)*
Sunday
  воскресенье *(vas-kri-SEN-yuh)*

January
  январь *(yan-VAR)*
February
  февраль *(fev-VARL)*
March
  март *(mart)*
April
  апрель *(ap-REL)*
May
  май *(my)*
June
  июнь *(ee-YOON)*
July
  июль *(ee-YOOL)*
August
  август *(AV-gust)*
September
  сентябрь *(seen-TYAB-r)*
October
  октябрь *(ok-TYAB-r)*
November
  ноябрь *(nah-YAB-r)*
December
  декабрь *(dek-AHB-er)*

Museum Dates

Centuries are written with Roman numerals.

century(ies)
  в (в)
year(s)
  г (г)
beginning, middle, end
  начало, середина, конец
AD (lit: our era)
  н.э.
BC (lit: before our era)
  до н.э.
10th century AD
  X в. н.э.
7th century BC
  VII в. до н.э.

Numbers

How many?   Сколько? *(SKOL-ka)*

1	один *(ah-DYIN)*
2	два *(dva)*
3	три *(tree)*
4	четыре *(chi-TIR-yeh)*
5	пять *(pyaht)*

6	шесть *(shest)*
7	семь *(syem)*
8	восемь *(VO-syim)*
9	девять *(DYEV-yut)*
10	десять *(DYES-yut)*
100	сто *(stoh)*
1000	тысяча *(TIH-suh-chuh)*
one million	один миллион *(ah-DYIN mi-li-OHN)*

Emergencies

Help!
  На помощь! *(na POH-mushch!)*
I need a doctor.
  Мне нужен врач. *(mnyeh NU-zhin vrahch)*
Police!
  Милиция! *(mi-LEET-si-yuh!)*
Thief!
  Вор! *(vor!)*
Fire!
  Пожар! *(pa-ZHAR!)*

Glossary

aeroport – airport
aerovokzal – air terminal in city
apteka – pharmacy
avtobus – bus
avtovokzal – bus station

babushka – grandmother
banya – bathhouse
benzin – petrol
bilet – ticket
bufet – snack bar, usually in a hotel, selling cheap cold meats, boiled eggs, salads, bread, pastries etc
bulochnaya – bakery
buterbrod – open sandwich

dacha – country cottage, summer house
deklaratsia – customs declaration
Detsky Mir – Children's World (department store)
dezhurnaya – woman looking after a particular floor of a hotel
dom – house
duma – parliament

elektrichka – suburban train
etazh – floor (storey)

GAI – State Automobile Inspectorate (traffic police)
gazeta – newspaper
glavpochtamt – main post office
gril-bar – grill bar, often limited to roast chicken
gorod – city, town
gostinitsa – hotel

ikra – caviar
izveshchenie – notification

kafe – café
kassa – ticket office, cashier's desk
khleb – bread
klyuch – key
kniga – book
krazha – theft

kvartira – flat, apartment
kvitantsia – receipt

magazin – shop
magizdat – underground recording illegally distributed under Communist rule
manezh – riding school
marka – postage stamp or brand, trade mark
marshrutnoe taxi – minibus that runs along a fixed route
mashina – car
matryoshka – set of painted wooden dolls within dolls
mesto – place, seat
militsia – police
mineralnaya voda – mineral water
morskoy vokzal – sea terminal
most – bridge
muzey – museum
muzhskoy – men's (toilet)

naberezhnaya – embankment
novy – new

obed – lunch
oblast – area, region
obmen valyuty – currency exchange
ostanovka – bus stop
ostrov – island

Pashka – Easter
pereryv – break, recess
pereulok – lane
plan goroda – city map
ploshchad – square
pochtamt – post office (*glavpochtamt* is the town's main post office)
poezd – train
poliklinika – medical centre
posylki – parcels
prospekt – avenue

rechnoy vokzal – river terminal
reka – river

remont – closed for repairs (a sign you'll see all too often)
restoran – restaurant
Rozhdestvo – Christmas
rubl – rouble
rynok – market

samizdat – underground literary manuscript (similar to *magizdat*)
samovar – urn
sanitarny den – literally 'sanitary day'; the monthly day on which establishments shut down for cleaning (these days vary and often occur with little forewarning)
schyot – bill
sever – north
sobor – cathedral
stary – old
stolovaya – canteen, cafeteria

tapochki – slippers
teatr – theatre
tserkov – church
tsirk – circus

tualet – toilet
tuda i obratno – 'there and back', return ticket
troyka – horse-drawn sleigh

ulitsa – street
uzhin – dinner

vkhod – way in, entrance
voda – water
vokzal – station
vostok – east
vorovstvo – theft

yug – south

zakaznoe – registration of mail
zal – hall, room
zaliv – gulf, bay
zapad – west
zavtrak – breakfast
zhensky – women's (toilet)
zheton – token (for metro etc)

LONELY PLANET

Guides by Region

Lonely Planet is known worldwide for publishing practical, reliable and no-nonsense travel information in our guides and on our web site. The Lonely Planet list covers just about every accessible part of the world. Currently there are nine series: travel guides, shoestring guides, walking guides, city guides, phrasebooks, audio packs, travel atlases, diving and snorkelling guides and travel literature.

AFRICA Africa – the South • Africa on a shoestring • Arabic (Egyptian) phrasebook • Arabic (Moroccan) phrasebook • Cairo • Cape Town • Central Africa • East Africa • Egypt • Egypt travel atlas • Ethiopian (Amharic) phrasebook • The Gambia & Senegal • Kenya • Kenya travel atlas • Malawi, Mozambique & Zambia • Morocco • North Africa • South Africa, Lesotho & Swaziland • South Africa, Lesotho & Swaziland travel atlas • Swahili phrasebook • Trekking in East Africa • Tunisia • West Africa • Zimbabwe, Botswana & Namibia • Zimbabwe, Botswana & Namibia travel atlas
Travel Literature: The Rainbird: A Central African Journey • Songs to an African Sunset: A Zimbabwean Story • Mali Blues: Traveling to an African Beat

AUSTRALIA & THE PACIFIC Australia • Australian phrasebook • Bushwalking in Australia • Bushwalking in Papua New Guinea • Fiji • Fijian phrasebook • Islands of Australia's Great Barrier Reef • Melbourne • Micronesia • New Caledonia • New South Wales & the ACT • New Zealand • Northern Territory • Outback Australia • Papua New Guinea • Papua New Guinea (Pidgin) phrasebook • Queensland • Rarotonga & the Cook Islands • Samoa • Solomon Islands • South Australia • Sydney • Tahiti & French Polynesia • Tasmania • Tonga • Tramping in New Zealand • Vanuatu • Victoria • Western Australia
Travel Literature: Islands in the Clouds • Sean & David's Long Drive

CENTRAL AMERICA & THE CARIBBEAN Bahamas and Turks & Caicos • Bermuda • Central America on a shoestring • Costa Rica • Cuba • Eastern Caribbean • Guatemala, Belize & Yucatán: La Ruta Maya • Jamaica • Mexico • Mexico City • Panama
Travel Literature: Green Dreams: Travels in Central America

EUROPE Amsterdam • Andalucia • Austria • Baltic States phrasebook • Berlin • Britain • Central Europe • Central Europe phrasebook • Czech & Slovak Republics • Denmark • Dublin • Eastern Europe • Eastern Europe phrasebook • Estonia, Latvia & Lithuania • Finland • France • French phrasebook • Germany • German phrasebook • Greece • Greek phrasebook • Hungary • Iceland, Greenland & the Faroe Islands • Ireland • Italian phrasebook • Italy • Lisbon • London • Mediterranean Europe • Mediterranean Europe phrasebook • Paris • Poland • Portugal • Portugal travel atlas • Prague • Romania & Moldova • Russia, Ukraine & Belarus • Russian phrasebook • Scandinavian & Baltic Europe • Scandinavian Europe phrasebook • Slovenia • Spain • Spanish phrasebook • St Petersburg • Switzerland • Trekking in Spain • Ukrainian phrasebook • Vienna • Walking in Britain • Walking in Italy • Walking in Switzerland • Western Europe • Western Europe phrasebook
Travel Literature: The Olive Grove: Travels in Greece

INDIAN SUBCONTINENT Bangladesh • Bengali phrasebook • Bhutan • Delhi • Goa • Hindi/Urdu phrasebook • India • India & Bangladesh travel atlas • Indian Himalaya • Karakoram Highway • Nepal • Nepali phrasebook • Pakistan • Rajasthan • South India • Sri Lanka • Sri Lanka phrasebook • Trekking in the Indian Himalaya • Trekking in the Karakoram & Hindukush • Trekking in the Nepal Himalaya
Travel Literature: In Rajasthan • Shopping for Buddhas

LONELY PLANET

Mail Order

Lonely Planet products are distributed worldwide.They are also available by mail order from Lonely Planet, so if you have difficulty finding a title please write to us. North and South American residents should write to 150 Linden St, Oakland CA 94607, USA; European and African residents should write to 10a Spring Place, London NW5 3BH; and residents of other countries to PO Box 617, Hawthorn, Victoria 3122, Australia.

ISLANDS OF THE INDIAN OCEAN Madagascar & Comoros • Maldives • Mauritius, Reúnion & Seychelles

MIDDLE EAST & CENTRAL ASIA Arab Gulf States • Central Asia • Central Asia phrasebook • Iran • Israel & the Palestinian Territories • Israel & the Palestinian Territories travel atlas • Istanbul • Jerusalem • Jordan & Syria • Jordan, Syria & Lebanon travel atlas • Lebanon • Middle East on a shoestring • Turkey • Turkish phrasebook • Turkey travel atlas • Yemen
Travel Literature: The Gates of Damascus • Kingdom of the Film Stars: Journey into Jordan

NORTH AMERICA Alaska • Backpacking in Alaska • Baja California • California & Nevada • Canada • Florida • Hawaii • Honolulu • Los Angeles • Miami • New England USA • New Orleans • New York City • New York, New Jersey & Pennsylvania • Pacific Northwest USA • Rocky Mountain States • San Francisco • Seattle • Southwest USA • USA phrasebook • Washington, DC & the Capital Region
Travel Literature: Drive Thru America

NORTH-EAST ASIA Beijing • Cantonese phrasebook • China • Hong Kong • Hong Kong, Macau & Guangzhou • Japan • Japanese phrasebook • Japanese audio pack • Korea • Korean phrasebook • Kyoto • Mandarin phrasebook • Mongolia • Mongolian phrasebook • North-East Asia on a shoestring • Seoul • South West China • Taiwan • Tibet • Tibet phrasebook • Tokyo
Travel Literature: Lost Japan

SOUTH AMERICA Argentina, Uruguay & Paraguay • Bolivia • Brazil • Brazilian phrasebook • Buenos Aires • Chile & Easter Island • Chile & Easter Island travel atlas • Colombia • Ecuador & the Galapagos Islands • Latin American (Spanish) phrasebook • Peru • Quechua phrasebook • Rio de Janeiro • South America on a shoestring • Trekking in the Patagonian Andes • Venezuela
Travel Literature: Full Circle: A South American Journey

SOUTH-EAST ASIA Bali & Lombok • Bangkok • Burmese phrasebook • Cambodia • Hill Tribes phrasebook • Ho Chi Minh City • Indonesia • Indonesian phrasebook • Indonesian audio pack • Jakarta • Java • Laos • Lao phrasebook • Laos travel atlas • Malay phrasebook • Malaysia, Singapore & Brunei • Myanmar (Burma) • Philippines • Pilipino (Tagalog) phrasebook • Singapore • South-East Asia on a shoestring • South-East Asia phrasebook • Thailand • Thailand's Islands & Beaches • Thailand travel atlas • Thai phrasebook • Thai audio pack • Vietnam • Vietnamese phrasebook • Vietnam travel atlas

ALSO AVAILABLE: Antarctica • Brief Encounters: Stories of Love, Sex & Travel • Chasing Rickshaws • Not the Only Planet: Travel Stories from Science Fiction • Travel with Children • Traveller's Tales

Index

Text

Boxed Text

Name Changes in St Petersburg

Streets

Old Name	New Name	Old Name	New Name
nab Kanala Krushteyna	nab Admiraltelsky Kanala	pl Kommunarov	Nikolskaya pl
ul Krasnogo Elektrika	Atamanskaya ul	Krasnogvardeysky pr	Novocherkassky pr
ul Zhelyabova	Bolshaya Konyushennaya ul	ul Pestelya	Panteleymonovskaya ul
ul Skorokhodova	Bolshaya Monetnaya ul	ul Soyuza Svyazy	Pochtamtskaya ul
pr Karla Marxa	Bolshoy Sampsonevsky pr	per Podbelskogo	Pochtamtsky per
ul Petra Lavrova	Furshtadtskaya ul	ul Anny Ulyanovoy	Polozova ul
Krasnaya ul	Galernaya ul	Radishcheva pl	Preobrazhenskaya pl
ul Dzerzhinskogo	Gorokhovaya ul	Kodatskogo ul and	
ul Marii Ulyanovoy	Grafsky per	Pogranichikov pr	Pribrezhnaya ul
ul Rakova	Italyanskaya ul	pr Ogorodnikova	Rizhsky pr
Kirovsky pr	Kamennoostrovsky pr	pl Mira	Sennaya pl
ul Tolmacheva	Karavannaya ul	ul Voynova	Shpalernaya ul
ul Krasnoy Konnitsy	Kavalergardskaya ul	Pelshe ul	Sirenevy bulvar
ul Plekhanova**	Kazanskaya ul	pr Gaza	Staro-Petergofsky pr
bulvar Profsoyuzov	Konnogvardeysky bulvar	pl Revolutsii	Troitskaya pl
		ul Gertsena	ul Bolshaya Morskaya
pr Maxim Gorkogo	Kronverksky pr	ul Brodskogo	ul Mikhailovskaya
pr N I Smirnova	Lanskoye shosse	ul Voytika	Vitebskaya ul
ul Sofie Perovskoy	Malaya Konyushennaya ul	pr Mayorova	Voznesensky pr
ul Gogolya	Malaya Morskaya ul	ul Olega Koshevogo	Vvedenskaya ul
Bratev Vasilevykh ul	Malaya Posadskaya ul	nab Kanala Griboedova**	nab Kanala Yekatarinski
pr Shchorsa	Maly pr (Petrogradskoy storony)	ul Fotevoy	Yeletskaya ul
ul Bratstva	Maly Sampsonievsky pr	ul Fofanovoy	Yenotaevskaya ul
ul Khalturina	Millionnaya ul	ul Kalyaeva	Zakharevskaya ul
Zaporozhsky per	Moshkov per		

** This street is still generally referred to only by its Soviet-era name; in this book we bow to general usage and use the old name.

Bridges

Old Name	New Name	Old Name	New Name
Komsomolsky most	Kharlamov most	Pionersky most	Silin most
most Pestelya	Panteleymonovsky most	Kirovsky most	Troitsky most
most Svobody	Sampsonevsky most		

Parks

Old Name	New Name	Old Name	New Name
Sad imeni A M Gorkogo	Alexandrovsky Sad	Chelyuskintsev Park	Udelny Park
Sad imeni F E Dzerzhinskogo	Lopukhinsky Sad		

Metro Stations

Old Name	New Name	Old Name	New Name
Komsomolskaya	Devyatkino	Pl Mira	Sennaya Pl
Krasnogvardeyskaya	Novocherkasskaya		

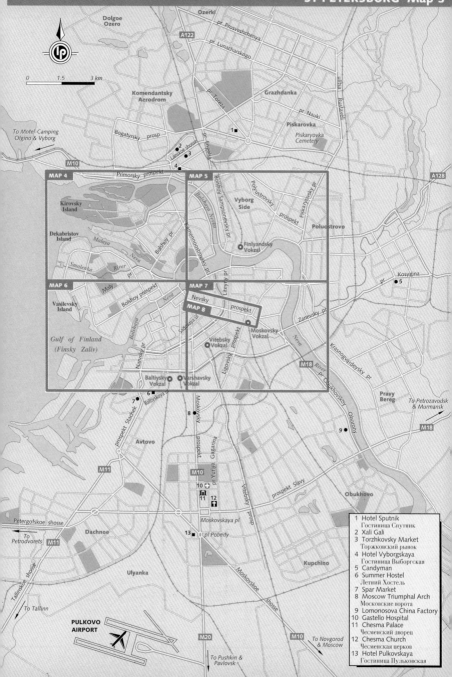

1 Hotel Sputnik
Гостиница Спутник
2 Xali Gali
3 Torzhkovsky Market
Торжковский рынок
4 Hotel Vyborgskaya
Гостиница Выборгская
5 Candyman
6 Summer Hostel
Летний Хостель
7 Spar Market
8 Moscow Triumphal Arch
Московские ворота
9 Lomonosova China Factory
10 Gastello Hospital
11 Chesma Palace
Чесменский дворец
12 Chesma Church
Чесменская церковь
13 Hotel Pulkovskaya
Гостиница Пульковская

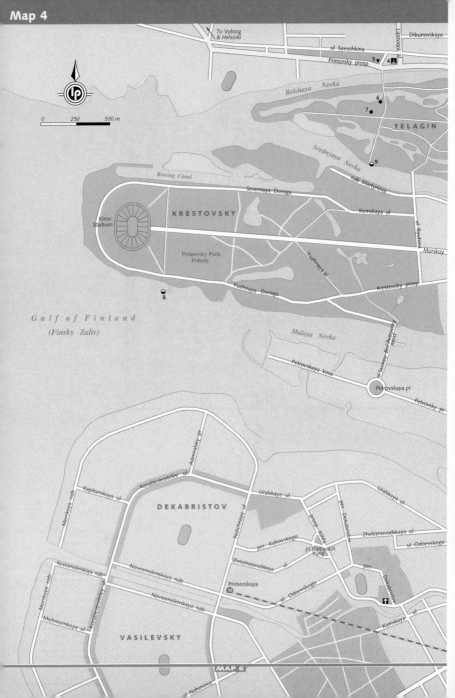

Map 4

To Vyborg
& Helsinki

ul Savushkina

Primorsky prosp

Bolshaya Nevka

YELAGIN

Srednyaya Nevka

nab Martynova

Rowing Canal

Severnaya Doroga

KRESTOVSKY

Kemskaya ul

ul Ryubina

Morskoy

Kirov
Stadium

Primorsky Park
Pobedy

Yuzhnaya ul

Krestovsky prosp

Yuzhnaya Doroga

Gulf of Finland
(Finsky Zaliv)

Malaya Nevka

ul Severny Bol Petrovsky most

Petrovskaya kosa

Petrovskaya pl

Petrovsky pr

Admiralteysky pr

Korablestroitelei ul

Kapitanskaya ul

Morskaya nab

DEKABRISTOV

Nalichnaya ul

Uralskaya ul

Uralskaya ul

prosp KIMa

per Dekabristov

Zheleznovodskaya ul

per Kakhovskogo

pl Baltiyskih
Yung

ul Odoevskogo

Zheleznovodskaya ul

per Dekabristov

Novosmolenskaya nab

Novosmolenskaya nab

Primorskaya
Ⓜ

ul Odoevskogo

Kamskaya ul

Novosmolenskaya nab

Morskaya nab

Korablestroitelei ul

Michmanskaya ul

VASILEVSKY

ul Nahimova

MAP 6

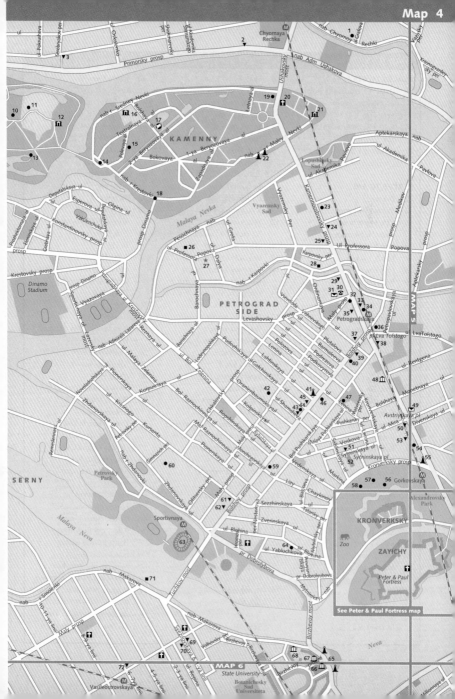

Map 4

Map 4

Domes of the Catherine Palace

Catherine Palace, Pushkin

Cathedral, Kizhi Island

Birch House, Gatchina

Great Palace and statue of Paul I, Pavlovsk

Map 5

Map 5

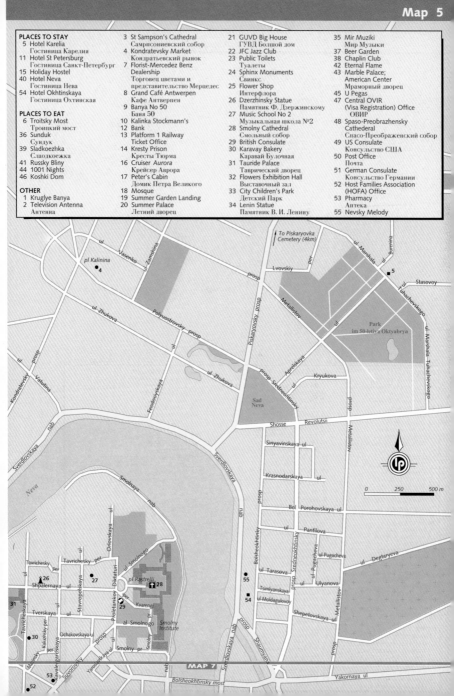

Map 6

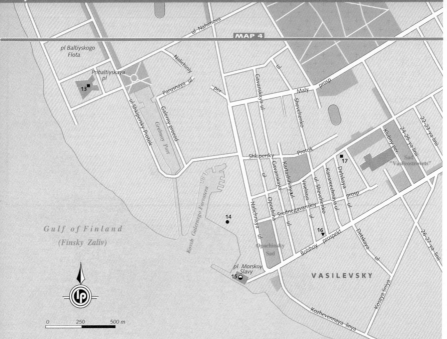

MAP 4

pl Baltiyskogo Flota

Pribaltiyskaya pl

13

Gulf of Finland

(Finsky Zaliv)

14

Shkipersky

Protok

17

Sad "Vasileostrovets"

Opachinsky Sad

pl Morskoy Slavy

18

VASILEVSKY

0   250   500 m

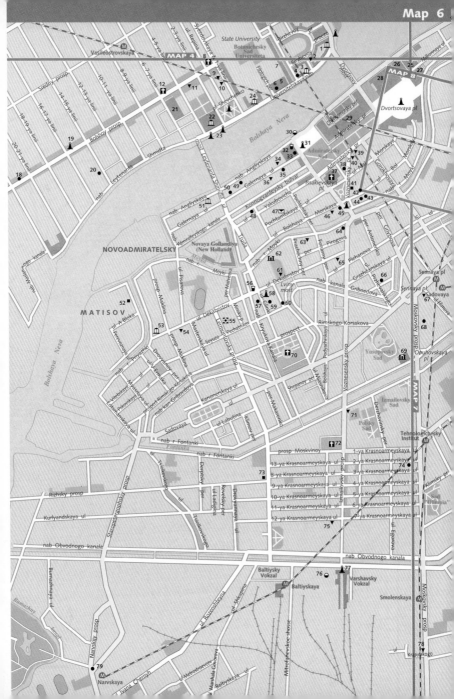

Map 6

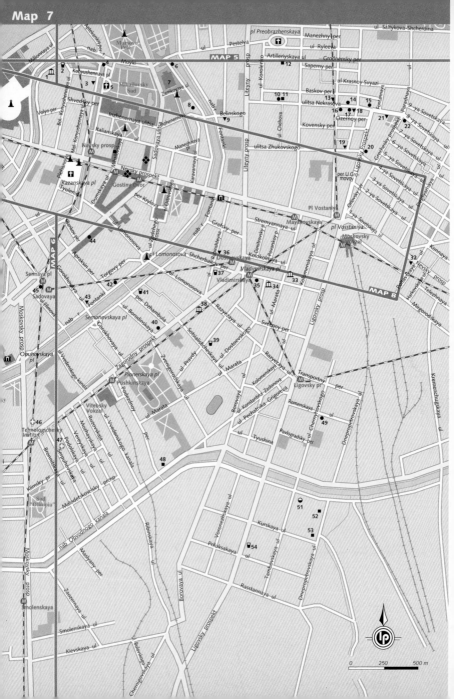

Map 7

MAP 5

MAP 6

MAP 8

Map 7

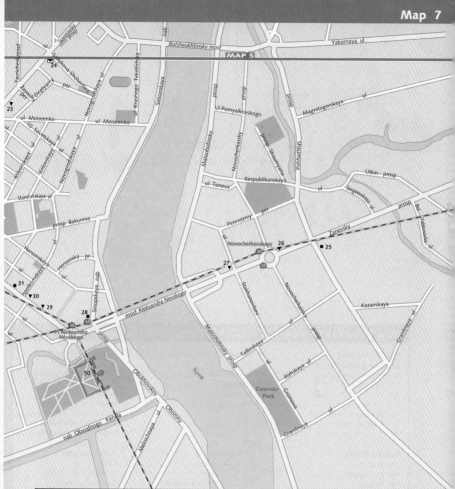

Map 8 NEVSKY PROSPEKT НЕВСВКИЙ ПРОСПЕКТ

Map 8 NEVSKY PROSPECT НЕВСКИЙ ПРОСПЕКТ

PLACES TO STAY

24 Grand Hotel Europe
53 Student Dormitory
   Общежитье
85 Hotel Oktyabrskaya
   Гостиница Октябрьская
88 St Petersburg Hostel &
   Sindbad Travel
95 Sheraton Nevskij Palace Hotel

PLACES TO EAT

13 Milano
19 Grillmaster
25 Sadko's
28 Gino Ginelli
29 Sakura
37 La Strada
38 Minutka
   Минутка
39 Kafe Literaturnoe
   Кафе Литературное
49 Taleon Club
50 Pizza Hut
55 Nevsky 27
78 Galeo
79 Pizza Hut/KFC
83 Carrols
84 Koshki Dom
87 Skazka

89 Bahlsen-Le Café; Bahlsen
   Bakery
91 Baskin Robbins
93 Grillmaster
94 Restoran Nevsky
   Ресторан Невский
97 Carrols
100 La Cucuracha

OTHER

1 Winter Palace
   Зимний дворец
2 Glinka Capella
   Хоровая капелла имени
   Глинки
3 Ipris (copy centre)
   Иприс
4 British Airways
5 Imperial Policeman Statue
6 Marstall
7 Benois Building
   Корпус Бэнуа
8 Maly Theatre
   Малый театр
9 Brodsky House-Museum
10 Pushkin Statue
   Памятник А. С. Пушкину
11 Russian Museum
   Русский музей

12 Museum of Ethnography
   Музей Этнографии
14 LOT Polish Airlines Office
15 Zimny Stadion
   Зимний Стадион
16 Yeliseevsky Food Shop
   Гастрономая Елисеевский
17 Teatr Kukol-Marionetok
18 Passazh Department Store
20 Armenian Church
   Армянская церков
21 ATM
22 Promstroy Industry &
   Construction Bank;
   St Petersburg Savings Bank
23 Big Hall (Philharmonia)
   Большой зал филармонии
26 Maly Zal Philharmonii im. M.
   I. Glinki (Small Hall)
   Малый зал филармонии
27 Chayka Bar
30 Dom Knigi
   Дом книги
31 Valhall
32 24-Hour Pharmacy
   Аптека (24-Часа)
33 Beer Garden
34 Lutheran Church
   Лутеранский церковь

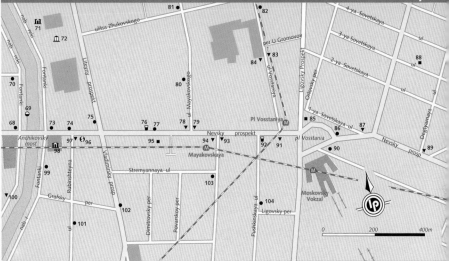

Map 9 PETRODVORETS ПЕТРОДВОРЕЦ

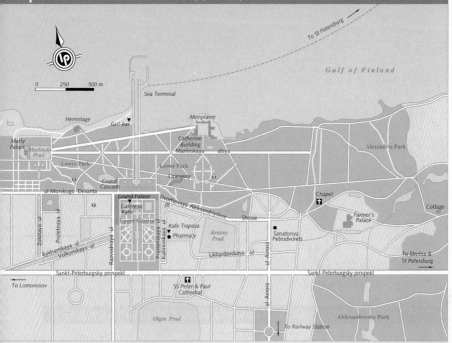

Gulf of Finland

To St Petersburg

0   250   500 m

Sea Terminal

Hermitage
Gril-bar
Monplaisir

Marly
Palace
Marlinsky
Prud

Catherine
Building
Marlinskaya   aleya

Alexandria Park

Lower Park
Lower Park
Orangery
Grand
Cascade

ul Morskogo Desanta

Grand Palace
Galereya
Kafe
Upper Garden

Dvortsovaya Aleksandryskoe
pl

Chapel

Cottage

Farmer's
Palace

Kafe Trapeza
Pharmacy

Krasny
Prud

Shosse

Sanatoriya
Petrodvorets

To Strelna &
St Petersburg

Zolotaya ul
Proletnaya ul
Eykhanskaya ul
Volkonskaya ul
Razvodnaya ul
Pravlenskaya ul
Kalininskaya ul

Likhardovskaya ul

ul Avrora

Sankt-Peterburgsky prospekt
Sankt-Peterburgsky prospekt

To Lomonosov

SS Peter & Paul
Cathedral

Olgin Prud

ul Avrora

Aleksandrovsky Park

To Railway Station

NICK SELBY

Grand Cascade (with water off) and Grand Palace, Petrodvorets